Copyright © 2024 by Artvoices Books & Nanette Smalley
All Rights Reserved; no portion of this work may be reproduced without the permission of the publisher.
Library of Congress Control Number: 2024935313
ISBN: 9798986841397
Printed in China

Project Management by Oak Porcelli, and Gina Pennock (cooking tools)
Written by Nanette Smalley, Oak Porcelli, and Kevin Cain
Copyedited by Hannah Grajko
Photography by Roxanne Turpen, Peter Farr and Gina Pennock (cooking tools)
Designed by Tanya Jessica, Jessica Creative Co.


First Artvoices Books Publishing Edition 2024
Baton Rouge, Louisiana USA

ARTVOICES COOKBOOKS PUBLISHING
www.artvoicesbooks.com

# FAVORITE

## CHEF NANETTE SMALLEY

A LIFE IN FOOD TO INSPIRE THE HOME CHEF

# ACKNOWLEDGEMENTS

When a person sets out to create a book, it starts with an idea, and then that idea may stay dormant until it is spoken out loud to the supportive and loving people around them.

Throughout my career, I have had the privilege of learning from and creating with so many talented chefs, sous chef, prep cooks, sommeliers, front of the house staff, butlers, and house managers; the list goes on and on. They are in my thoughts every time every time I pick up to get to work or sit at a perfectly laid out table surrounded by family and friends, Specifically, it was a group of talented and dedicated individuals who came together in a commercial kitchen in May 2023 in Buffalo N.Y. that brought my dream into reality. I would like to express my gratitude to them with a few words.

Let me thank my son Oak, who has been my constant encouragement and given me the support to finally see my dream of creating a generational cookbook come to fruition. You were my best critic in those early days and my biggest supporter. I love you with all my heart.

Thank you Michael, my husband, who encourages me with a gentle smile and an affectionate nature; always there with a glass of wine and a thoughtful conversation after a long day. Our life together is an adventure and I wake up relishing each day with you.

To the creative and artist team, Gina Pennock, Roxanne Turpen, and Peter Farr brought these recipes to life without the use of stabilizers or additives; they helped to beautifully capture authentic examples of these recipes that I have made throughout my career with their creativity, poise, and professionalism.

My creative director, Tanya Harding, brought everything together with her exceptional layout and graphic design skills and her endless patience. her ability to see my vision and execute it with clarity was astounding.

The kitchen staff of Steve Mallory (Estabon) Jake Whitfield, Christine Aguglis and Diego Castillo contributed, their know how and wonderfully developed palates to make sure each recipe was accurate and executable.

Hannah Graijko and Kevin Cain helped to give me a voice for this book and made the recipes concise and clear for the home chef.

The team at Curate Hospitality of Jodi Battaglia and Katherine Giacobbe did an amazing job organizing the initial phases of production. Their thoughtfulness made getting the project off the ground possible.

They connected us with sponsorships from Le Creuset and D'Artagnan, two excellent companies.

Byron Shuttleworth shared his broad knowledge of wine and wine regions as well as his nuanced palette for pairing food and wine.

Wendy York, reinvigorated my desire to write this book in 2020. Her encouragement was the jump start that I needed.

Lastly I would l like to thank my dear friends Chef Steve and Chef Trudie Anige, with whom I have spent countless hours. The three of us learning and growing from one another was a beautiful experience. You were always there for me with support and friendship.

Looking back, I feel a sense of immense gratitude. Your knowledge and passion for friendship, innovation, and shared experience has left an indelible mark on my professional and private life.

- Nanette

# CONTENTS

- 05 ACKNOWLEDGMENTS
- 08 FOREWORD
- 09 INTRODUCTION

## 13 BREAKFAST
- 14 Baked Eggs la Querencia
- 16 French Quiche
- 20 Summer Roulade
- 22 Tomatillo Shakshuka
- 24 Chimayó Chile Sauce
- 26 Homesick Southwest Breakfast
- 28 Blueberry Muffins
- 30 Cream Scones

## 32 STARTERS
## 32 SOUP
- 34 Watermelon Gazpacho
- 36 Spring Tonic
- 38 Cream of Watercress
- 40 Russian Cabbage Borscht
- 42 Smoked Trout Chowder
- 44 Portuguese Stew

## 46 SALADS
- 46 Palo Alto Salad
- 47 Escarole, Gruyére and Walnut
- 48 Exotic Curry Chicken Salad
- 50 Old-Fashioned Coleslaw
- 52 Tomato and Mango Salad
- 54 Herbed Egg Ribbons and Crab
- 58 Bitter Greens Goat Cheese Soufflé
- 60 Smoked Trout with Apples
- 64 Radicchio Salad with Chestnuts and Prosciutto
- 66 Radicchio, Oranges, and Charred Grilled Onion
- 68 Marinated Vegetable Salad

## 70 SANDWICHES
- 70 Open-Faced Crab Sandwiches
- 72 Provençal Stuffed Sandwich Loaf

## 74 ENTERTAINING
## 76 LITTLE BITES
- 76 Roquefort Grapes with Pistachios
- 78 Pickled Celery, Apple & Celery Root Salad with Endive
- 80 Sage Fritters
- 82 Retro Cheese Puffs
- 84 Phyllo Triangles with Goose Liver Mousse and Pistachios
- 86 Corn Cakes with Smoked Black Cod
- 88 Smoked Salmon Tartare
- 92 Thai Chicken Salad
- 94 Cashew Sesame Chicken
- 96 Chicken Satay
- 98 Caramelized Bacon
- 100 Golden Spiced Chèvre Cheese
- 102 Jacqueline's Baked Brie with Curry and Chutney
- 104 Red Wine Biscuits

## 106 DRINKS
- 106 Smalley Family Eggnog
- 108 French 75
- 109 Brunch Punch

## 110 TEA PARTY
- 112 Cheddar Chutney
- 113 Queen Elizabeth's Smoked Salmon
- 113 Lime Butter, Cucumber, and Pickled Ginger
- 113 Pecan, Cream Cheese, and Olive

## 114 ENTREÉS
## 116 BEEF, PORK & LAMB
- 116 Cognac Marinated Filet of Beef
- 118 Filet of Beef with Blue Cheese and Pistachios
- 120 Filet of Beef with Green Peppercorn Sauce
- 124 Spicy Zinfandel Meatballs
- 126 Braciole
- 130 Spiced Dusted Lamb Chops with Cherry Tomatoes
- 134 Lamb Meatballs with Tahini
- 136 Grilled Tenderloin of Pork with Cherry Salsa
- 140 Pan Roasted Pork Loin with Balsamic Vinegar Onions

## 142 POULTRY
- 142 Herb Chicken Paillard
- 144 Chicken with Salad on Top
- 146 Chicken Breast Françoise Paul Boucse
- 148 Pan Roasted Chicken with Sage Vermouth Sauce
- 150 Provençal Chicken
- 154 Persian Black Lime Chicken
- 156 Stuffed Poussin with Roasted Grape Cluster
- 158 Roasted Chicken with Foie Gras Butter

- 162 Old-Fashioned Southern Fried Chicken
- 164 Grits
- 168 Duck a L'orange
- 172 Pheasant in Salt Crust with White Peppercorn Sauce
- 174 Braised Pheasant Legs with Dried Morels and Chestnuts
- 176 Peppercorn Marinated Quail with Cranberry, Cherry, and Tomato Relish
- 178 Cranberry, Cherry, and Tomato Relish

## 180 SEAFOOD

- 182 Scallops with Grapefruit and Onion Salad
- 184 Crab Cakes and Tartar Sauce
- 186 Shrimp Thai Curry
- 188 Chili-Rubbed Prawns with Barbeque Hollandaise Sauce
- 190 New Orleans Shrimp
- 192 Italian Breaded Shrimp
- 194 Salmon with Scallion Ginger Sauce
- 196 Seared Salmon with Corn and Shiitake Mushrooms
- 200 Chilean Sea Bass with Honey Soy Glaze and Ginger Butter Sauce
- 202 Seafood Crêpes

## 204 PASTA

- 204 Angel Hair Pasta with Garlic, Olive Oil, and Red Pepper
- 206 Penne Saint Martin
- 208 Penne Pasta with Beets, and Gorgonzola
- 212 Rotolo with Spinach Stuffing and Creamy Tomato Sauce

## 214 VEGETABLE

- 214 Cheese Soufflé
- 216 Lisa's Stuffed Portobello Mushrooms

## 220 SIDE DISHES

- 220 Jerusalem Artichoke and Vegetable Tagine
- 224 Indian Spiced Cauliflower
- 228 Cauliflower Steaks with Caper Pancetta Sauce
- 230 Glazed Miso Eggplant
- 232 Sweet Potatoes in Orange Shells
- 234 Bliss Potatoes
- 236 Cilantro Risotto
- 238 Cornbread

## 240 DESSERTS
## 242 CAKES

- 242 French Lemon Cake
- 244 Rosemary Olive Oil Orange Cake
- 246 Castagnaccio Chestnut Flour Cake
- 250 Nanette's Creamy Chocolate Cake
- 252 Financiers
- 254 Christmas Fruit Cake

## 256 COOKIES

- 256 Oak's White Bark Cookies
- 258 Pecan Lemon Shortbread
- 260 Walnut Shortbread Cookies
- 262 Saffron Shortbread
- 264 Cowboy Cookies
- 266 Flourless Chocolate Cookies
- 268 Mocha Cookies

## 270 TARTS AND OTHER DELECTABLES

- 270 Bittersweet Chocolate Tart
- 274 French Apple Tart
- 278 Rhubarb Galette
- 280 Oak's Chocolate Mousse
- 282 My Favorite Chocolate Truffles
- 284 Ricotta Doughnuts with Chocolate Sauce
- 286 Coeur a La Creme
- 288 Matcha Ice Cream Sundaes with Chocolate
- 290 Sesame Pistachio Brittle

## 292 SAUCES

- 294 Pickled Cherries
- 294 Lemon Confit
- 295 Shio Koji Marinade
- 295 Homemade Mayonaise
- 296 All Purpose Butter for Stuffing Under Poultry Skin

## 298 APPENDIX A: OBSERVATIONS
## 302 APPENDIX B: MENUS
## 307 LIST OF PURVEYORS
## 308 INDEX
## 316 MEMORIES

# FOREWORD

**In New York City, mix together one gorgeous, passionate west-coast chef, add two transplanted Australian chefs, slowly blend together over celebrations at an Englishman's apartment in the East Village, and watch the friendship rise for decades.**

Over the course of 20 years, we shared an extraordinary journey working together in NYC, marked by the perfect blend of camaraderie, laughter and professionalism with plenty of memorable eating along the way.

This enticingly delicious cookbook that our dear friend Nanette has created, a gift from her son Oak, is a testament of dreams fulfilled.

It is a celebration of her culinary artistry, a reflection of her boundless creativity, and an outpouring of the love and admiration of her family and friends.

It completes her lifelong culinary journey of nurturing, caring and comforting all those who have come into her orbit, with her creations that are chock full of love.

Before NYC was her beloved restaurant in Santa Fe, New Mexico. La Querencia was so named as this translates to a favorite place, where people feel most secure, feel at home and go to be fed and nourished.

Choose any recipe, put out the invite, and you will instantly have many new and eager friends hanging about and feeling right at home!

The transformative power of sharing and caring through the beautiful food in these pages will feed your soul, nourish your body and be a feast for all your senses.

Delve right in, cook with love, share generously, and revel in the connection and enrichment these pages will bring.

With all our love and admiration,

*Trudy + Steve Ainge*

# INTRODUCTION

First off, I want to thank you for picking up a copy of *Favorite*. This book is a labor of love that has taken 50 years to realize, and your support means the world to me. *Favorite* is meant to be a book of utility and evolution. It is here to help you grow through experimentation. These recipes are tried and true, and are meant as a guide as you prepare for your own journey in the kitchen.

Curiosity is paramount when setting out in any endeavor. Have fun, make mistakes, and find the joy that I and countless other chefs have discovered through our lives in food. Everyone's journey in the kitchen is unique, and the path is made through the enthusiasm of exploration, not by comparison. I have been a chef most of my life and through my experiences I have learned the most important things in the kitchen are to have fun, love the experience, and savor the moments that create lasting friendships around a table.

My mother, Jacqueline, was an incredible woman who supported my curiosity and sense of play throughout my childhood. When I was 15 years old, she gifted me a copy of *Laroussse Gastronomique*, which is considered by many to be one of the foundational resources of culinary knowledge. Cooking recipes from it became the spark that ignited my love of french cooking, learning the processes and techniques that would become the building blocks for my life in food. I fervently read it cover to cover, discovering what has become a passion for creating aromas, flavors, and smiles for the people I love. I hope this book can be a bridge for future generations of explorers in the kitchen.

Whenever I found a new recipe, my mother would help me every step of the way. We would make the trip to the only gourmet store in Hollywood from Palos Verdes, an hour drive in those days. She filled every moment of the journey with adventure and support, instilling a joy for the process as much as the product. It also helped that she would always clean up after me, sparing me the horror of a mountain of dirty dishes.

# THE MOST IMPORTANT PART OF BEING IN THE KITCHEN? LEARNING... MAKE MISTAKES AND CONTINUE ON.

Top to Bottom: Chef Nanette at the Bidwell Farmer's Market, having a laugh with her beloved son Oak, and putting the final touches on the Scallops with Grapefruit Salad at bottom.

In 1974, I became a mother. The responsibility and joy was like a lightning bolt that struck me dead in my tracks. As a single parent at 23 years old, I had to learn how to create a life not only for myself but for my newborn son, Oak. Everyone has hopes and dreams for what they expect their life to be at that age, and I was no different. I wanted to become a massage therapist, helping people heal and feel good. Once Oak arrived all of that changed. Knowing that I could provide for him through working in the food service industry, I reimagined those dreams and began my professional life in food. Working with people to feel good was still my focus so I just figured out a different approach.

Growing up by the Pacific Ocean in southern California, the rich soil offered what would become another lifelong love, gardening. In her remarkably progressive manner, my mother kept an organic garden at our home. Seeing things grow and experiencing fresh, succulent flavors in the summer is one of the greatest pleasures a chef can create for themselves. I strongly encourage anyone with a love for food to cultivate a small garden plot of your own or join a community garden. These experiences can be life changing.

When I set out on my career, I never thought of it as a career. I was doing what came naturally. In order to survive these early years of motherhood in Santa Fe, I took a job at Howard Johnson's working the 4am to noon shift. While I was there the lessons learned from *Laroussse Gastronomique* came flooding back and I started to do things from scratch, making my own stocks, adding touches of flavor to extremely bland and gray food. This is also when I started the beginning of my catering career, informally cooking for dinner parties my friends would throw which eventually lead to making the connections to start my first restaurant.

10

Chef Nanette preparing to plate Duck a L'Orange.

Through practice and patience you will be able to make all of the recipes in this book. I have spent countless hours preparing and reviewing these recipes to make sure that even the most novice home chef can execute them to their surprise and delight.

I have included notes on each recipe to give you more insight into why these recipes are my "Favorites." I hope they will become your favorites as well. Also, I have included a section of tips and tricks to help make your time in the kitchen more enjoyable as well as a list of purveyors for some of the harder to find items in this book.

The recipes in this book are a culmination of my love of food and shared experience. Over the last 50 years I have collected, created and developed the recipes that you are about to learn. This is truly the most important part of being in the kitchen: learning. Learning about what food you like, learning what your tastes are, and learning about how to cultivate your skillset.

Make mistakes and continue on.

# WHEN I SET OUT ON MY CAREER I NEVER THOUGHT OF IT AS A CAREER, I WAS DOING WHAT CAME NATURALLY.

French Lemon Cakes, page 243.

# FAVORITE BREAKFAST

# BAKED EGGS LA QUERENCIA

**Prep time**
10 min.

**Actual time**
22 min.

**Serves**
1

### Step 1
Preheat oven to 400 degrees. Butter a custard dish well.

### Step 2
Break the eggs into the custard dish. Pour in the cream. Add a dash of salt and pepper. Sprinkle with the herbs, followed by the breadcrumbs. Cover with the grated cheese (push down if you need to). Transfer to a baking sheet. Cook for 10 to 12 minutes until the eggs are set, golden brown, and bubbly. Keep an eye on them because it is easy to overbake them. Take out and cool before enjoying.

**Ingredients**

2 eggs

Butter at room temperature
(to coat the custard dish)

¼ cup heavy cream

Pinch of sea salt

5 grinds freshly ground white pepper

2 tablespoons grated cheese
(I use Gruyère, but you can use Parmesan or any favorite cheese of yours, as long as it is suitable for grating)

1 tablespoon fresh breadcrumbs
(Not dried)

½ tablespoon fresh herbs
(I like chervil, thyme, or tarragon)

**Difficulty level: Easy**

**Wine pairing:**
A rosé, gamay, or sauvignon blanc

When I embarked on the journey of opening my restaurant, La Querencia in Santa Fe, I noticed that most establishments in town were primarily focused on Southwestern cuisine. Inspired to bring a wider range of flavors to the area, I sought out an easy yet rich French recipe to add to our menu for breakfast and lunch. With the delicately herbaceous and creamy flavors, it's no wonder why it swiftly became the most sought-after item on our menu. The beauty of this dish lies in its versatility. You can add an elegant touch by incorporating a teaspoon of white truffle paste to the cream, or sprinkle finely minced fresh black truffle for a truly heavenly experience. Whether you're enjoying a leisurely weekend brunch or savoring a light lunch, these aromatic baked eggs are an easy introduction to a world of exquisite taste.

It doesn't get better than an old-world French classic. This recipe came with the first quiche pan I bought when I was 15 years old and it is still the one I use today. Often, a certain magic is imbued in the tools you use over the years. Creating a familiar relationship with one's tools leads to dishes such as these turning out perfectly time and time again, allowing your creative confidence to flourish. This recipe allows for so much innovation—you can add many other wonderful ingredients such as bacon, ham, spinach, mushrooms, or various cheeses. Also, you can bake the filling in a soufflé dish if you want to make this gluten-free.

# FRENCH QUICHE

| **Prep time** | **Actual time** | **Serves** |
| 15 min. | 45 min. | 8 |

### Ingredients
**Pastry dough**

8 ounces butter, cut into 1 inch pieces and well chilled

2 ⅔ cup flour

¾ teaspoons salt

2 tablespoons sugar

½ cup ice water (you might need more)

Herbs and spices to taste and preference (optional)

Tart pan

**Quiche**

3 whole eggs

3 egg yolks

2 cups heavy cream

½ to 1 teaspoon, kosher salt

Ground long pepper, to taste

Pinch nutmeg

1 packed cup shredded Gruyère cheese

½ cup shredded Colby cheese

2 tablespoons fresh thyme

**Wine pairing**

Champagne, an Alsace riesling, or Beaujolais

### Step 1
Preheat oven 350 degrees.

In a food processor with a metal blade, process flour, sugar, salt, and butter until it resembles a fine meal, 8 to 10 seconds.

### Step 2
Have your ice water at hand. With the motor running, pour in the water in a steady stream and process using quick pulses until it forms a ball. Be careful not to over process it or it will be tough. Remove from the food processor bowl and give it a pat with your hand to form into a disk. Chill for at least 1 hour.

Roll out to a circle larger than the tart pan to ¼ inch thick.

Fold into thirds, transfer to the middle of the tart pan, unfold, and press to fit. Chill in the refrigerator at least 1 hour before baking. Prick the bottom of the tart shell all around with a fork, to prevent bubbling.

### Step 3
Line with parchment paper and fill with pie weights. Bake in the oven for 20 minutes, rotating the pan once after 10 minutes. Let cool and remove the pie weights. The pastry shell can be made a day in advance, just be sure it is at room temperature before adding the filling.

### For the quiche
**Step 1**

Preheat oven to 375 degrees. Whisk together the eggs and egg yolks until well incorporated. Add cream, salt, pepper, nutmeg, and thyme. Mix until combined.

### Step 2
Sprinkle the cheeses over the pre-baked crust and pour in filling. It might not take all the filling. Place the quiche dish on a sheet pan and bake for 25 minutes. Let cool for 10 minutes before serving.

Culturally, we are in a constant flux, expressing our tastes and preferences through various fads. This recipe is one that was very en-vogue when I was first catering in the mid 90's in New York. It has since fallen out of fashion, but like Day-Glo, baggy pants, and all great things from the 90's, it should not be forgotten. The silkiness of the cream cheese paired with the aromatic blend of herbs and fresh tomatoes will leave your guests dreaming of tastes from a summer day. Once you have the basic recipe for the roulade down, be creative and come up with fillings that suit your individual palette. Pack it for a picnic, pair it with a fantastic wine, and enjoy those summer days.

# SUMMER ROULADE WITH TOMATOES, HERBS & CREAM CHEESE

| Prep time | Actual time | Serves |
|---|---|---|
| 40 min. | 30 min. | 6 |

## Ingredients

**Soufflé base for roulades**

- 5 eggs
- 1 ½ cups milk
- 5 tablespoons flour
- ½ teaspoon salt
- ½ teaspoon freshly ground white pepper
- Pinch cayenne pepper
- ¼ teaspoon grated nutmeg
- ½ cup Parmesan cheese

**Filling**

- 1 pound ripe tomatoes
- 2 to 3 tablespoons extra virgin olive oil
- Pinch sugar
- Salt and freshly ground white pepper, to taste
- 8 ounces cream cheese, at room temperature
- 1 to 2 tablespoons milk (to thin out cream cheese)
- 1 tablespoon high-quality balsamic vinegar
- 1 bunch scallions, white part only, finely chopped
- ½ cup mixed minced herbs (parsley, basil, tarragon, or dill)

**Difficulty level: Difficult**

**Wine pairing:** A crisp vin gris or a chilled Beaujolais

## For the soufflé base

**Step 1**

Preheat oven to 400 degrees.
Line a 10 by 15 inch baking pan with parchment paper and add butter and flour to coat.

**Step 2**

Separate the yolks from the whites. Lightly beat the yolks and set aside.

**Step 3**

In a small saucepan, melt the butter until it is bubbling. Add flour and cook for 3 minutes, stirring occasionally. Add cayenne, salt, pepper, and nutmeg. Gradually, add the yolks to the mixture, stirring until well incorporated. Set aside.

**Step 4**

In a large bowl with a handheld mixer, beat the egg whites until stiff but not dry. Fold in ¼ of the yolk mixture into the beaten egg whites. Fold in the cheese and the rest of the egg whites until well incorporated.

**Step 5**

Pour into the prepared baking sheet and even out well with a spatula. Bake for 15 minutes until it is lightly browned. When the roulade is completely cool, lay a piece of parchment larger than the sheet pan on top and carefully flip the roulade over. Remove sheet pan. Now it is ready to fill and roll.

## For the filling

**Step 1**

To skin your tomatoes, fill a medium saucepan ¾ full with water and bring to a boil. On each tomato, make a small "X" on the bottom with a knife. On top, remove the core from the center. Carefully drop into the boiling water until the skins start to burst. Drain. When cool enough to handle, remove skin and chop tomatoes into ½ inch pieces.

**Step 2**

In a medium skillet, heat the olive oil over medium heat. Add the tomatoes and sauté them over medium-high heat to evaporate the juices, about 20 minutes. Stir in a pinch of sugar. Remove from heat and add salt, pepper, and vinegar to taste. Set aside to cool.

## To construct the roulade

**Step 1**

In a small bowl, whisk the milk and cream cheese until it is spreadable. With a spatula, carefully spread onto the roulade to cover the entire surface.

**Step 2**

Cover the roulade with the scallions, herbs, and tomatoes (in that order). Roll the roulade tightly starting at one end. If you are not serving it right away, wrap it well in plastic wrap and put in the refrigerator until ready to serve.

Take out 20 minutes before serving to bring it to room temperature. Slice thinly and serve.

# TOMATILLO SHAKSHUKA

| Prep time | Actual time | Serves |
|---|---|---|
| 20 min. | 40 min. | 4 |

### Step 1
Fill a medium saucepan halfway with water and bring to a boil. Add the tomatillos and jalapeño pepper, stirring occasionally. Cook until softened, about 10 minutes. Strain into a colander. Transfer to a food processor and add the cilantro stems, 1 teaspoon of cumin, and the tortillas. Add a big pinch of salt and pepper and ½ cup of water. Blend until smooth (you may need more water).

### Step 2
In a large, non-stick skillet, heat the olive oil over medium heat. Add the onion, poblano, and a pinch each of salt and pepper. Occasionally stirring, cook until lightly browned, 6 to 8 minutes. Gradually add the spinach, stirring to wilt before adding more; cook until all the spinach has wilted. Taste and add more salt if needed. Pour the sauce from the food processor into the skillet and stir to combine. Reduce heat to low and gently simmer until thickened. You might need to add a little water.

### Step 3: Two ways to cook the eggs: the traditional method for Shakshuka or pan poached. I use the poached method if I only want to make one or two servings.

#### Traditional method
Preheat oven to 375 degrees.

One at a time, crack each egg into a small bowl. Make wells in the sauce and add 1 egg to each well. Drag the edge of a rubber spatula through the egg whites, being careful not to break the yolks. Season with salt and pepper, and bake until the egg whites are just beginning to set, about 10 minutes. Turn the broiler to high and cook until the egg whites are set, 1 to 2 minutes. Remove from the oven and sprinkle with cheese.

#### Poaching method
In a small, non-stick skillet, heat 1 teaspoon olive oil over medium heat. When the skillet is hot, add 2 eggs, then add two tablespoons of water and cover. Turn heat to medium and cook until eggs are just set. In a soup bowl, add the sauce and make a well. Add an egg to the well and top with the cheese. Add salt to taste and serve hot.

## Ingredients
- 1 pound tomatillos, husks removed, rinsed, and cored
- 2 jalapeño peppers, stemmed and seeds removed, cut in half
- ½ bunch of cilantro, stems separated and leaves chopped
- 3 cloves garlic, minced
- ½ cup torn corn or flour tortillas
- 1-1 ½ teaspoons of salt
- 12 grinds freshly ground black pepper
- 3 teaspoons ground cumin, divided
- 2 tablespoons extra virgin olive oil
- 1 small onion, chopped
- 2 large poblano Chilis, seeded, chopped
- 8 ounces baby spinach
- 1 cup shredded Monterey Jack cheese
- 8 eggs

**Difficulty Level: Moderate**

**Wine pairing:** An Albariño from Portugal or a grüner veltliner

One of my fondest memories from childhood is harvesting fresh vegetables beside my mother in our family garden. There is nothing better than taking the time to grow your own food. By cooking whatever you have cared for that season, a deep rooted bond is created between the chef, the land, and the dish. Once, the shared plot in my community garden produced an overabundance of tomatillos and I wanted to make sure none went to waste, which is the inspiration that led to this dish. Tomatillos both provide a light foundation to hold the other ingredients, as well as provide a citrusy pop with a touch of heat. If you're looking for a superb and flavorful dish to share with friends for brunch, look no further than shakshuka.

All thanks to the garden.

I was born in Santa Fe, New Mexico, and later owned a restaurant there, which has made me *very* fond of Southwest cuisine, particularly the chilis from the region. The food we grow up with often becomes our comfort food later in life. This recipe is what I make when I am feeling homesick for the Southwest. You can use this sauce on top of chili relleno, grilled chicken, or with eggs.

The historic village of Chimayó, located in the heart of New Mexico, is approximately a 30-minute drive north of Santa Fe, nestled at the foothills of the crimson-hued Sangre de Cristo mountains. Established by Spanish settlers in the late 17th century, this tight-knit community of 3,000 inhabitants lies near the Santa Cruz river and is best known for El Santuario de Chimayó. However, the most prized culinary item of the region is its distinctly reddish-orange chili, which attracts purveyors from all corners of the globe seeking a combination of sweetness and spice highlighted by an understated smokiness that can only be found in the Chimayó chili.

Despite its worldwide fame, these chilis are grown exclusively in Chimayó in small batches by farmers who harvest the crop each fall and primarily use it for their family recipes. While these chilies may be hard to find in your local market, they can be purchased online.

# CHIMAYÓ CHILI SAUCE

**Actual time** 40 min.

**Serves*** 1

### Step 1
Melt butter or drippings in a medium saucepan over low heat. When it is bubbling, stir in the flour and chili powder to mix well. Sauté, stirring for 2 minutes. Add the garlic.

### Step 2
Turn the heat to low and slowly add the broth to the pan while whisking with a wire whisk until it thickens. Add the tomato sauce, cumin, salt, and oregano. Simmer for at least 15 minutes to 30 minutes. Taste and adjust seasoning if needed.

**Ingredients**

2 tablespoons unsalted butter or bacon drippings

2 tablespoons flour

¼ cup Chimayó chili powder or substitute ancho chili powder

2 cups beef stock (You can use chicken or vegetable stock if you prefer; I like the richness the beef stock adds)

2 to 4 ounces tomato sauce

¾ teaspoon salt

1 clove garlic, crushed

¼ teaspoon dried oregano

2 teaspoons ground cumin

**Difficulty level: Easy**

*makes about 2 cups of sauce so you will have leftover

# HOMESICK SOUTHWEST BREAKFAST

| Prep time | Actual time | Serves |
| 10 min. | 40 min. | 1 |

### Ingredients
2 corn tortillas, preferrably blue corn if you can find them
2 eggs, poached or steamed
½ cup shredded cheddar cheese
1 tablespoon minced cilantro
½ cup Chimayó chili sauce

### Step 1
In a steamer, steam eggs for 6 minutes. When cool enough to handle, peel and set aside.

### Step 2
Microwave 2 tortillas covered with a paper towel for 30 seconds. Take out and top with the eggs.

To serve, pour about ½ cup of sauce over the eggs. Top with cheese and cilantro.

**Difficulty level: Easy**

# BLUEBERRY MUFFINS

**Prep time**
15 min.

**Actual time**
40 min.

**Serves**
12

### Step 1
Preheat oven to 400 degrees. Grease muffin tins with butter. Melt butter.

In a large bowl, sift together flour, ⅔ cup sugar, baking powder, baking soda, and salt. In a smaller bowl, whisk together yogurt, butter, egg, lemon rind, and vanilla.

### Step 2
Make a well in the center of the dry ingredients, pour in the yogurt mixture and stir just to combine (don't over-mix). Fold in the blueberries. Spoon the batter into the muffin cups and sprinkle with the remaining sugar.

### Step 3
Bake for 20 to 25 minutes until a cake tester is inserted in the center of a muffin and comes out clean. Remove tins from the oven onto a cooling rack. Cool at least 5 minutes until removing muffins.

### Ingredients
- 2 cups all-purpose flour
- ⅔ cup sugar, plus 1 tablespoon for sprinkling on the muffins before baking
- 1 teaspoon baking soda
- 1 teaspoon baking powder
- 1 teaspoon kosher salt
- 1 8-ounce container of lemon or lime whole milk yogurt (you can substitute buttermilk, sour-cream, or crème fraîche if you like)
- ½ cup unsalted butter, melted
- 1 egg, lightly beaten
- 2 teaspoons grated lemon rind
- 1 teaspoon vanilla extract
- 2 cups blueberries, fresh or frozen and drained

**Difficulty Level: Easy**

If you're intimidated by baking, this is a *perfect* recipe for you! This recipe is an excellent one for building your confidence and create an unbelievably delicious treat. These muffins have always been a huge hit with clients and friends alike. Another perk of this recipe is that you can easily make a double batch and freeze half to have on hand. However, after trying them, you'll understand why they never last long in storage.

# CREAM SCONES

| Prep time | Actual time | Serves |
|---|---|---|
| 15 min. | 40 min. | 12 |

### Step 1
Preheat oven to 400 degrees.

Using an electric stand mixer with a paddle attachment, mix the flour, baking powder, salt, sugar, and butter to a mealy consistency. Add the currants, cream, and eggs. Do not over-beat.

### Step 2
Turn out the dough on a floured surface and pat it down by hand until it is ¾ inch thick. Cut the scones with a round cookie cutter, occasionally dipping the cutter in flour to keep the dough from sticking to the cutter. Place the scones on a large cookie sheet lined with parchment. Brush the scones with the egg wash and sprinkle with sugar. Bake for about 10 minutes until golden brown.

Serve scones with a quality butter, crème fraîche, or clotted cream and a preserve.

**Ingredients**

2 cups all-purpose flour

1 tablespoon baking powder

½ teaspoon sea salt

1 tablespoon sugar

12 tablespoons (1 ½ stick) unsalted butter, chilled and cut into ½ inch pieces

1 cup heavy cream

2 eggs, lightly beaten

1 egg mixed with 1 tablespoon water for the egg wash

⅓ cup currants dusted with ½ teaspoon flour

Sugar to dust the scones

**Difficulty level: Easy**

If you're looking for a classic, yet unique morning treat to start your day, look no further than this scone recipe. Years of catering allowed me to spend time testing the perfect combination of ingredients to create a fluffy, moist delight. Say farewell to dry scones!

In search of variety? Swap the traditionally used currants for chopped apricots, flavorful dried cherries, or even a vibrant burst of fresh strawberries or blueberries to fit your morning cravings. Let your culinary creativity guide you in selecting the perfect additions to infuse an extra touch of magic into these delectable baked treats. Up your breakfast game and create a blissful morning.

# FAVORITE STARTERS

Soups, Salads, & Sandwiches

# WATERMELON GAZPACHO

| **Prep time** | **Actual time** | **Serves** |
|---|---|---|
| 30 minutes | 40 minutes plus overnight chill | 4-6 |

### Ingredients

5 cups diced watermelon, 4 cups cut into 1-inch cubes, 1 cup small diced watermelon for serving

½ teaspoon salt

15 grinds freshly ground white pepper

Pinch cayenne

1 tablespoon red wine or sherry vinegar

2 tablespoons fresh lime juice, plus lime wedges for serving

1 cup honeydew melon, ¼ inch cubes

1 small jalapeno minced fine, about 1 ½ tablespoons

1 cup diced cucumber, ¼ inch cubes

1 tablespoon extra-virgin olive oil

1 tablespoon snipped chives

2 tablespoons minced basil leaves

2 tablespoons minced mint leaves

Pinch crushed red pepper (optional)

Pinch flaky salt such as Maldon or fleur de sel (optional)

**Difficulty level: Moderate**

**Wine pairing:**

Dry French rosé or a California Zinfandel

### Step 1
### For Gazpacho

Put 4 cups of diced watermelon in a food processor or blender and pulse to a purée. Strain purée through a fine-meshed sieve into a bowl. You should have about 4 cups of purée. Season with salt, pepper, cayenne, 1 tablespoon vinegar of choice, and 2 tablespoons lime juice and minced jalapeño. Taste and adjust seasoning.

Refrigerate overnight.

### Step 2
### For feta cream

2 ounces french feta (I like the taste of the french feta), about ½ cup crumbled

¼ cup sour cream

2 tablespoons milk

Mash feta and sour cream together in a small bowl until mostly smooth. Whisk in the milk.

### Step 3
### For serving

Place remaining diced watermelon, honeydew melon, and cucumber in a small mixing bowl. Toss with a bit of salt and pepper, 2 tablespoons of lime juice, and 2 tablespoons of olive oil. Divide the mixture evenly into chilled soup bowls.

Ladle watermelon purée into each bowl. Sprinkle with chives, basil, and mint. Add a sprinkle of crushed red pepper and flaky salt if desired. Pass lime wedges separately. Serve with feta cream.

This recipe has become a fantastic choice whenever I have the pleasure of hosting a summertime dinner party with friends. The combination of flavors, carefully selected, adds a touch of fruity sweetness from the melon and subtle heat from the pepper. Its vibrant presentation captivates the eye and refreshes the palette as a great start to a summer meal.

# SPRING TONIC

| Prep time | Actual time | Serves |
|---|---|---|
| 20 min. | 1 hr., 25 min. | 4-6 |

### Ingredients
- 3 cans whole tomatoes, preferably San Marzano
- 2 stalks of celery
- 2 carrots, peeled
- 1 green pepper, deseeded
- 1 large yellow onion
- 3 black peppercorns
- 2 whole cloves
- 1 teaspoon salt
- ½ teaspoon dried basil
- ½ teaspoon sugar
- ⅓ cup port
- 1 ½ tablespoons fresh lemon juice

### Cheese croutons for garnish
- 10 slices of white bread, crusts removed and cut into 1-inch squares
- ¼ cup unsalted butter
- ¼ cup extra virgin olive oil
- 5 tablespoons grated Parmesan
- 1 teaspoon kosher salt
- 1 teaspoon paprika
- 1 teaspoon garlic powder

**Difficulty level: Easy**

**Wine pairing:** port, dry sherry, or pinot noir

### Step 1
Put the contents of the canned tomatoes, juice and all, in a large stockpot, breaking the solids chunks up with a knife. Cut the vegetables into chunks, 1 inch wide, and add to the pot. Stir in the peppercorns, clove, salt, basil, and sugar.

Cover the pot with a lid and, on high heat, bring to a boil. Once it reaches a boil, lower heat and simmer for 1 hour, covered until the vegetables are soft, stirring a few times during cooking.

### Step 2
When it is cool, strain the soup through a fine mesh strainer lined with multiple sheets of cheesecloth, into a small stock pot, squeezing out all the juices from the vegetables.

### Step 3
Return the pot to the stove and add the port and lemon juice. Add salt and pepper to taste. Bring gently to a boil and serve hot.

### Cheese croutons
### Step 1
In a medium size skillet, melt butter until hot and bubbling. Add olive oil, salt, paprika, garlic powder, and bread. Cook and toss over low heat until the bread is crisp and golden brown. Drain on paper towels.

### Step 2
Place warm bread in a large bowl and toss with cheese.

To serve, pour the hot soup into a bowl, adding a few croutons on top. It can also be served cold.

This recipe holds a special place in my heart due to its history in my family. My mother and I would often prepare it together, especially for Christmas dinner. Not only is it nutritious and delicious, but it also serves as a perfect starter for any meal. Whenever I make it now, memories of my mother at the stove, diligently preparing this soup, flood back and remind me of the cherished moments we shared in the kitchen. The recipe itself is easy to follow, resulting in a vibrant and flavorful vegetable broth. The addition of a splash of lemon juice and port unites all the flavors perfectly, creating a well-balanced first course.

# CREAM OF WATERCRESS

| Prep time | Actual time | Serves |
|---|---|---|
| 30 min. | 45 min. | 6-8 |

### Step 1
Melt the butter in a large saucepan until it is bubbling. Turn the heat to low. Add the onion, cover, and cook slowly until they are tender and translucent, about 5 to 10 minutes. Stir often and do not let it brown.

### Step 2
Stir in the watercress and salt, cover with a lid, and cook, about 5 minutes or until the watercress is wilted.

Sprinkle with flour and stir occasionally over medium heat for 3 minutes.

### Step 3
Bring the chicken stock to a boil. Put it in a measuring cup and microwave it. You can also bring it to a boil on the stovetop. Take the pan off heat, add 4 cups chicken stock, and return to the burner stirring until it comes to a boil. Lower heat and simmer for 5 to 8 minutes. Pour into a blender or Vitamix blender, blend until smooth. Add the cream and blend one more time. Taste and if too bitter add another more broth. Serve with a garnish of croutons.

## Ingredients
- ⅓ cup minced onion
- 3 tablespoons unsalted butter
- 3 tablespoons flour
- 4 cups fresh watercress; I use some of the stems and leaves, but remove the tough part of the stem
- 1 teaspoon salt
- Freshly ground white pepper
- 5 ½ cups chicken stock
- ½ to ¾ cup heavy cream

**Difficulty level: Easy**

**Wine pairing**

A cabernet, white Burgundy, or a New Zealand pinot noir

When serving this cherished creation to guests, I undoubtedly will be asked for the recipe. This particular soup recipe has been adapted from one by the culinary genius, Julia Child. Its preparation is straightforward and doesn't require a lot of time for the flavors to meld together. Lately, I've noticed that the only watercress available in supermarkets is the hydroponic kind, which I don't recommend using because of its price point and doesn't provide the same complexity of flavor. If you can find it from a local purveyor or farmer's market, that will undoubtedly create the best end result. As versatile as it is delicious, it can be enjoyed cold in the summer or warm in the winter.

# Russian Cabbage Borscht

| Prep time | Actual time | Serves |
|---|---|---|
| 20 min. | 55 min. | 4 |

### Step 1
Place the potatoes and beets in the water or stock, and cook until just barely tender, about 5 to 8 minutes. Strain the water off and set aside both the vegetable and cooking water.

### Step 2
In a large sauté pan, heat the butter over medium heat and sauté the onions and caraway seeds until the onion is translucent. Add the carrot, celery, cabbage, and dill. Bring to a simmer, cover, and turn the heat to low. Sweat the vegetables until tender, about 5 minutes.

### Step3
Stir in the tomato purée, honey, vinegar, salt, and pepper. Add cooking water from step 1, the potatoes, and beets, and bring to a boil. Turn heat to low and simmer for about 20 minutes. Taste and adjust if needed.

Serve in bowls and top with sour cream and minced dill.

**Ingredients**

2 tablespoons butter
2 cups chopped onion
1 cup thinly sliced potato
1 cup thinly sliced red beets
1 large carrot
2 stalks of celery
3 cups thinly sliced white or red cabbage
1 cup tomato purée
2 teaspoons caraway seed
6 cups water or chicken broth
2 teaspoon kosher salt
15 grinds freshly ground white pepper
2 teaspoons fresh minced dill
1 tablespoon apple cider vinegar
1 tablespoon honey
Sour cream for garnish

**Difficulty level: Moderate**

**Wine pairing:**
Pinot gris, dry rosé, dolcetto, or chilled vodka

Family recipes are the best recipes, and this particular one was given to me by my Russian friend, Boris, whose family has enjoyed this soup for many generations. The reason why generational recipes excel is because they have been refined over time, with small mistakes being corrected and flavor intricacies becoming fully developed. I have experimented with numerous borscht recipes, but *this* one stands out for its delicate nature, perfect balance of ingredients, and exquisite taste. Notably, the technique described in step 2, the gentle sweating of the vegetables, ensures that they soften and release their flavors, further enhancing the overall brilliance of this recipe.

# SMOKED TROUT CHOWDER

**Prep time**
15 min.

**Actual time**
45 min.

**Serves**
4

### Ingredients

1 tablespoon butter

3 ribs of celery, chopped

3 large leeks, only the white part, chopped

2 filets of smoked trout, skin removed and flaked

2 cloves garlic, minced

2 potatoes, peeled and cut into ½ inch pieces

¼ to ½ cup white wine

4 cups chicken broth

1 teaspoon fresh thyme leaves

1 bay leaf

1 ¼ teaspoon salt

10 grinds freshly ground white pepper

1 cup heavy cream

**Difficulty level: Moderate**

**Wine pairing**

A fruity chardonnay from Napa or Sonoma Valley, an albarino, or a white pinot noir

### Step 1

In a large stock pot, heat butter over low heat. Add leeks, celery, garlic, and ¼ teaspoon salt, stirring occasionally until vegetables start to soften, about 10 minutes.

### Step 2

Turn heat up to medium, add potatoes, wine, broth, thyme, and bay leaf. Bring to a boil, reduce heat, and simmer partially covered until potatoes are tender, about 15 minutes.

### Step 3

Stir in the cream and cook over medium heat until the soup starts to thicken, 2 to 3 minutes. Add the white pepper. Taste and adjust if needed. Stir in the smoked trout. Cook another minute or two so the trout gets heated and impart its flavor into the soup.

Serve in heated soup bowls.

> "COOKING REQUIRES CONFIDENT GUESSWORK AND IMPROVISATION—EXPERIMENTATION AND SUBSTITUTION, DEALING WITH FAILURE AND UNCERTAINTY IN A CREATIVE WAY."
> — PAUL THEROUX

This recipe is born from the conundrum of having a craving for clam chowder but no clams in the pantry. Going out on a limb, I decided to use smoked trout in the traditional recipe. To my pleasant surprise, the outcome exceeded my expectations. This experience exemplifies the kind of kitchen experimentation I encourage you to try whenever you can; the trope of necessity being the mother of invention is all the more true when applied to culinary creations such as this. The subtle smokiness of the trout pairs wonderfully with the creamy broth, resulting in a comforting and flavorful soup.

On a crisp winter's day, when the chill in the air sends shivers down your spine, there's nothing quite like the comforting embrace of a homemade, hearty stew. Its tantalizing aroma envelops your kitchen, filling it with warmth and inviting you to escape the frosty world outside. One such day, my dear friend Maggie shared with me this tried and true recipe. Every spoonful of her stew was a taste of pure delight, as it brought forth *all* the elements of a cozy gathering with cherished companions—laughter, heartfelt conversations, and a genuine sense of friendship.

# PORTUGUESE STEW WITH LINGUIÇA SAUSAGE AND KALE

| Prep time | Actual time | Serves |
|---|---|---|
| 20 min. | 1 hr., 10 min. | 6-8 |

### Ingredients
1 can (20 ounces) garbanzo beans
2 tablespoons olive oil
1 pound spicy linguiça or spicy Italian sausage
1 large yellow onion, cut in half and sliced into ¼ inch thick pieces
2 cups chicken stock
1 green or red bell pepper, deseeded, de-ribbed, cut in half lengthwise, and then into crosswise strips, ¼ inch thick
2 cups peeled butternut squash, in 1 inch pieces
1 can whole tomatoes in purée; strain the purée and chop the tomatoes into 1 inch pieces
1 tablespoon tomato paste
1 teaspoon dried thyme
1 teaspoon dried oregano
¼ teaspoon ground cayenne
1 bouquet (6 peppercorns, 1 bay leaf, 1 clove sliced garlic, 3 fresh sprigs of parsley—tied together in a piece of cheesecloth)
1 bunch of kale, thick stems removed, and torn into pieces

**Difficulty level: Moderate**
**Wine pairing:**
Alvarinho vinho verde, South African chenin blanc, pinot noir, or a Portuguese red Douro reserva

### Step 1
In a stock pot large enough to hold all ingredients for the stew, warm the olive oil over medium-high heat. Add the sausages and lightly brown on all sides, about 5 minutes. Using tongs, transfer to a dish and cut crosswise into pieces ½ inch thick. Set aside.

### Step 2
Add the onions to the pot and sauté until soft. Add the stock to the pot, scraping the bottom of the pot with a large spoon to get the browned bits up. Return the sausages to the pot, along with the pepper, squash, tomatoes and their juice, tomato paste, thyme, oregano, bouquet, cayenne, garbanzo beans, and kale. Cover and lower heat and gently simmer the stew until the kale is tender and the flavors of the vegetables have developed, about 45 minutes.

Serve with hearty Italian bread.

# PALO ALTO SALAD

**Prep time**: 10 min., plus time to chill
**Serves**: 4
**Difficulty level: Easy**

### Ingredients
6 tablespoons extra virgin olive oil
2 tablespoons white wine vinegar
½ teaspoon salt
1 small garlic clove, minced
1 small head of butter lettuce
2 heads of Boston Bibb lettuce
½ cup endive, cut into ¼ inch strips
2 tablespoons minced fresh parsley
2 tablespoons minced fresh chives
1 tablespoon minced fresh dill
2 teaspoons chopped fresh thyme
1 avocado, cut into cubes right before serving
Toasted sunflower seeds

### Step 1
Add the olive oil, vinegar, salt, and garlic to the bottom of your salad bowl.

### Step 2
Wash and dry all the lettuce. Tear into bite-size pieces and place on top of the dressing. Add the endive. Do not toss. Sprinkle the herbs over the top of the lettuce leaves. Cover the bowl tightly with plastic wrap and chill in the refrigerator until ready to serve.
Just before serving, peel the avocado and add to the greens. Toss, add the sunflower seeds on top, and serve.

Whenever I'm going to dinner at a friend's house, I never want to show up empty handed. I often choose to make this salad because of the ease of preparation and the herbaceous freshness that shines through in every bite. It is a true example of Californian cuisine as I found it in the *Private Collection: Recipes from the Junior League of Palo Alto*. The avocado is often synonymous with California cuisine, which is an essential component of this salad.

# ESCAROLE, GRUYÈRE & WALNUT

**Prep time**: 25 min.
**Serves**: 4
**Difficulty level**: Moderate
**Wine pairing**:
Pinot grigio or dry riesling.

### Ingredients
**Dressing**
1 ½ tablespoons olive oil
1 ½ tablespoons walnut oil
1 ½ tablespoons sherry vinegar
1 shallots, finely minced
Kosher salt and freshly ground black pepper

**Salad**
½ cup walnuts
2 heads escarole, pale hearts only
½ pound gruyère, trimmed of any rind and cut into matchstick-size pieces
¼ cup Italian parsley

### Step 1
Preheat oven to 350 degrees.
Toast the walnuts on a baking sheet until fragrant and lightly colored, about 12 minutes. Cool and break up any large pieces.

### Step 2
Combine the escarole, walnuts, cheese, and parsley in a salad bowl. Add enough dressing to coat the salad lightly so the leaves glisten but are not drenched; you may not need it all. Toss well, season with salt and pepper to taste, and toss again. Serve immediately.

Traditionally in French cuisine, the cheese is served after the main course and before the salad. The salad is typically served at the end of the meal to assist in digestion after the other courses. This recipe exemplifies these quintessential aspects with contemporary twist by combining the salad and cheese course in a seamless fusion. It combines the unexpected pairing of gruyère, escarole, and walnuts, resulting in a simple salad that is absolutely delicious.

During my teenage years, I loved preparing this delectable salad for my family at lunchtime. A discovery from a Sunset Cookbook dating back to the 1950s, this particular recipe captured my attention immediately.

The unique combination of crisp water chestnuts, sweet grapes, and fruity lychee, paired with the savory curry dressing, results in the perfect lunch. It is worth noting that this salad is best savored on the day of its creation, ensuring optimal freshness and taste.

# EXOTIC CURRY CHICKEN SALAD

**Prep time** 20 min.

**Actual time** 30 min. 1 hr. to chill

**Serves** 4–6

### Ingredients

**Salad**

2 pounds poached turkey or chicken, cut into 1-inch chunks; this can be done the day before making the salad

1 can water chestnuts, drained and sliced thin

1 pound green grapes, stems removed and cut in half

2 cups sliced celery, soaked in ice water for 30 minutes

1 can lychee nuts (this can be omitted if too difficult to find)

2 ½ cups roasted, slivered almonds

2 heads butter lettuce

**Poached chicken breast**

4 cups cold water

One bunch of herbs, your choice

2 boneless, skinless chicken breasts

1 teaspoon kosher salt

**Dressing**

2 cups homemade mayonnaise (see page 295) (store bought works also)

2 to 3 tablespoon Madras curry powder (or other curry powders)

1 tablespoon soy sauce

2 teaspoons fresh lime juice

2 tablespoons fresh lemon juice

1 to 1 ½ tablespoons Major Grey chutney

1 teaspoon sugar

**Difficulty Level: Moderate**

**Wine pairing:** If you are a red wine lover, try a pinot noir. For a white wine option, try a German riesling or a French Vouvray.

### For the poached chicken breasts

In a large saucepan, add cold water, bunch of herbs, salt, and chicken breasts. Turn heat to medium and bring the water to a gentle boil. As soon as the surface of the water starts to roll, flip the breasts over with tongs, and remove the pot from heat and cover with a tight-fitting lid. The breasts will continue to cook gently in hot water.

Once the breasts register an internal temperature of 150 degrees, remove them from the water to cool. This will take 5 to 10 minutes. Remember, it will depend on the size of the breast; smaller will cook faster than a larger breast, so check intermittently. Let rest for at least 5 minutes.

### For the dressing

**Step 1**

In a medium bowl whisk together the mayonnaise, curry powder, soy sauce, chutney, and lemon juice. Add salt and pepper, taste and adjust if needed.

**Step 2**

Drain the celery and pat dry. Soaking in cold water then drying makes them nice and crispy.

Add the chicken, water chestnuts, grapes, celery, and lychee nuts in a large bowl. Gently toss until well incorporated and chill for at least an hour so the flavors can mingle.

When ready to serve, make a bowl of the lettuce leaves on your serving plate. Top with the curry chicken salad and sprinkle with the almonds.

49

# OLD FASHIONED COLESLAW

| **Prep time** | **Actual time** | **Serves** |
|---|---|---|
| 10 min. | 50 min. | 6-8 |

### Step 1
In a small saucepan over medium heat, whisk together the egg yolk, vinegar, mustard, salt, pepper, cayenne, sugar, and flour. Add the water and continue to whisk. Bring the mixture to a boil and let simmer for a few minutes until it thickens, 6 to 8 minutes. Take the saucepan off the heat and stir in the cream until blended. Taste and adjust seasoning if needed. Sometimes I add more mustard. Let cool to room temperature.

### Step 2
In a serving bowl, combine the cabbage, carrot, scallions, and herbs. Toss with the dressing. Let it sit for 30 minutes to allow the flavors to mingle together before serving.

## Ingredients
### Dressing
1 egg yolk
¼ cup apple cider vinegar
½ to 1 teaspoon English-style dry mustard (I like to use Colemans)
½ teaspoon salt
½ teaspoon freshly ground white pepper
Pinch cayenne
2 tablespoons sugar
1 tablespoon flour
¼ cup water
2 tablespoons cream

### Slaw
6 cups shredded cabbage (you can use red and green)
½ cup shredded carrots
½ cup finely sliced scallions
1 tablespoon minced fresh dill
1 tablespoon finely minced fresh parsley
½ tablespoon minced fresh tarragon

**Difficulty level: Moderate**

I love old recipes, as they have stood the test of time. This particular recipe dates back to the 1940s. Coleslaw originates from the Dutch term *koolsla* meaning *cabbage salad*. It's heartwarming to think of the numerous families who have gathered around the dinner table or enjoyed sunny day picnics with this scrumptious and uncomplicated side dish as a part of their shared memories. Over the course of my career, I have served this coleslaw hundreds of times, always receiving rave reviews.

# TOMATO AND MANGO SALAD

**Prep time**
15 min.

**Actual time**
20 min.

**Serves**
4-6

### Ingredients
1 ½ tablespoons fresh lemon juice
1 teaspoon curry powder
½ teaspoon kosher salt
2 pinches sugar
3 tablespoons extra virgin olive oil
2 pounds fresh ripe tomatoes, cored and cut into ¾ inch wedges
2 mangos, peeled, pitted, and cut into ½ inch strips
½ cup pistachio, shelled and roasted
10 basil leaves (I like to use purple basil when I can find it)

**Difficulty level: Easy**

### Step 1
Whisk together the lemon juice, curry powder, salt, and sugar. Slowly whisk in olive oil until emulsified.

To serve, place tomato wedges and mango strips on a serving platter. Drizzle with the dressing. Top with basil and pistachios.

> "COOKING IS LIKE PAINTING OR WRITING A SONG. JUST AS THERE ARE ONLY SO MANY NO[TES] OR COLORS, THERE ARE ONLY SO MANY FLAVORS—IT'S HOW YOU COMBINE TH[EM] THAT SETS YOU APART."
> — WOLFGANG PUCK

This refreshing, one-step salad is perfect for hot summer days when the tomato harvest is in full swing. Its vibrant colors are reminiscent of a beautiful summertime sunset when everything feels content and right with the world. **Its sweetness and acidity complements curry dishes splendidly.** Be sure to use the freshest tomatoes available for ideal flavors. For presentation, it is recommended to serve it on a large platter rather than individual servings.

# HERBED EGG RIBBONS AND CRAB

**Prep time:** 40 min.
**Actual time:** 50 min.
**Serves:** 4

## Ingredients

**For the pasta**
- Olive oil spray
- 8 eggs
- ¼ cup chopped Italian parsley
- 2 teaspoons minced fresh basil
- 2 teaspoons minced fresh thyme
- 1 teaspoon kosher salt, more to taste
- 2 teaspoons fresh lemon juice
- 4 teaspoons extra virgin olive oil
- 1 cup lump crab meat, without shells

**For the salsa**
- 5 small blood oranges, peeled, sections cut from the membrane (you can use regular oranges)
- 1 small red or yellow bell pepper, cored, seeded, and diced small
- 1 small jalapeño, seeded and minced
- 1 tablespoon fresh lime juice

**For the slaw**
- 3 tablespoons whole-fat yogurt
- 2 teaspoons Dijon mustard
- ¼ teaspoon kosher salt
- 15 grinds freshly ground white pepper
- ½ teaspoon cracked coriander seed
- 4 cups shredded iceberg lettuce

**Difficulty level: Difficult**
**Wine pairing:**
Chablis, chardonnay, or a dry riesling

## For the pasta
### Step 1
To make the pasta, spray a non-stick skillet with olive oil and place on low heat. Whisk the herbs, eggs, salt, and pepper until well incorporated. Pour enough mixture into the skillet to thinly cover the bottom and move around the egg to coat the pan evenly. Cook until the top has set, about 3 minutes. Slide the omelet onto a large plate, invert it back into the pan and cook the other side for about 20 seconds. This is a tricky process so don't get discouraged if your eggs don't come out perfectly flat; you will be slicing them later on anyway. Slide onto a large piece of parchment paper. Repeat with the remaining mixture.

### Step 2
Once they've cooled, slice the omelets into very thin strips. Place in a bowl and toss with 2 teaspoons lemon juice, olive oil, crab meat, salt and pepper to taste. Taste and adjust if needed.

## For the salsa
### Step 3
To make the salsa, toss all ingredients together in a medium bowl. Set aside.

## For the slaw
### Step 4
To make the slaw, whisk together the yogurt, mustard, salt, pepper, and coriander. Toss with the lettuce until well incorporated.

To serve, mound the egg pasta in the center of 4 plates. Make a ring around the pasta with the slaw. Place 3 spoonfuls of the salsa around the slaw. Drizzle with extra virgin olive oil.

Eggs are an incredibly versatile ingredient. One particularly unusual approach I've discovered is adding egg ribbons to a salad, which has been met with praise and curiosity whenever I've served it. In this recipe, the egg ribbons almost resemble a pasta, and when added to crab, creates a creamy and rich blend that complements the crunch of the fresh slaw and spicy citrus salsa marvelously.

This salad recipe is truly unique. The velvety texture of the goat cheese soufflé perfectly complements the bitter greens, while the tangy shallots vinaigrette adds an extra layer of flavor. I never tire of preparing this dish for dinner parties, as it is always met with rave reviews from my guests. It makes the perfect dish for an aesthetically-pleasing first course or a satisfying lunch.

# BITTER GREENS GOAT CHEESE SOUFFLÉ

**Prep time:** 30 min.

**Actual time:** 1 hr 10 min.

**Serves:** 6 to 8, depending on the size of the soufflé dish

## Ingredients

**For the soufflés**

¼ cup plus 3 tablespoons freshly grated Parmesan cheese

1 11-ounce log of mild fresh goat cheese, such as Montrachet

¾ cup milk

2 tablespoons unsalted butter

3 tablespoons all-purpose flour

1 teaspoon, kosher salt

10 grinds freshly ground pepper

Pinch nutmeg

Pinch cayenne

3 egg yolks

6 egg whites

3 tablespoons chopped mixed fresh herbs, such as chives, tarragon, thyme, and parsley

Boiling water for water bath

**Salad**

4 Belgian endives

1 head of frisée

1 small head of escarole

1 small head of radicchio

**For the vinaigrette**

¼ cup minced shallots

¼ cup sherry vinegar

2 teaspoons dry mustard

¾ teaspoon freshly ground black pepper

½ teaspoon kosher salt

Pinch sugar

¾ cup extra virgin olive oil

¾ cup vegetable oil (I use avocado oil)

### Step 1

Start soaking the shallots before making the soufflés (that way, your timing will work out for the salad). To do this, combine shallots and sherry vinegar. Set aside, Set aside.

### Make the soufflés

Preheat oven to 350 degrees. Generously butter your ramekins and sprinkle with a little parmesan in each ramekin; tilt to coat all sides of the ramekin.

### Step 2

Cut ⅓ of the goat cheese log into even pieces, about ¼ inch thick. One slice per ramekin. You will add this to the soufflés before baking. Crumble the remainder of the log and set it aside.

### Step 3

Bring the milk to a boil in a small saucepan or microwave it. Meanwhile, in a medium saucepan, melt the butter over medium heat. Add the flour and cook for 2 to 3 minutes, stirring constantly. Pour in boiling milk and whisk vigorously until smooth and thickened. Remove the pan from heat and mix the crumbled goat cheese and the remaining ¼ cup of Parmesan cheese, salt, pepper, nutmeg, and cayenne into the base of the soufflé. Let it cool for 10 minutes.

### Step 4

Place the egg yolks in a medium bowl. Stir in a few tablespoons of the warm soufflés base until blended. With a large spatula, gently fold in the remaining base. Stir in the fresh herbs.

### Step 5

In a medium bowl, beat the egg whites with a pinch of salt until stiff peaks form. Gently stir ⅓ of the beaten egg whites into the base to lighten it. Gently fold in the remaining whites until just incorporated.

### Step 6

Spoon 2 tablespoons of the soufflé mixture into each prepared ramekin and top with the reserved slice of goat cheese. Fill the rest of the remaining soufflé mixture and place them in a baking dish big enough to accommodate all the ramekins ½ inch apart. Pour enough boiling water to reach ½ way up the ramekins.

### Step 7
Bake the soufflés for about 40 to 50 minutes, or until they are browned on top and beginning to shrink away from the sides of the ramekins. Remove from the oven. Remove the ramekins from the water bath and let cool on a rack for about 15 minutes.

**Note:** The soufflés can be made up to 4 hours ahead. Simply set aside at room temperature and reheated in a 325-degree oven for 7 minutes.

### Step 8
While the soufflés are baking, make the dressing and prepare the salad greens.

### Step 1
After steeping the shallots, add the dry mustard, salt, pepper, and sugar. Slowly whisk in oils to emulsify.

### Step 2
Wash and dry all greens and tear into bite-sized pieces. Toss with enough dressing to coat the leaves until they glisten, but are not drenched.

To serve, unmold the soufflés onto a salad plate. Surround with the salad and drizzle a little of the vinaigrette on top of the soufflés.

**Difficulty level: Difficult**
**Wine pairing:**
Sancerre, a Pouilly-Fumé, or dry riesling

# SMOKED TROUT WITH APPLES, AND BLACK TRUFFLE VINAIGRETTE

**Prep time:** 20 min.

**Actual time:** 25 min.

**Serves:** 4

### Step 1
Peel and cut up the apples into bite-sized pieces.

In a large bowl, fold together the apples, crème fraîche, celery, horseradish, parsley, thyme, salt, and pepper. Set aside.

### Step 2
**For the vinaigrette**

In a small bowl, mix together the mustard, vinegar, thyme, sugar, salt, and pepper. Slowly whisk in the truffle oil to emulsify.

### Step 3
Toss the greens with the vinaigrette until the leaves glisten, but are not drenched.

On a chilled salad plate or large platter (if you are not doing individual servings), place a mound of dressed greens. Place apple salad in the center and top with the flaked smoked trout.

### Ingredients
- 3 unpeeled, firm apples like Gala, Cortland, or Northern Sky
- ½ cup crème fraîche
- ½ cup thinly sliced celery, plus a few leaves, soaked in cold water for 30 minutes then drained
- 2 tablespoons prepared white horseradish, drained
- 2 tablespoons minced flat leaf parsley
- 1 teaspoon fresh thyme leaves, removed from stem
- ½ teaspoon of kosher salt
- 15 grinds freshly ground black pepper
- 3 cups watercress, 2 bunches stemmed
- 3 cups baby arugula
- 3 cups Boston lettuce
- 2 smoked trout, bones & skin removed

### Black truffle vinaigrette
- 2 teaspoons Dijon mustard
- 2 tablespoons white wine vinegar
- 1 teaspoon kosher salt
- 8 grinds freshly ground black pepper
- 1 teaspoon sugar
- 1 teaspoon thyme
- 6 tablespoons black truffle oil (use a quality brand such as Spécialités D'Huile); buy in small quantities since their aroma and flavor start to dissipate once opened

### Wine pairing:
A California chardonnay, such as Robert Young, a dry rosé, or a Pouilly-Fumé

60

This salad is a wonderful choice for the fall season, when apples are at their prime. I like to incorporate 2 to 3 different types of apples into this recipe to create a nuanced combination of flavors, adding crunch to every bite. This salad is substantial enough to be enjoyed as a main course, especially when accompanied by a warming soup. What makes it even better is the truffle vinaigrette, which is a personal favorite of mine. This versatile dressing can be used to elevate other green salads.

When a chef discovers an ingredient that captivates their senses, it often marks the beginning of a lifelong love affair. For me, chestnuts are precisely one of those ingredients. I eagerly await their arrival every winter, knowing that their presence will spark my culinary creativity throughout the year. The inspiration behind this dish emerged from the pages of a British magazine, and I added a personal touch with the additions of cheese and prosciutto to create an additional layer of salty complexity. Radicchio Salad with Chestnuts, Thyme, and Prosciutto is versatile and can be enjoyed as a quick lunch or a delightful first course.

> "COOKING IS LIKE LOVE.
> IT SHOULD BE ENTERED
> INTO WITH ABANDON
> OR NOT AT ALL."
> — HARRIET VAN HORNE

# RADICCHIO SALAD WITH CHESTNUTS, AND PROSCUTTO

**Prep time**
15 min.

**Actual time**
30 min.

**Serves**
4

### Ingredient
1 cup extra virgin olive oil
10 sprigs fresh thyme leaves, removed from the stem
15 cooked French chestnuts
1 head Castelfranco or radicchio
½ cup high quality ricotta
8 slices prosciutto
2 teaspoons high quality aged balsamic vinegar
10 thin slices of manchego cheese (to slice, I use a small Japanese mandoline)

### For the vinaigrette
¼ cup Champagne or chardonnay vinegar
1 tablespoon sherry vinegar
2 tablespoons finely minced shallots
2 teaspoons honey or maple syrup
10 grinds freshly ground white pepper
Kosher salt
¾ cup of the olive oil you poached the chestnuts in

**Difficulty level:** Moderate
**Wine pairing:** Mourvèdre or syrah

### Step 1
Over low heat, warm the olive oil in a small saucepan, then add half of the thyme leaves. The oil should be just warm to the touch. Add the chestnuts, cover with a lid and leave to poach and soften over low heat for a few minutes. Taste one; if it is dry and starchy, they need to poach a little longer. When they are soft and creamy, they are done. Set aside and strain the olive oil to use for the vinaigrette.

### Step 2
Cut the core off the radicchio, allowing you to separate the leaves. Wash and set aside to dry; cover with a paper towel until you are ready to use them.

### Step 3
In a medium-sized bowl, combine the vinegar and shallots, then add 1 teaspoon salt. Mix well and let marinate for at least 15 minutes.

### Step 4
Mix the honey or maple syrup with a whisk, and slowly add the olive oil to emulsify. You will probably have leftover vinaigrette. I strain out the shallots if I am going to save it for later.

### Step 5
To assemble, arrange the ricotta on four plates or one large platter. In a salad bowl, toss the radicchio with enough of the dressing to coat the leaves lightly. Add salt and pepper to taste. You don't want them to be too acidic; the chestnuts and prosciutto must shine through. Arrange the leaves on the ricotta, then place the chestnuts in and around the leaves. Add the prosciutto and drizzle the balsamic over the whole salad. Add a bit of salt and white pepper, and sprinkle with the rest of the thyme leaves. Top with slices of manchego.

# RADICCHIO, ORANGES, AND CHARRED GRILLED ONION

| Prep time | Actual time | Serves |
|---|---|---|
| 30 min. | 1 hr. | 4 |

### Ingredients

4 medium oranges (if you can find them, I like to use Cara Cara oranges)

2 teaspoons sherry vinegar

3 tablespoons extra virgin olive oil, divided

¼ teaspoon sea salt

10 grinds freshly ground white pepper

1 large head Ricicchio, washed and cored, cut in half and cut into thin slices.

1 medium red onion, ½ inch slices separated

¼ cup roasted pistachios

Pinch sugar

**Difficulty level: Moderate**

### Step 1

Preheat oven to 450 degrees.

Create eight 2 by ½ inch strips of zest from the oranges with a vegetable peeler, leaving the bitter white pith. Cut the zest into tiny slivers with a small knife and set it aside. Slice off the top and bottom of the orange, then cut away the remaining pith with a paring knife. Holding the oranges over a bowl, cut between the membranes to release the orange sections and set aside for salad. Squeeze the remaining membranes over the bowl with your hands to collect the rest of the juice.

### Step 2

To make the dressing, strain the orange juice into a small bowl. Whisk in the vinegar, salt, sugar, and pepper. Continue whisking in 1 tablespoon olive oil until well emulsified, taste and adjust if needed.

### Step 3

In a medium bowl, toss the radicchio with ½ the dressing. Separately, toss the orange sections with the other half of the dressing.

### Step 4

Place the onions on a baking sheet and brush with remaining oil. Add salt and pepper to taste. Place in the oven and bake until almost soft.

### Step 5

Set the broiler to medium heat. Place onions on the middle rack and broil until charred, about 2 minutes.

On a platter, layer the radicchio, oranges, and then onions (in that order). Sprinkle with pistachios and orange slivers.

Serve.

I love when bitterness meets sweetness. During the chilly winter months, when fresh flavors are scarce, this aesthetically-pleasing dish emerges as a true gem, offering not only a burst of freshness but also a comforting warmth. The bitterness of the radicchio and the acidic tanginess from the oranges is complemented wonderfully by the mellow sweetness of the charred onions. I am consistently awestruck by the transformation that occurs when heat and time work their magic on ingredients, with the red onion serving as a prime example of this culinary alchemy.

During my journey of catering, I often looked for recipes I could easily use for varied events. Creating a dish fit for catering requires a few important characteristics to be met; notably its ability to withstand travel, preserve its integrity over hours, and above all, tantalize the taste buds. This recipe effortlessly fulfills all those criteria. With its medley of vegetables, readily available year-round, it boasts the versatility to serve as a hearty side dish, perfect for adding festive flair to the holiday season or a potluck with friends.

# MARINATED VEGETABLE SALAD

**Prep time** 10 min.

**Actual time** 20 min.

**Serves** 6

### Ingredients

1 large bunch of broccoli, trimmed and separated into small florets

1 large head of cauliflower, trimmed and separated into small florets

3 medium-sized carrots, peeled and sliced into ¼ inch rounds

1 10-ounce package frozen edamame

1 10-ounce package frozen peas

¾ cup Dijon mustard

¾ cup sour cream

¾ cup homemade mayonnaise (see page 295)

2 teaspoons celery seeds

2 tablespoons minced fresh tarragon leaves

½ cup minced fresh Italian parsley

**Difficulty level: Moderate**

### Step 1
In a large bowl, add ice and water for a water bath. Bring a large pan of salted water to a boil. Drop the broccoli into the boiling water and bring the water back to a boil. Blanch for 2 minutes. Lift broccoli from the water with a slotted spoon. Drop into the ice water bath. This process stops the vegetable from overcooking.

### Step 2
Drop the cauliflower into the boiling water and blanch for 2 minutes; lift it from the boiling water and put it into the ice water bath. Repeat with the carrots and blanche for 1 minute. Do the same with the peas and edamame for 1 minute. Dry all the vegetables thoroughly on a towel. This is very important, otherwise the vegetables get soggy.

### Step 3
Whisk the remaining ingredients together in a small bowl. Toss with the vegetables gently but thoroughly. Chill for at least an hour or overnight.
To serve, place on a platter and take to a gathering.

# OPEN-FACED CRAB SANDWICHES

**Prep time**
10 min., plus marinating time

**Actual time**
20 min.

**Serves**
2

### Ingredients

6 ounces fresh-cooked king crab or Dungeness crab, picked over and flaked

¼ cup lemon juice

6 ounces cream cheese, at room temperature

¼ cup mayonnaise (preferably homemade)

¼ cup heavy cream

1 tablespoon grated onion

1 garlic clove, minced

2 teaspoons snipped chives

1/4 teaspoon for Worcestershire

A few drops of Tabasco

Sea salt and freshly ground white pepper

2 English muffins, separated

**Difficulty level: Easy**

**Wine pairing:** chardonnay, roussanne, or Chablis

### Step 1

In a medium size bowl, marinate the crab in the lemon juice for about 1 hour.

In another medium bowl, cream together the cream cheese, heavy cream, and mayonnaise. Stir in the grated onion, garlic, and chives.

Drain the crab meat and add to the cream cheese mixture. Add the Worcestershire, Tabasco, and salt and pepper to taste. Adjust if needed.

### Step 2

Set the oven to high broil.

Toast the English muffins until golden. Put the crab mixture on the English muffin, piling a little high. Broil until bubbly and the tops turn golden brown.

Serve.

I have worked as a chef in various settings throughout the years, and some of my most cherished memories revolve around the restaurant I once owned in Santa Fe. One dish that holds a special place in my heart is this recipe from our lunch menu, which was incredibly popular then and continues to be a favorite now whenever I prepare it for others. In fact, it garnered significant attention and praise, earning its own spotlight as the most sought-after item at La Querencia. In December 1979, *Gourmet* magazine even featured it in their "You Asked For It" section. This crab sandwich is simple, nostalgic, and truly satisfying. I sincerely hope you find as much joy in it as I do.

# PROVENÇAL STUFFED SANDWICH LOAF

| Prep time | Actual time | Serves |
|---|---|---|
| 40 min. | Overnight to sit | 4 |

### Ingredients

1 cup chopped Kalamata olives

4 roasted red peppers, minced (you can use jarred ones or fresh ones you have roasted)

1 pint cherry tomatoes, seeded and chopped

6 scallions, minced

3 tablespoons minced capers

⅓ cup minced fresh parsley

1 cup watercress

1 loaf Italian or French bread, preferably a batard

### Dressing

1 cup parsley leaves

½ to 1 cup fresh basil

⅓ cup watercress

1 clove garlic, crushed

3 tablespoons lemon juice

4 anchovies, rinsed and patted dry

½ cup extra virgin olive oil

Reserved breadcrumbs

**Difficulty level: Moderate**
**Wine pairing:**
A rosé from Provence or a French pinot noir

### For the loaf filling

**Step 1**
In a medium bowl, combine the olives, red peppers, scallions, tomatoes, anchovies, capers, parsley, and watercress. Add salt and pepper to taste and adjust if needed.

**Step 2**
Remove the soft interior of your bread, leaving a 1/4 inch thick shell of the loaf. Set aside the crumbs for the dressing.

**Step 3**
To make the dressing, combine all the dressing ingredients in a food processor and blend. Taste and adjust if needed.

**Step 4**
Spread half the dressing on each half of the hollowed-out bread. This coats the bread; creating a barrier so the bread doesn't get too soggy.

**Step 5**
Fill the half loaves with the filling. Put the two halves back together, wrap tightly with tin foil and refrigerate overnight.

Take out of the refrigerator for an hour or so to bring to room temperature before serving. Cut into 2 inch thick slices and serve.

Another way of serving is to add a layer of provolone cheese on each half before wrapping it in tin foil. You can heat it up in an oven at 350 degrees for 30 minutes. The cheese will be melted and it will be warm and delicious.

This sandwich is the perfect option for a picnic lunch. When I used to live in California, my family and I would frequently spend our days on the coast, enjoying meals together while relishing in the delights of nature. I've found that this dish is best when made the night before so all the flavors can blend together. This sandwich is not only incredibly simple to prepare, it is also pleasing to the eye.

# FAVORITE ENTERTAINING

Little Bites, Drinks, and Entertaining

# ROQUEFORT GRAPES WITH PISTACHIOS

| Prep time | Actual time | Serves |
| --- | --- | --- |
| 30 min. | 3 hrs. | 20 grapes |

### Step 1
Add the cream cheese and Roquefort cheese to a bowl and mix until creamy and well blended. You can use a food processor or an electric mixer.

Cover the bowl with plastic wrap and chill for at least 2 hours in the refrigerator; you want the mixture to be firm. If the mixture is loose, add more cream cheese and chill again.

### Step 2
In a food processor, finely chop the nuts by pulsing the machine a few times. You want them fine enough to adhere to the grapes.

Remove the grapes from the refrigerator. Remove the stems from the grapes.

### Step 3
Take the cheese mixture out of the refrigerator and wet your hands. Put enough of the cheese mixture in your palm to cover the grape. Wrap the cheese all around the grape and put it on a plate. Return to the refrigerator to chill for at least 30 minutes. After the final chill, take out and roll in the ground nuts to cover.

Chill until ready to serve.

## Ingredients
- ½ pound Roquefort cheese, or you can use any variety of blue cheese or gorgonzola cheese
- ½ pound cream cheese
- ¼ pound pistachios, or you can use roasted pecans
- 1 bunch seedless green grapes, chilled

**Difficulty level: Difficult**

**Wine pairing:**
Sancerre or Champagne

When it's hot out and you are entertaining or wanting a snack on hand, these pretty little bites of cheese and sweetness deliver a refreshing moment. I often serve them on a plate covered with rose petals, as it adds a bit of color.

# PICKLED CELERY, APPLE & CELERY ROOT SALAD WITH ENDIVE

**Prep time** 20 min.

**Actual time** 10 min.

**Serves** Approximately 20

### Step 1
Heat the vinegar, sugar, fennel, and bay leaf in a small saucepan over medium heat until the sugar is dissolved. Taste and adjust if needed. If too acidic, add more sugar or honey.

### Step 2
Place the celery in a bowl and pour the liquid over the celery. Allow to pickle, stirring occasionally. Set aside while you make the salad.

### For the salad
### Step 1
In a small bowl, mix together mustard, pickling juice, salt, and pepper. Add the olive oil, slowly whisking until emulsified. In another bowl, add the apple, celery root, some of the pickled celery, and the dressing. Taste and adjust seasoning if needed. Fold in the blue cheese.

One way of serving is to put salad in an endive leaf and top with a bit of blue cheese as a little bite. Another way is to serve on a bed of thinly sliced endive, top with the salad, and sprinkle with the hemp seeds.

### Ingredients
**For the pickled celery**

¼ cup sherry vinegar

2 tablespoons sugar or honey

1 bay leaf

1 teaspoon fennel seed

2 to 4 celery sticks, sliced thin

**For the salad**

½ of a celery root, peeled and diced small

¾ cup apples, peeled and cut into same size as the celery root

2 tablespoons pickled celery

3 tablespoons fresh lemon juice

3 tablespoons extra virgin olive oil

1 tablespoons of the pickling liquid

1 tablespoon Dijon mustard

Salt to taste

8 to 10 grinds freshly ground white pepper

½ cup of a high-quality blue cheese (I like Bleu d'Auvergne or Saint Agur)

2 endive

1 to 2 tablespoons hemp hearts, for garnish

**Difficulty level: Moderate**

**Wine pairing:** Chablis or an unoaked chardonnay

Achieving a harmonious balance between acidity and savory flavors can prove to be challenging. Within this recipe, the interplay between the pickled celery and apple produces a fusion of taste that traverses the entire palate. This culinary creation is exceptionally suitable for wintertime, as it imparts a vibrant burst of freshness.

# SAGE FRITTERS

**Prep time** 15 min.

**Actual time** 1 hr., 25 min.

### Ingredients
Sage leaves, washed and dried (stems in tact)
2 tablespoons butter
1 cup water
½ cup whole milk
1 cup all-purpose flour
Sea salt
15 grinds freshly black ground pepper
2 large egg whites
Vegetable oil for frying

**Difficulty level: Moderate**

### Step 1
Preheat oven to 270 degrees.

In a medium saucepan, heat water, butter, and milk over low heat until the butter has melted. Mix flour, salt, and pepper in a medium mixing bowl.

### Step 2
Take the water mixture off the heat and slowly add the flour, stirring with a spoon until it is smooth. You can put it in a food processor and add a little water if it gets lumpy. It should be the consistency of pancake batter. Cover and let sit for at least 1 hour before adding the egg whites. You can also leave it in the refrigerator overnight.

Bring the batter to room temperature when ready to prepare the fritters.

### Step 3
In a small bowl, add the egg whites and beat until they are stiff but not dry. Fold the egg whites into the flour mixture.

### Step 4
In a skillet, add oil to 1 inch. Heat oil to around 375 degrees. Dip the leaves into your batter until the leaves are well covered. Add to the oil; do not crowd the leaves, so you have room to turn them easily. Cook until they are golden brown, turning once. Remove them with a slotted spoon onto paper towels to drain.

Sprinkle with sea salt before serving.

You can keep them warm in the oven for up to 15 minutes.

This recipe creates a wonderful little bite out of an overlooked and underutilized herb: sage. When we think of herbs, we often think of them as an addition to a dish, but this recipe makes sage the focus of an aromatic and light first bite. The batter is airy and compliments not only sage, but other leaves and flowers such as parsley leaves, nasturtium flowers, or squash blossoms.

# RETRO CHEESE PUFFS

| Prep time | Actual time | Serves |
| --- | --- | --- |
| 10 min. | 14 min. | 16 |

### Step 1
Heat oven to 350 degrees.

Remove crusts from the bread and cut them into your desired shape. I like rounds, no bigger than 1 ½ inches.

### Step 2
In a small mixing bowl, mix all ingredients except for the bread.

Lay bread pieces on a sheet pan. Toast in the oven until just golden on one side. Remove from the oven. Let cool. Turn broiler on low. When the bread has cooled, spread the mixture on toasted pieces to about ¼ inch high.

Broil for 3 to 4 minutes until golden brown and bubbly.

Serve warm.

### Ingredients
½ cup mayonnaise or make your own (recipe on page 295)

½ cup high-quality, freshly grated Parmesan cheese

¼ cup finely minced spring onion

1 tablespoon finely minced scallions

Dash cayenne

8 grinds of freshly ground white pepper

A loaf of quality white bread, sliced

**Difficulty level: Easy**

**Wine pairing:**

A full-bodied chardonnay or Champagne

Ranging from social elites to kindergarteners, cheese is universally adored. This delectable creation stems from a cherished family recipe, imparted to me by one of my esteemed clients in Manhattan. It consistently receives resounding acclaim on every occasion she hosts. When seeking a swift and gratifying option, this dish proves exemplary, boasting a preparation time of under 15 minutes. What's not to like about that?

# PHYLLO TRIANGLES WITH GOOSE LIVER MOUSSE AND PISTACHIOS

| Prep time | Actual time | Serves |
|---|---|---|
| 25 min. | 1 hr. | 20 little bites |

### Ingredients
1 cup finely minced cremini mushrooms
2 tablespoons butter
4 tablespoons Mousse Royale au Sauternes
2 tablespoons cognac
2 tablespoons minced chives
¾ cup pistachios, finely minced
1 teaspoon sea salt
15 grinds freshly ground black pepper

### Phyllo pastry
½ pound unsalted butter, melted
⅔ cup extra virgin olive oil

**Difficulty level: Moderate**
**Wine pairing:**
Port, mourvèdre, or a Sancerre for white

### Step 1
Preheat oven to 350 degrees.

In a food processor, add mushrooms and pulse until finely minced. In a medium sized skillet, melt butter over medium heat until the butter starts to bubble, about 2 minutes. Add the minced mushrooms and a dash of salt. Sauté until no liquid remains, about 5 to 8 minutes.

Add the cognac and stir until the cognac reduces completely, about 3 minutes. Remove from the heat and set aside to cool.

### Step 2
Transfer the mushroom mixture to a medium size bowl. When cool, add the mousse, chives, and pistachios. Mix until combined. Add salt and pepper to taste.

### Step 3
**For the phyllo**

Combine the melted butter and olive oil. Prepare your phyllo. Unwrap and lay out on parchment paper. Keep the dough you are not working with covered by a damp towel so it does not dry out.

Cut a strip 2 ½ inches wide. Take off 2 pieces of the phyllo and butter lightly. Add another 2 layers of Phyllo and butter lightly. Do this 3 times, so you have 6 layers of phyllo. At the top corner of the dough, add 1 tablespoon of filling and fold into a triangle like you would fold a flag.

Put on a parchment lined baking sheet.

Bake for 10 to 12 minutes until golden brown.

Serve slightly warm.

Working as a caterer in a large market like New York City creates a lot of pressure to make a name for oneself. Over the years, I joined many culinary associations for networking opportunities. Back in the days before the internet and social media, self-branding largely relied on contests. I learned about a contest sponsored by Les Trois Petits Cochons at the James Beard House. Having previously utilized their products in my recipes and deeply admiring their work, I decided to enter a recipe for a unique bite-sized creation. I was honored to be awarded a place in their catalog of recipes. The celebration at the James Beard House was an evening I will always remember; one filled with great wine and engaging conversations with fellow chefs.

# CORN CAKES WITH SMOKED BLACK COD
*And Lemon Confit Crème Fraîche*

| Prep time | Actual time | Serves |
|---|---|---|
| 30 min. | 1 hr. | 20 little bites |

### Ingredients
2 cups fresh corn kernels, taken off the cob
1 cup finely minced red pepper, deseeded
½ cup finely minced scallions
¼ cup finely minced mixed fresh herbs such as dill, chives, and thyme
1 tablespoon fresh lemon juice
1 teaspoon salt
¼ teaspoon baking powder
1 teaspoon honey or sugar
½ cup heavy cream
3 eggs, separated into separate bowls
½ cup flour
4 to 6 ounces of black cod or smoked salmon, deboned and carefully pulled from the skin, flaked into small pieces
Fresh dill sprigs, for garnish
Extra virgin olive oil

### Lemon confit crème fraîche
1 cup crème fraîche or sour cream
1 ½ tablespoons finely minced lemon from the preserved lemon confit recipe (See recipe page 294)

**Difficulty level:** Moderate

**Wine pairing:** A light, fruity pinot noir, chardonnay, or Soave

### Step 1
In a large bowl, combine corn kernels, red pepper, scallions, herbs, lemon juice, and salt.

### Step 2
In a small bowl, whisk together flour, salt, and baking powder. Set aside.

### Step 3
In a medium bowl, whisk together cream, egg yolks, and honey or sugar.

### Step 4
In a medium bowl with a hand held mixer, beat the egg whites until stiff but not dry. Fold in ¼ of the beaten egg whites into the cream mixture to combine. Fold in the rest of the egg whites. Transfer this mixture into the corn mixture bowl and fold in until incorporated.

### Step 5
Fold in the dry ingredients from step 2 into the corn mixture until well incorporated.

### Step 6
In a 12 inch skillet, preferably cast iron, heat 2 tbsp of oil over medium heat. Drop the batter from a spoon into the skillet. If it will be a little bite, make small cakes, about 1 ½ inch. If it is for a first course, make the cakes about 3 inches. Cook until golden brown and then turn to cook the other side. You might have to keep adjusting the heat to keep the right temperature. These can be made ahead and served warm or at room temperature.

To serve, top corn cakes with some of the flaked cod or smoked salmon, a dollop of the lemon crème fraîche, and a sprig of fresh dill.

It was crucial for me to have recipes that were versatile in terms of serving size. These delectable corn cakes are perfect for serving as a bite-sized starter during a cocktail hour or as a first course in a more formal sit-down setting. While working on the central coast of California, I developed this recipe using smoked black cod due to its availability. However, if you find yourself in a place where black cod is unavailable, smoked salmon serves as an excellent substitute.

OBSERVATIONS FOR SAUCES PG 300 FROM NANETTE
APPX A
APPX A

# SMOKED SALMON TARTARE

**Prep time** 10 min.

**Actual time** 20 min.

**Serves** 2 to 4 depending on serving size

### Ingredients

6 ounces salmon or salmon trout, skinned and trimmed

2 ounces quality smoked salmon (not lox, as it is too salty)

1 tablespoon finely minced red onion

1 tablespoon finely minced cornichons

1 tablespoon finely minced fresh parsley

1 teaspoon finely minced fresh tarragon

1 tablespoon extra virgin olive oil

1 teaspoon fresh lemon juice

½ teaspoon Worcestershire sauce

½ teaspoon Dijon mustard

Two drops of hot sauce (more to taste)

**Difficulty level: Easy**

**Wine pairing:** Gavi di Gavi or a roussanne

### Step 1

Chop the salmon coarsely with a knife and place it in a bowl. Chop the smoked salmon coarsely and add to the bowl. Mix the two together. Be sure to hold back on the smoked salmon at first as the saltiness varies from brand to brand. You can always add more.

### Step 2

Mix the remaining other ingredients in a small bowl until well combined. Stir into the salmon mixture. Taste and adjust seasoning if needed.

Refrigerate until ready to serve.

To serve as a little bite: separate endive leaves and top with the salmon tartare, or place it on a slice of cucumber or a slice of buttered, toasted French baguette.

**To serve as a first course:** put on a chilled salad plate and arrange endive leaves as if they were petals of a flower. In the center of the plate, mound the tartare. Sprinkle with parsley. Drizzle with olive oil.

While I was living in New York, André Soltner was the chef at Lutece. This recipe is an adaptation of one of his signature dishes. The combination of smoked salmon and fresh salmon makes this recipe unique. The aromatics of the smoked salmon creates a delightful marriage between flavor and texture. You can serve this as a little bite before dinner or as a first course with toasted slices of a French baguette.

Before the internet, magazines were a great resource for finding recipes. I have filing cabinets full of clippings from my many years as a chef and food lover; so many such that it is hard to recall where they all came from. But the special ones stick out.

This recipe is one of my favorite sandwiches, which I often used as a little bite when I had my catering business. If you are planning on using this recipe for a little bite, use a small aluminum bread pan; they usually are 6x3. The cumin bread and Thai chicken salad are a perfect flavor match. The chicken salad keeps well and you will have leftover bread. Serve on warmed (not toasted) cumin bread.

# THAI CHICKEN SALAD
## On Cumin Quick Bread

### Ingredients
**Cumin bread**
3 cups all-purpose flour
¼ cup sugar
2 tablespoons double-acting baking powder
4 teaspoons ground cumin seed
2 teaspoons cumin seed, roasted and crushed lightly
½ teaspoon dry mustard
2 teaspoons salt
1 ½ cups milk
⅓ cup vegetable oil (I use a quality olive oil, but you can use grapeseed, safflower, or avocado)

**Chicken salad**
¼ cup fresh lime juice
1 teaspoon salt, to taste
½ teaspoon chili powder
⅓ cup finely chopped fresh cilantro
⅓ cup finely chopped fresh mint leaves
3 ½ teaspoons salt
1 teaspoon ground cumin
1 teaspoon ground coriander
⅓ cup finely chopped shallots
⅓ cup thinly sliced scallions
⅓ cup mayonnaise
2 poached boneless, skinless chicken breasts (about 1 ¼ pounds), cut into ¼ inch cubes; approximately 3 cups (see recipe below)
4 cups water

**Poached chicken breast**
**Ingredients**
4 cups cold water
2 tablespoons cumin seeds
2 Thai chilis
2 boneless, skinless chicken breasts
1 teaspoon kosher salt

**Difficulty level: Moderate**
**Wine pairing:**
A dry riesling or a sparkling white.

| Prep time | Actual time | Serves |
| --- | --- | --- |
| 35 min. | 1 hr., 40 min. | 10 to 15 |

**For the cumin bread**

**Step 1**

Preheat oven to 350 degrees.
Butter a loaf pan or individual 3 x 6 loaf pans well and set aside.

**Step 2**

In a large bowl, stir together flour, sugar, baking powder, ground cumin seed, cumin seed, mustard, and salt.

**Step 3**

In another bowl, whisk together the eggs, milk, and oil. Stir this mixture into the dry ingredients until combined and moist. Pour the batter into the loaf pan.

**Step 4**

If you are using a regular bread pan, bake for 1 hour or until a tester comes out cleanly. If you are using small pans, bake for 40 minutes and test. Place on a wire rack to cool for 15 minutes, then turn out of the pan to cool completely.

**For Poached Chicken Breast**

**Step 1**

In a large saucepan, add cold water, cumin seeds, Thai chilies, salt, and chicken breasts. Turn heat to medium and bring the water to a gentle boil. As soon as the surface of the water starts to roll, flip the breasts over with tongs, and remove the pot from heat and cover with a tight-fitting lid. The breasts will continue to cook gently in hot water.

Once the breasts register an internal temperature of 150 degrees, remove them from the water to cool. This will take 5 to 10 minutes. Remember, it will depend on the size of the breast; smaller will cook faster than a larger breast, so check intermittently. Let rest for at least 5 minutes.

**For chicken salad**

**Step 1**

Dice the poached chicken into ¼ inch squares.

**Nanette's Note:** This method of poaching chicken will result in a tender, moist, and succulent chicken breast. The ratio of water-to-meat is essential. Larger breasts will take longer to cook, and smaller breasts will overcook more quickly. If you want to cook more chicken, add another 2 cups of water per breast. The cold water is critical here because it allows the chicken to cook more gradually than it would if you just put it into boiling water.

**Step 2**

In a large bowl, whisk together the lime juice, salt, chili powder, cumin, coriander, mint, cilantro, and sugar until well combined.

**Step 3**

Stir in the chicken, shallots, and scallions. Fold in the mayonnaise. Taste and adjust if needed. You may make this a day in advance.

To serve, slice cumin bread, top with chicken salad, and garnish with cilantro sprig.

Find the homemade mayonnaise recipe on page 295.

93

# CASHEW SESAME CHICKEN

**Prep time:** 40 min.

**Actual time:** 1 hr., plus marinating time

**Serves** Makes about 36 little bites

### Ingredients
**Marinade for chicken**

1 clove garlic

1 inch piece of fresh ginger, peeled

1 egg

2 tablespoons dry sherry

1 tablespoon lemon or lime juice

1 teaspoon soy sauce

1 to 2 teaspoons ground cumin

1 teaspoon sugar

1 pound boneless, skinless chicken breasts, cut into 1-inch pieces

½ to 1 cup dry roasted cashews

½ cup white sesame seeds

¼ cup cornstarch

**For the sauce**

1 12-ounce jar of apricot jam

1 to 2 teaspoons dry English or Chinese hot mustard, dissolved in 1 tablespoon hot water

1 tablespoon grated lemon rind

1 tablespoon grated lime rind

1 to 2 teaspoons fresh lime juice

Vegetable oil for frying

**Difficulty level: Moderate**

**Wine pairing:**
A French Chablis or a dry riesling

### Step 1
To make the marinade, finely chop garlic and ginger in a food processor for about 10 seconds. Add remaining ingredients and pause until combined, about 4 times. Place the chicken in a zip lock plastic bag. Pour in the marinade. Seal and turn to coat the chicken pieces. Place the bag in a large bowl and marinate at room temperature for 3 hours or overnight in the refrigerator.

### Step 2
Process the cashews in the food processor for about 10 seconds, or until they are finely chopped. Combine with the sesame seeds in a small bowl and set aside.

### Step 3
Put a sieve over a bowl, add chicken, and drain into the bowl. When well drained, transfer chicken to a small bowl and stir in the cornstarch. Let it sit while you make the sauce.

### Step 4
In a food processor, place all of the sauce ingredients and process until smooth, about 15 seconds. Taste and adjust if needed.

### Step 5
In a large skillet, heat 2 inches of vegetable oil to 375 degrees.

Dip the chicken pieces into the cashew-sesame mixture to coat and fry in batches (without crowding the chicken pieces) until golden brown, about 3 minutes per batch. Transfer with a slotted spoon to paper towels to drain.

To serve, place the chicken pieces on toothpicks and put on a serving tray with the sauce in a bowl and a little spoon.

Catering in New York is a dynamic and competitive industry, where chefs must constantly strive to stay fresh and captivating. In this spirit, I decided to modernize our offerings by introducing the concept of *little bites* instead of using the traditional term *hors d'oeuvres.* One standout example of these *little bites* is our flavorful and crispy chicken bites. They provide a comforting and familiar experience, while the addition of apricot mustard sauce adds a sophisticated twist, satisfying all who try it.

# CHICKEN SATAY

**Prep time:** 15 min.

**Actual time:** 40 min., plus overnight for the marinade

**Serves** 20 skewers

### Step 1
Trim chicken of any fat and cut into strips 3 inches long and ¼ inch thick.

In a food processor, combine remaining ingredients, pulsing until the marinade is smooth. In a large zip lock plastic bag, add the chicken and pour the marinade to cover. Marinate overnight.

### For the sauce
### Step 2
In a food processor, combine the peanut butter, sesame oil, garlic, sambal, and sugar, and process until well incorporated. Add the lemon juice and zest, followed by the coconut milk to thin. If the mixture is still thick, add more coconut milk or water. Taste and adjust if needed.

### Step 3
Heat grill or broiler.

Thread a piece of the chicken lengthwise on each skewer. Grill for 2 to 3 minutes on each side until done, basting with the marinade once on each side. If you are broiling the skewers, cook about the same time and baste on each side. Serve while they are warm. Place on a platter with peanut sauce in a bowl with a spoon.

**Ingredients**
Bamboo skewers (soaked on a sheet pan with water for 30 minutes so they will not burn)
1 ½ pounds boneless, skinless chicken breasts
1 tablespoon chopped fresh ginger
1 onion, cut into chunks
3 cloves garlic
1 cup low-sodium soy sauce
1 to 2 teaspoons sambal to taste
Juices of 1 lemon and 1 lime
1 tablespoon sugar
1 teaspoon ground cumin
2 tablespoons sesame oil

**Peanut sauce**
1 cup smooth creamy peanut butter
2 tablespoons dark sesame oil
3 tablespoons soy sauce
1 clove garlic
1 teaspoon sambal
1 tablespoon sugar
Juice of one lemon and rind for zesting
½ cup coconut milk to thin (more if needed)

**Difficulty level: Moderate**
**Wine pairing:**
Gavi di Gavi or pinot gris

These delightful little bites serve as an impeccable start to an Indian or Thai-themed dinner. The savory chicken marinade infuses the morsels with exquisite tenderness, while the creamy peanut sauce flawlessly accompanies their flavors. Together, they create a well-balanced South Asian inspired experience that is sure to impress your guests.

# CARAMELIZED BACON

**Prep time:** 10 min.

**Actual time:** 45 min.

**Serves:** 10, 2' pieces of bacon

### Ingredients
½ cup brown sugar, lightly packed
½ cup chopped or whole pecans
1 teaspoon black pepper
1 teaspoon salt
⅛ teaspoons cayenne pepper
2 tablespoons maple syrup or agave
½ pound thick-cut apple-smoked bacon

**Difficulty level:** Easy

**Wine pairing:** Gamay or cabernet franc

### Step 1
Preheat oven to 375 degrees.
Line a sheet pan with alumin.um foil for easy cleaning (this is a messy process). Place a wire rack on top.

### Step 2
Combine the brown sugar and pecans in a food processor and pulse until the pecans are coarsely ground. Be sure to not over process, as the texture and taste will be off if the mixture is too fine. Add the salt, pepper, and cayenne and pulse until well combined. Add the maple syrup and pulse again to moisten the mixture.

### Step 3
Cut bacon into the desired size. I like them to be 2 inches when I am serving them as a little bite.

### Step 4
With a small spoon, evenly spread the pecan mixture on top of each piece of bacon, using all the mixture. Place bacon on the prepared sheet pan and bake for 25 to 30 minutes, until the topping is browned, but not burned. If it is underbaked, the bacon will not crisp as it cools.

While it's still hot, transfer the bacon to a sheet pan lined with paper towels to cool.

Serve at room temperature.

Dear readers, I must ask you to brace yourselves for what lies ahead. The recipe I present here is so dangerously good, it should really have a Surgeon General's warning with it. With each savored bite, you are lured deeper into a state of addiction, where your taste buds will be overjoyed with flavor and texture. This is the type of recipe that you either praise or curse the day you first try it. Proceed with caution as you approach this tantalizing and habit-forming little bite!

# Golden Spiced Chèvre Cheese

**Prep time:** 15 min.

**Actual time:** Marinate overnight

**Serves:** 6-8

### Ingredients

½ to 1 teaspoon saffron

1 tablespoon hot water

1 teaspoon cumin seed

1 teaspoon black peppercorns

½ teaspoon crushed red pepper

½ cup high-quality extra virgin olive oil

3 cloves garlic, smashed

½ teaspoon kosher salt

11-ounce log of a French chèvre

### Wine pairing:

Chardonnay, sauvignon blanc, or sparkling wine.

**Step 1**

In a small bowl, cover the saffron with 1 tablespoon of hot water. Set aside.

**Step 2**

In a small skillet, combine the cumin, peppercorns, and crushed red pepper. Toast over medium-high heat, shaking the pan until aromatic, about 1 minute. Transfer the spices to a mortar and grind until it is a coarse powder.

**Step 3**

In a small bowl, add olive oil, salt, garlic, and spices. Stir to combine.

**Step 4**

Arrange the cheese on a serving platter. Spoon half of the saffron mixture on top of cheese, turn over and add the remaining saffron mixture on top. Pour over the olive oil mixture and roll the cheese to coat. Let marinate for at least 5 hours, basting the cheese often.

You can refrigerate overnight if you are serving it the next day. Bring to room temperature and baste before serving.

When preparing this dish, don't be surprised if you feel transported to a foreign land. The fragrant, brilliantly colorful combination of saffron, black pepper, and garlic will bring visions of distant marketplaces to your mind and palette. This is a wonderful way to marinate chèvre cheese. I often serve this with crackers or pappadums before an Indian-inspired meal. Everyone who has tasted it wants the recipe. Now, you my dear readers, have it at your fingertips.

# JACQUELINE'S BAKED BRIE WITH CURRY AND CHUTNEY

**Prep time**
10 min.

**Actual time**
25 min.

**Serves**
10-15

### Step 1
Preheat oven to 350 degrees.

Sprinkle curry powder over the top and sides of the brie; rub the curry powder into the rind to thoroughly coat the surface. Place the brie wheel in a large pie plate or oven-proof dish lined with parchment paper. Spread a generous layer of chutney over the top and evenly sprinkle with pecans.

### Step 2
Bake for 10 to 15 minutes in the preheated oven or until the pecans are slightly golden and the cheese inside the rind is melted. Sometimes the rind collapses and the cheese flows out onto the parchment. If that happens, use scissors to cut the parchment away from the cheese after you have moved it to a serving dish.

To serve, transfer to a round serving dish and surround with grapes and slices of baguette.

## Ingredients
1 8-ounce wheel French brie, at room temperature
¼ cup Major Grey chutney
¼ cup chopped roasted pecans
1 to 2 teaspoons of curry powder

**Difficulty level: Easy**

**Wine pairing:**
Pinot noir or Champagne

Generational recipes are a great source of inspiration for me. This one is my mother's recipe, which she passed down to me. Whenever she and her friends gathered to play Mahjong, she would prepare it for them. The fragrant spices of the curry filled the room, captivating everyone's senses. The combination of the curry's spice, the chutney's sweetness, and the creaminess of the brie creates an alluring opening dish for any party.

I frequently carry these delectable accompaniments when attending wine tastings, appreciating the delicate infusion of pepper's gentle warmth and a touch of sweetness that beautifully complements a fine red wine. Moreover, it brings me great pleasure to present these delectable treats on a platter when hosting guests for an evening of wine indulgence, providing them with an exquisite nibble to enhance their overall experience.

OBSERVATIONS FOR BAKING PG 298 FROM NANETTE
APPX B — APPX B

# RED WINE BISCUITS

| **Prep time:** | **Actual time:** | **Yields** |
| 15 min. | 40 min. | 60 biscuits |

### Step 1
Preheat oven to 350 degrees.

### Step 2
Mix together all of the ingredients in an electric mixer until it forms a ball.

Place the ball on a board and divide into quarters. Take each quarter and roll into logs 2 inches in diameter. Wrap in plastic wrap (don't worry if it feels oily at this point). Refrigerate for a few hours.

### Step 3
Take out the dough and cut into ¼ inch slices. Put slices onto a baking sheet and bake for about 25 to 30 minutes until golden brown on the bottom.

Store in an airtight container. These can also be easily frozen to have on hand for the future.

### Ingredients
4 to 4 ½ cups of all-purpose flour
¾ cup sugar
2 teaspoons salt
1 tablespoon baking powder
1 tablespoon coarsely ground black peppercorns
1 cup quality red wine
1 cup vegetable oil

My grandfather was a real-deal cowboy. As a child, I fondly remember visiting his house in Santa Fe during Christmas, where a large punch bowl was always filled with this incredibly delicious nectar for the adult guests to enjoy.

This eggnog recipe has been passed down in my family for three generations, and it has become a cherished Christmas morning tradition that I am thrilled to share. One of the remarkable aspects of eggnog is that its flavor deepens over time, resulting in a wonderfully intricate drinking experience. To really ring in the celebrations, it's a great idea to have ample amounts of this iconic beverage available throughout the holiday season, as it is perfect for both ageing and gifting. Feel free to use any brown liquor of your choice, such as rum, cognac, whiskey, or bourbon.

# SMALLEY FAMILY EGGNOG

**Prep time:** 30 min.
**Actual Time:** 2 days
**Serves:** 16 to 20
**Difficulty level: Moderate**

### Ingredients
12 eggs, separated
1 lb powdered sugar
2 cups Irish whiskey
4 cups bourbon
8 cups heavy cream
6 grates of freshly grated nutmeg for garnish

### Step 1
Separate the egg yolk from the whites. Place whites in a separate bowl, cover, and refrigerate overnight.

### Step 2
In a stand mixer, add egg yolks and beat on medium high setting until light in color. Gradually beat in powdered sugar. Turn speed to low and slowly beat in 2 cups of Irish whiskey. Cover and refrigerate overnight.

### Step 3
Transfer egg yolks, bourbon, and powdered sugar mixture to a large mixing bowl. Slowly whisk in 4 cups bourbon and 8 cups heavy cream until well incorporated. Cover and refrigerate overnight.

### Step 4
Transfer egg whites to a stand mixer bowl, beat by starting on medium and increasing the speed to high, until egg whites are stiff but not dry. Gently fold egg whites into egg yolk mixture until incorporated.
Serve with freshly grated nutmeg in a festive glass.

# FRENCH 75

**Prep time:** 5 min.
**Actual time:** 5 min.
**Serves:** 1
**Difficulty level: Easy**

### Ingredients
1 ounce gin
1/2 ounce lemon juice, freshly squeezed
1/2 ounce simple syrup
3 ounce Champagne

### Step 1
Place gin, simple syrup, and lemon juice in a cocktail shaker over ice. Shake until the metal of the shaker is cold to the touch, about 20 to 30 seconds.

### Step 2
Strain through a tea strainer into a champagne flute. Top with Champagne. Garnish with a lemon peel.

The first time I enjoyed this effervescent delight, I was at the Campbell, an off-the-beaten-path bar located in the majestic Grand Central Station in Midtown Manhattan. The Campbell was originally an opulent apartment of John W. Campbell, a financier who was a member of the New York Central Railroad board of directors. I visited the Campbell in 2007 after the final restoration to return it to original splendor. I ordered this exquisite cocktail, the combination of the bite of the lemon juice and the sweetness of the simple syrup is highlighted by the herbaceous notes of the botanicals in the gin. A perfect cocktail to transport you back in time. It is perfect for any occasion.

# BRUNCH PUNCH

**Prep time**: 5 min.
**Serves**: 1
**Difficulty level: Easy**

**Ingredients**
1 ¼ ounces Cynar
¼ ounce yellow Chartreuse
¼ ounce fresh lemon juice
1 ½ ounce fresh orange juice
2 ounces of sparkling wine or cava

Serve over ice and garnish with a slice of orange. Cheers!

"COME QUICK,
 I AM TASTING STARS."
— DOM PERIGON

Hosting afternoon tea parties for my friends is one of the simple joys in life that I truly enjoy planning for. It gives me an excuse to bring out my collection of fine China teacups and elegant linens, as well as an opportunity to savor delicate sandwiches in the company of those dear to my heart. Such afternoons of pleasure and leisure are a rarity in today's busy world, often only found in tearooms of yesteryear.

Typically, I offer 3 to 4 different types of sandwiches, a selection of 3 teas (including at least one herbal infusion), freshly baked scones, and a variety of jams. An exquisite finishing touch are the Chocolate Truffles on page 282. The options listed here are just some of the many combinations you can serve for such a delightful occasion.

# TEA PARTY SANDWICHES

### CHEDDAR CHUTNEY
**Actual time**: 15 min.
**Serves**: 6 sandwiches

**Ingredients**

½ cup Major Grey Chutney, large pieces minced

½ pound sharp cheddar cheese (preferably white)

½ cup sour cream

3 ounces cream cheese, at room temperature

¼ teaspoon kosher salt

5 to 10 grinds of white pepper

12 thin slices of whole wheat bread

½ cup finely minced cilantro

⅓ cup mayonnaise

**Step 1**

In a bowl, add the chutney, cheddar cheese, cream cheese, salt, and pepper. Using a handheld mixer, beat until well incorporated. Taste and adjust as needed.

**Step 2**

Remove crusts from bread. On 6 slices of bread, spread the chutney mixture evenly, about a ¼ inch thick. Top with another piece of bread and press slightly. With a round 1 ½ inch cookie cutter, cut circles from each sandwich. You will get 3 to 4 rings.

To serve, put the minced cilantro on a small plate, spread the mayonnaise on the edges of each sandwich and roll the edges in cilantro.

Difficulty level: Moderate

## QUEEN ELIZABETH'S SMOKED SALMON

**Actual time:** 20 min.
**Serves**: 4 sandwiches

### Ingredients

8 ounces cream cheese, at room temperature
1 tablespoon finely minced fresh dill
1 tablespoon finely minced chives
Juice of ½ a lemon
¼ teaspoon kosher salt
5 to 10 grinds of black pepper
16 slices of thin white bread, crusts removed (Pepperidge Farm bread is the best if you can find it)
8 ounces smoked salmon
1 English cucumber, peeled and sliced very thin (I use a mandoline for this)

### Step 1

Make the herbed cream cheese
In a medium bowl, using a handheld mixer, beat the cream cheese, dill, chives, and lemon juice together. Season with salt and pepper, taste and adjust if needed. Set aside.

### Step 2

Assemble the sandwiches
Lay out 4 slices of bread on a flat surface. Spread the herbed cream cheese on each slice of bread. Lay slices of salmon over the bread and top with cucumbers, pressing them gently into the cream cheese. Lay a slice of bread on top. Gently press the top bread slice. Cut into the desired shape.

## LIME BUTTER, CUCUMBER, AND PICKLED GINGER

**Actual time:** 16 min.
**Serves**: 4 sandwiches

### Ingredients

2 English cucumbers
Zest and juice of 1 fresh lime
1 stick quality, unsalted butter, at room temperature
Pinch salt
Pickled ginger, drained and laid out on a paper towel
Thin white bread (Pepperidge Farm, if available)

### Step 1

In a food processor, add the softened butter, lime juice, lime zest, and dash of salt, and pulse to blend well. Taste and adjust if needed.

### Step 2

Peel cucumbers, and with a mandoline, thinly slice the cucumbers and place on a plate.
Cut the crusts off the bread.
With a butter knife, spread the butter mixture on one slice of bread. Lay cucumbers on top of the butter, covering the whole slice of bread. Layer the pickled ginger evenly on top of the cucumbers. Top with a slice of buttered bread and cut into desired shape.

## PECAN, CREAM CHEESE, AND OLIVE

**Actual time:** 30 min.
**Serves**: 4 sandwiches

### Ingredients

1 cup green Spanish olives with pimento, plus a few for garnish
1 cup roasted pecans
1 cup cream cheese
Thin white bread

### Step 1

Remove crusts from the bread.

### Step 2

Hand chop the olives and pecans separately. With a hand mixer, beat the cream cheese until light and fluffy. Fold in the olives and pecans. Spread on a slice of thin white bread and top with another slice to form a sandwich.

To serve, cut sandwiches into small squares. Thinly slice a few green olives and top each sandwich with an olive slice.

# FAVORITE ENTRÉES

Beef, Pork, and Lamb

# COGNAC-MARINATED FILET OF BEEF OR TRES MAJOR

| Prep time | Actual time | Serves |
|---|---|---|
| 15 min. | Overnight, plus 30 min. | 6 |

### Ingredients
3 pounds center-cut beef filet
  *or* 3 pounds teres major
1 clove garlic, finely minced
2 medium shallots, minced
1 tablespoon fresh rosemary, minced
1 ½ tablespoons fresh thyme leaves, minced
Kosher salt
10 grinds freshly ground black pepper
3 tablespoons cognac
⅓ cup extra virgin olive oil, divided

**Difficulty level: Easy**
**Wine pairing:**
Cabernet or merlot

### Step 1
Mix the garlic, shallots, herbs, cognac, and ¼ cup olive oil (reserve the rest). Mix well until incorporated.

### Step 2
On a sheet pan lined with parchment paper, lay your filet on top. Salt and pepper all sides of the filet, then cover the filet with the marinade, rolling so you cover all sides.
Put in your refrigerator overnight, uncovered.

### Step 3
Preheat oven to 450 degrees.
Remove meat from the refrigerator and pat dry, rubbing off the herbs. Rub with the remaining olive oil. Let it come to room temperature. Transfer the filet to a roasting pan. Roast for 15 to 20 minutes or until it reaches 125 degrees. Remove from the oven and let rest for 10 to 15 minutes.
Carve and serve.

During my time in New York as a chef, I forged relationships with renowned food purveyors. One such gem was Lobel's butcher shop, located on the lively upper east side of Manhattan. Lobel's is celebrated for its exemplary customer service, and it was through them that I discovered the culinary marvel known as **teres major**. This delightful cut of beef is the second most tender part of the cow. This marinade serves as a perfect companion to enhance the exceptional qualities of this cut. By allowing the meat to marinate overnight, the cognac acts as a tenderizing agent, resulting in a melt-in-your-mouth texture. It's worth noting that this marinade can be employed with any cut of beef, boosting both flavor *and* tenderness.

# FILET OF BEEF WITH BLUE CHEESE AND PISTACHIOS

| Prep time: | Actual time: | Serves |
|---|---|---|
| 30 min. | 45 min. | 2 |

### Step 1
Preheat oven to 400 degrees.
Rub the filets with salt and pepper, then coat with olive oil and brandy. Let rest for at least 1 hour (this step is part of the magic that makes the filets so tender). In a large sauté pan (ideally, cast iron), heat the oil over medium heat until it shimmers, add the filets, and sear on both sides. Finish off in the oven until a thermometer reads 125 degrees, about 5 to 10 minutes in the oven. Take out of the oven and place on a serving platter, cover with tin foil, and let rest while you prepare the sauce.

### Step 2
Pour out the fat from the pan and return it to medium heat until warm. Add the butter to the pan to melt. Add the shallots, a pinch of salt, and sauté until golden brown and soft, about 3 minutes. Add the wine and beef stock. Reduce until it starts to thicken. Add the pistachios. Cook over medium heat, stirring until the liquid has mostly evaporated. Remove the pan from the heat and stir in the blue cheese until melted and creamy. Add salt and pepper to taste.

Top filet with the sauce and serve.

**Ingredients**
2 filets of beef, 4 to 6 ounces each
1 shallots, minced
Sprinkle of sea salt
10 grinds freshly ground black pepper
2 tablespoons brandy or cognac
1 tablespoon olive oil
1 tablespoon unsalted butter, plus 1 tablespoon for sautéing the fillet
½ cup red wine
2 to 3 tablespoons of pistachios, dry roasted
¼ cup of Saint Agur blue cheese or gorgonzola
¼ to ½ cup stock beef stock (I use homemade)

**Difficulty level: Moderate**

**Wine pairing:**
A nice, rich California chardonnay such as Caymus (any which works with blue cheese), a big red Napa cabernet, or a red Bordeaux.

Finding traditional recipes with an unusual twist is a beloved pastime of mine. It's truly a delight to discover how different flavors and ingredients can come together to transform a classic dish. When it comes to preparing beef, there are so many opportunities to be adventurous! The creamy richness of the blue cheese in this recipe harmonizes beautifully with the nutty undertones of the pistachios. As you savor the interplay of flavors, you'll find that they elevate the dish, providing a delightful contrast that captivates the the palate.

# FILET OF BEEF WITH GREEN PEPPERCORN SAUCE

| Prep time | Actual time | Serves |
|---|---|---|
| 30 min. | 50 min., plus marinating time | 6-8 |

### Ingredients
4 pound, center cut filet of beef, trimmed and tied (have your butcher do this)

### Beef marinade
3 tablespoons cognac
Kosher salt
15 grinds freshly ground black pepper
1 ½ cup good beef stock (see recipe below)
1 cup heavy cream
2-3 tablespoons green peppercorns
3 tablespoons fresh lemon juice
3 tablespoons butter, cut into pieces, room temperature

### Brown Stock
2 pounds stewing beef
2 pounds veal shanks
2 pounds veal bones
2 onions, sliced
1 carrot, sliced
2 stalks celery, sliced
1 ½ teaspoon salt
1 ½ teaspoon fresh or dried thyme
4 sprigs parsley
1 bay leaf

**Difficulty level: Moderate**

**Wine pairing:**
Canvasback cabernet from Walla Walla, French syrah, a grand cru Saint-Émilion

### Prepare marinade
Prepare the marinade and marinade filet in the refrigerator overnight.

### For the brown stock (It is best to make the stock the night before.)

**Step 1**
Preheat oven to 450 degrees.
On a tin foil lined sheet pan, add the meat and brown in the oven on all sides, about 20 minutes. In a separate pan, do the same with the vegetables. When you brown your meat and vegetables it creates a richer stock.

**Step 2**
Transfer meat, bones, and vegetables to a large stock pot and add 3 quarts cold water. Add the celery, salt, thyme, parsley, and bay leaf. Over medium heat, bring the water to a boil, skimming off the foam as it rises to the surface. Simmer stock uncovered for 4 hours, adding more water if necessary until it has reduced to 2 quarts, or in half. Strain the stock into a stock pan and bring to a boil, turn heat to low, and simmer for another hour. Taste and adjust if needed.

### To roast the beef
Preheat oven to 450 degrees. Take the beef out of the marinade and dry in paper towels before searing.
Season the filet with salt and pepper on all sides. In a large, heavy skillet over medium-high heat, add 2 tablespoons olive oil and heat until sizzling. Brown the filet on all sides. Transfer to a baking dish and roast for 20 to 25 minutes until the thermometer reads 125 degrees.

**Step 2**
Transfer to a cutting board and let rest while you make the sauce. In the skillet you used to brown the filet, pour off all the fat. In a small saucepan, heat the cognac until hot. Pour the cognac into the skillet to ignite, shaking the pan until the flames go out. Scrape the brown bits clinging to the bottom and sides.

**Step 3**
Add the 1 ½ cup stock and the cream, reducing the sauce over medium-high heat to 2 cups.

**Step 4**
Add the peppercorns, lemon juice, salt, and pepper. Simmer for 1 minute. Remove skillet from heat and swirl in the butter. Taste and if too hot or astringent add more beef stock.

It's incredible how a recipe discovered in an old issue of *Gourmet* magazine in 1975 has stood the test of time. This dish holds a special place in my heart as it has always been my son's absolute favorite.

On the last night of the fulfilling and winding journey that was the creation of this book, I was planning the final meal with my talented and dedicated staff; serendipitously, it coincided with my son's birthday. The stars aligned and I knew this recipe had to be included. That evening, the flavors mingled with laughter, camaraderie, and a shared appreciation for the culinary arts, encapsulating the very essence of our exploration together. While the passage of time has prompted me to make a few contemporary adjustments to the original recipe, the spirit of the dish remains faithfully intact.

If you want to try a *really* unusual wine pairing, a white Châteauneuf du Pape is delightful. This also would work with a red Châteauneuf du Pape.

# SPICY ZINFANDEL MEATBALLS

**Prep time**
1 hr.

**Actual time**
2 hr.

**Serves**
4; makes 15 meatballs (1 ½ inches)

### For the sauce
**Step 1**

Preheat oven to 350 degrees.

In a food processor, add the bell pepper and jalapeño and pulse until finely minced. Scrape into a bowl and set aside.

Add onion and garlic into the food processor and pulse until finely minced. Scrape into the same bowl as peppers. Set aside.

**Step 2**

In a large saucepan, heat olive oil until smoking. Add onion and pepper mixture. Sauté until translucent. Add the BBQ sauce, ketchup, red wine vinegar, cumin., chili powder and brown sugar and bring to a boil. Cook for about 10 minutes, stirring occasionally. Add the zinfandel wine, reduce heat, and simmer for 30 minutes until thickened. Taste and adjust if needed.

### For the meatballs
**Step 1**

In a food processor, pulse the parmesan and parsley until finely grated and transfer to a large bowl. Add onion and garlic into the food processor and pulse until finely minced. Add to the bowl along with the rest of the ingredients until well incorporated. Shape into 2-inch meatballs and dredge lightly with flour.

**Step 2**

Heat a large skillet over medium-high heat. Add 2 to 3 tablespoons of oil and brown the meatballs.

**Step 3**

Pour sauce into a baking dish, gently fold in the meatballs, and bake in the oven for about 30 minutes.

### Ingredients for sauce
1 tablespoon olive oil
1 onion, minced
8 cloves fresh garlic, minced
1 green bell pepper
1 jalapeño
1 cup BBQ sauce (your choice)
1 cup ketchup
1 cup red wine vinegar
1 teaspoon ground cumin
½ teaspoon chili powder (preferably Chimayó)
2 tablespoons brown sugar
2 cup quality zinfandel wine

### Nanette's Classic Meatballs
1 clove garlic
1 medium onion
½ cup packed fresh parsley
4 ounces Parmesan cheese in chunks
1 pound lean ground beef
½ cup breadcrumbs
1 large egg, lightly beaten
1 tablespoons tomato paste
½ teaspoon salt and pepper, to taste
Flour for dredging

**Difficulty level: Moderate**

**Wine pairing:**
Australian GSM, a zinfandel from Dry Creek, or a petite sirah.

While living in Paso Robles, California, I had the pleasure of learning about the beautifully complex wines of this region. As I became acquainted with some of the passionate winemakers of the area, they entrusted me with catering their wine tastings and special events. It was during this time that I had the opportunity to develop a recipe that would harmonize perfectly with a variety of red wines, showcasing their nuances and enhancing the overall tasting experience. **The true beauty of this recipe lies in its ability to pair with an array of red wines.** Every bite acts as a delightful counterpart, enhancing the flavors on your palate and leaving you with a lingering sense of satisfaction.

As the culinary enthusiast in my family, I understand the importance of preserving traditions and creating memorable experiences through food. This old-world Italian recipe has become a beloved tradition for us, especially during special occasions. **It's delightful aromas permeate our home, conjuring fond memories of generations past.** If you or anyone at your table has Italian heritage, it's likely that you'll hear lively exclamations on the different ways this dish has been prepared historically.

Italian cuisine is known for its regional variations and family traditions, so it's not uncommon for different families to have their own unique take on the recipe. With such a foundational dish, don't be surprised if you find yourself engaged in passionate discussions about the subtle nuances within the world of Italian cooking. My wish is that this recipe brings you and your loved ones joy as you savor the flavors and feel the cultural connections to another time. To complement this dish, I highly recommend pairing it with the angel hair pasta recipe found on page 208.

# BRACIOLE

| Prep time | Actual time | Serves |
|---|---|---|
| 25 hr. | 2 hrs. and 15 min. | 6 |

## Ingredients

1 to 2 pound flank steak
½ cup dried Italian breadcrumbs
1 clove garlic, minced
⅔ cup freshly grated pecorino romano
⅓ cup grated provolone
2 tablespoons fresh minced fresh parsley
2 teaspoon dried oregano, for sauce and flank steak
4 tablespoons extra virgin olive oil
Kosher salt
15 grinds freshly ground black pepper
1 cup red or white wine
3 ¼ cups simple tomato sauce (see recipe below), or you can use a good store bought sauce

### Sauce Ingredients

½ cup extra virgin olive oil
1 small onion, chopped
2 cloves garlic, minced
1 carrot, chopped
1 celery stalk, minced
2 bay leaves
2 (32 ounce) cans crushed tomatoes (I use San Marzano)
6 basil leaves
Kosher salt and freshly ground black pepper
4 tablespoons unsalted butter

**Difficulty level: Difficult**

**Wine pairing:** An Aglianico from Southern Italy, Montepulciiano d'Abruzzo, or a red from Campagna

Make sauce before proceeding to the flank steak and set aside.

### Step 1

In a large cast iron skillet with a lid, heat olive oil over medium heat. Add onion, garlic, and a pinch of salt. Sauté until soft and translucent, about 7 minutes. Add celery and carrot, and season with a bit more salt and freshly ground black pepper. Sauté until all the vegetables are soft, about 5 minutes. Add the tomatoes, basil, bay leaves, and oregano. Reduce heat to low and cover with a lid. Simmer for about 1 hour or until thick, stirring occasionally. Remove the bay leaves and taste. If it tastes too acidic, add the unsalted butter 1 tablespoon at a time to balance the flavor.

### Step 2

Working in batches, pour half of the sauce into the bowl of a food processor and pulse until smooth. Continue with the remaining sauce. If you have left over sauce, you can put it into freezer bags when it is cool and freeze. You can freeze for up to 6 months.

### To make the braciole

#### Step 1

In a medium bowl, stir the breadcrumbs, garlic, pecorino, provolone, and parsley together. Season with salt and pepper and set aside.

#### Step 2

Lay the flank steak between two pieces of plastic wrap and pound out to make it all even, a little less than ½ inch thick. Add salt and pepper to both sides. Your local butcher can usually do this step for you if ordered ahead of time.

#### Step 3

Remove from the plastic wrap and lay flat on a work surface. Sprinkle the bread crumb mixture evenly over the top of the steak. Starting with the short end, tightly roll up the steak, like a jelly roll, to enclose the filling completely. Using butcher's twine, tie the steak roll to secure. Sprinkle it with salt and pepper.

**Step 4**

Preheat oven to 350 degrees.

Heat the remaining 2 tablespoons of olive oil in a large, heavy, ovenproof skillet over medium heat. Add the braciole and braise until browned on all sides, about 8 minutes. Transfer the braciole to a plate. Add the wine to the skillet and bring to a boil, scraping up the browned pieces. Stir in about 3 cups of the tomato sauce and cook for 2 minutes. You want enough sauce to cover the braciole and then some. Return the braciole to the skillet and cover with foil. Bake until the meat is almost tender, turning the braciole and basting with the sauce every 30 minutes. After 1 hour, uncover and continue baking until meat is tender. Cooking time will be 1 ½ hours to 1 hour and 45 minutes. Check to see if it is tender by inserting the tip of a knife into the braciole; if the knife is easily inserted, the braciole is ready.

**Step 5**

Transfer the braciole to a cutting board and cut the string to remove. Cut the braciole into ½ inch thick slices.

Place on a platter, spoon sauce over the braciole, and serve.

# SPICED DUSTED LAMB CHOPS WITH CHERRY TOMATOES

**Prep time**
15 hr.

**Actual time**
40 min., plus resting time

**Serves**
4

### Ingredients

3 tablespoons ground coriander
2 ½ teaspoons ground ginger
2 teaspoons ground turmeric
1 teaspoon ground black pepper
1 teaspoon ground cumin
1 teaspoon ground cinnamon
½ teaspoon ground cloves
½ teaspoon cayenne
8 lamb chops
2 teaspoons sea salt
Olive oil
2 pints cherry tomatoes
1 to 2 tablespoons unsalted butter

**Difficulty level: Easy**

**Wine pairing:** a big zinfandel from Amado County, California, or a California petite sirah

### Step 1
Mix all the spices until well incorporated.

### Step 2
Rub the lamb chops with the spice mixture on both sides and let rest at room temperature for at least 1 hour.

### Step 3
In a medium bowl, toss the cherry tomatoes with 2 tablespoons of the spice mixture. Set aside.

When ready to grill, heat your grill 375 degrees. Drizzle olive oil over lamb chops on both sides. Grill chops for about 3 to 6 minutes on each side. Cook to 120 degree for rare and 130 degrees for medium rare. Transfer to a platter to rest for at least 10 minutes.

### Step 4
In a large sauté pan over medium heat, melt the butter until it is foaming. Add tomatoes and sauté until the skins start to burst. Taste and adjust seasoning if needed.

Serve cherry tomatoes on top of the lamb chops.

During my time running a catering business, I had the pleasure of teaching cooking classes to aspiring home cooks. One recipe that I often shared with my students was this versatile and mouthwatering dish that was not only easy to prepare, but was also packed with delightful flavors. The star of this dish is the unique spice mix, which is both delicious and handy to have in your pantry for various recipes. To achieve the best results, I would recommend rubbing the spice mix onto the lamb chops or whatever protein you're using and allowing it to marinate for about an hour. This resting period allows the flavors to penetrate the meat, creating a harmonious fusion that will make your taste buds dance with delight. I often serve this dish with the Tomato Mango Salad, page 52.

In this dish, the sumac-marinated onions bring a unique twist with its hint of citrus, which beautifully complements the creamy tahini sauce and savory lamb meatballs. Sumac is a spice derived from the dried and ground berries of the sumac plant. Its tangy, tart flavor profile adds a refreshing and slightly acidic note to dishes. Whether you're enjoying these lamb meatballs as a main course or as part of a mezze spread, the flavors of this dish are sure to transport you to a world of Mediterranean delight.

# LAMB MEATBALLS WITH TAHINI

**Ingredients**

**Lamb meatballs**

1 cup (2 ounces) crackers, Ritz or any cracker

2 tablespoons unsalted butter

1 medium yellow or white onion, finely chopped

6 garlic cloves, peeled, smashed, and finely chopped

1 teaspoon freshly ground black pepper

1 teaspoon ground coriander

1 teaspoon ground cumin

1 pound ground lamb

½ cup (lightly packed) roughly chopped parsley leaves and tender stems

1 large egg

1 teaspoon ground turmeric

1 teaspoon Kashmiri red chili powder (or ½ teaspoon cayenne pepper)

1 teaspoon kosher salt

½ teaspoon ground cinnamon

Neutral oil, such as safflower or grapeseed, for brushing

**Difficulty level: Moderate**

**Wine pairing:**

A French pinot noir or a dolcetto from Northern Italy

**Tahini sauce**

½ cup well-stirred tahini

⅓ cup fresh lemon juice

2 garlic cloves, peeled and finely grated

1 tablespoon extra-virgin olive oil

½ teaspoon (or more) kosher salt

4 to 5 tablespoons ice water

**Red onion and parsley salad**

½ medium red onion, peeled and thinly sliced

½ cup cherry tomatoes, cut in half

¼ cup (lightly packed) torn parsley leaves

3 tablespoons fresh lemon juice

1 tablespoon ground sumac

¼ teaspoon (or more) kosher salt

½ teaspoon sugar

| Prep time | Actual time | Serves |
|---|---|---|
| 30 min., plus time to chill | 1 hr. 20 min. | 4–6 |

### Step 1
Make the lamb meatballs.

In a large bowl, crush the crackers with your fingers into coarse pieces, ranging in size from large cornflakes to panko-sized bits. Add ½ cup of water and mix with your hands until moistened and incorporated but still lumpy. Let rest for 5 minutes.

### Step 2
In a medium sauté pan over medium heat, melt the butter. Sauté the onion, garlic, black pepper, coriander, and cumin, stirring occasionally for about 5 minutes, until tender, translucent, and fragrant. Scrape into the bowl with the Ritz cracker mixture. Let mixture cool.

### Step 3
To the Ritz cracker mixture, add the lamb, parsley, egg, turmeric, red chili powder, salt, and cinnamon. Using your hands, knead for 3 to 5 minutes until well combined, slightly sticky, and springy. Alternatively, mix the ingredients in the bowl of a stand mixer fitted with the paddle attachment on medium speed for about 1 minute, until well combined and springy. Wrap and chill in the refrigerator for ideally 24 hours—if you're in a rush, you can shorten that to 3 hours. If you want to plan ahead, you can refrigerate for up to 3 days.

### Step 4
Heat a grill to medium or a broiler to high with a rack 6 inches from the heat source. Portion the lamb mixture with a ¼ cup measure. You should get about 14 meatballs. Wet your hands, then roll the portions between your palms to form smooth balls. Rub or brush the meatballs all over with the oil.

### Step 5
Grill or broil the meatballs, carefully flipping once with a spoon or offset spatula halfway through, for 16 to 18 minutes, until browned on all sides. An instant-read thermometer inserted into the thickest part of the meatball should register at least 155°F (It's okay if they are cooked to a higher temperature) or no longer look pink in the center when split in half. Let the meatballs rest for 5 minutes before serving. While they are resting, baste with the pan drippings.

**While the meatballs rest, prepare the tahini sauce and red onion salad.**

### Step 1
In a medium bowl, whisk the tahini, lemon juice, garlic, oil, and salt until well combined. Whisk in 4 to 5 tablespoons of ice water until the consistency is smooth and as thick as pancake batter. Taste and add more salt or lemon juice if needed.

Make the red onion and parsley salad.

### Step 1
In another medium bowl, massage the onion, parsley, lemon juice, sumac, sugar, and salt with your hands until the onions have wilted. Taste and add more salt if needed. Stir in the tomatoes.

I like to serve it with curry couscous and a cucumber yogurt salad.

Put meatballs on top of couscous and the sumac onion salad on the side. Pass the tahini sauce.

# GRILLED TENDERLOIN OF PORK WITH CHERRY SALSA

**Prep time**
30 min.

**Actual time**
1 hr., plus marinade time the night before

**Serves**
2

### Ingredients
**Pork tenderloin**
3/4 to 1 pound, pork tenderloin
½ cup Shio Koji (see page 293)

**For the salsa**
1 cup pitted fresh cherries
1 tablespoon finely minced jalapeño pepper
¼ cup minced cilantro
1 to 2 tablespoons fresh lime juice
2 tablespoons finely minced shallots
1 heaping tablespoon pickled cherries
1 tablespoon pickling juice of cherries
2 tablespoons roasted hazelnuts, diced
½ teaspoon honey or sugar
Sea salt and freshly ground black pepper
2 tablespoons of extra virgin olive oil

**Difficulty level: Moderate**

**Wine pairing:**
A rich, French pinot noir, a mature Austrian grüner veltliner from the vineyards of Singerriedel or Achleiten, or a garnacha from Rioja, Spain

### Step 1
Line a sheet pan with parchment paper. Lay your tenderloin on parchment paper and cover with the Shio Koji to cover both sides. Cover with plastic wrap and marinate for 1 hour. Rinse Shio Koji from tenderloin and pat dry.

### Step 2
**For the second marinade**
¼ cup minced shallots
½ cup cilantro, minced
4 tablespoons fresh lime juice
¼ cup olive oil

**For the sauce**
¼ cup water or stock
2 tablespoon unsalted butter, divided

In a dish large enough to hold the pork tenderloin, mix the marinade ingredients. Lay the tenderloin on top and roll to cover. Alternatively, you can put all ingredients in a sealable plastic bag and toss to coat. Marinade for about 15 minutes, turning to coat 2 or 3 times. Avoid over-marinating, as the acid in the lime juice will start to cook the pork. .

### Step 3
Make your salsa. Combine all ingredients together. Taste and adjust salt and pepper, if needed.

### Step 4
Heat your grill to 400 degrees.

Remove pork from marinade, pat dry, and add salt and pepper. Set aside marinade to be used for the sauce. Grill pork to medium rare, turning once, to about 140 degrees (about 10 minutes). Let rest while you make the sauce.

### Step 5
In a small saucepan over medium heat, melt 1 tablespoon butter.

Add the marinade ingredients and cook until the shallots are soft, stirring occasionally. Add the water or stock and bring to a boil to reduce until you have 2 tablespoons left. Swirl in the remaining 1 tablespoon of butter.

To serve, slice the pork tenderloin into thin slices, pour over the sauce, and serve with the salsa.

Taste and adjust if needed

There's nothing quite like a summer evening spent around the grill, surrounded by cherished friends and refreshing cocktails. This recipe was made for nights like those. The cherry salsa, with its vibrant brightness, perfectly complements the succulent flavors brought out by the marinade. To save time and allow the flavors to enmesh, I prefer to make the salsa in the morning before dinner. To complete the experience, I serve this mouthwatering dish with Jalapeño Cilantro Risotto, page 233. The heat of the jalapeño adds a delightful contrast to the sweetness of the cherry salsa. The tenderloin, crowned with the vibrant cherry salsa and paired with wine or a favorite cocktail, is an embodiment of those special evenings we hold dear.

As a chef, I've had the privilege of working in various kitchens, some no larger than a shoebox. During my time at a hedge fund in Manhattan, the unique facility where I worked had a balcony overlooking bustling 5th Avenue, complete with a grill. Grilling food creates an olfactory magic, as the smells are woven into the whole experience. Up on that balcony, as the tantalizing aromas wafted through the air, it piqued the curiosity of the staff during their breaks. They would often gather there, observing my grilling techniques and eagerly anticipating the meal that awaits them. One particular dish that became a frequent request from the staff was this seared pork. The secret to its succulence lies in the combination of onions and balsamic vinegar. These two ingredients work harmoniously to both tenderize the pork and add a touch of sweetness, transforming it into a truly remarkable indulgence.

# PAN ROASTED PORK LOIN WITH BALSAMIC VINEGAR ONIONS

| Prep time | Actual time | Serves |
|---|---|---|
| 20 min. | 1 hr. 15 min. | 6-8 |

### Step 1
Preheat the oven to 425 degrees.

Cover the pork with salt and pepper. Grill on all sides. If you don't have a grill, you can sear it in a sauté pan over medium heat.

### Step 2
Place a large sauté pan to fit the pork over medium heat, melt the butter, add the onions, and sauté until softened, about 5 minutes. Stir in the rosemary. And add half of the balsamic vinegar. Add the pork and turn it so it is well coated on all sides.

### Step 3
Put into the preheated oven. Roast for 40 minutes. After the first 10 minutes, turn the pork and stir the onions once. After 35 minutes, add the remaining balsamic vinegar. The temperture should be 145 degrees.

### Step 4
Take out the pork and move it to a serving platter to rest while you make the sauce. Over medium heat, deglaze the pan juices with the red wine. Reduce till it is a concentrated sauce. Add the slurry, stirring until thickened and has a glossy look. Taste for seasoning and adjust if needed. Slice pork thinly and serve with the sauce.

### Ingredients
- 1 4-to-5-pound loin of pork
- Sea salt and freshly ground black pepper
- 2 red onions, peeled and cut into ⅛ inch slices
- ½ cup (one stick) unsalted butter
- 1 heaping tablespoon minced fresh rosemary
- 1 ½ cups quality balsamic vinegar
- 4 tablespoons red wine
- 1 teaspoon cornstarch dissolved in 1 tablespoon water to make slurry

**Difficulty level: Moderate**

**Wine pairing:**
A California pinot noir, Chianti Classico, a full-bodied white, or a pinot blanc from Friuli

# HERB CHICKEN PAILARD

| Prep time | Actual time | Serves |
|---|---|---|
| 15 min. | 20 min., plus marinating time | 4 |

### Step 1
In a small bowl, combine the mixed herbs, herbs de Provence, allspice, cayenne, and lemon peel. Add olive oil and mix well.

### Step 2
Pound the chicken breasts between 2 sheets of plastic wrap until ¼ inch thick. Line a sheet pan with parchment paper, lay breasts on the paper, and rub the herb mixture on both sides. Cover with a sheet of parchment and refrigerate for at least 4 hours or overnight.

### Step 3
When ready to eat, sprinkle the breasts with salt and pepper and grill over hot coals on a well-oiled rack for 2 to 3 minutes on each side. Avoid overcooking them, as this will make them tough. If sautéing, 3 minutes per side. If the tip of a knife can be inserted easily, the chicken is done and tender.

Serve with lemon wedges.

### Ingredients
2 boneless skinless chicken breasts
1 cup minced herbs (you can use a mixture of rosemary, thyme, dill, parsley, sage, and chives)
2 teaspoons dried herbs de Provence
Pinch allspice and cayenne
2 teaspoons lemon rind, finely chopped
Sea salt
15 grinds freshly ground black pepper
⅓ to ½ cup quality extra virgin olive oil

**Difficulty level: Easy**
**Wine pairing:**
A Chablis, sémillon, or pinot blanc

This summer dish is both easy to prepare and incredibly flavorful. It offers the flexibility of being made ahead of time and then grilled to perfection when you're ready to enjoy it. The tender and succulent chicken is the star of the dish, but it can also be sautéed if grilling isn't an option.

To serve alongside this delightful chicken, Angel Hair Pasta is an excellent choice. Its delicate texture and lightness complement the flavors of the dish, providing a satisfying and well-rounded meal. The leftovers can be repurposed in a variety of ways, adding a tasty twist to salads or sandwiches. Enjoy the taste of summer with this easy and tasty recipe!

Tomato season is a wonderful time of year; everything is slow and heavy on the vine. We take our time stretching out conversations and laughter over plates of fresh food, enjoying the reward for making it through the winter. This recipe is just that—a rewarding excursion into fresh tastes and colorful plates. The juicy and tangy tomatoes, along with other fresh ingredients, infuse the salad with a burst of freshness that beautifully contrasts with the crispy and savory chicken cutlet. The combination of the two creates a harmony of textures, flavors, and colors.

# CHICKEN WITH SALAD ON TOP

| Prep time | Actual time | Serves |
|---|---|---|
| 20 min. | 45 min. | 4 |

### Ingredients
**For the chicken**

1 ½ cup fresh breadcrumbs
2 teaspoons grated lemon peel
2 eggs
1 tablespoon white wine
4 boneless, skinless chicken breasts, pounded to ½ inch thick
10 grinds fresh ground white pepper
1 teaspoon kosher salt

**For the salad**

1 cup heirloom tomatoes, or any good tasting tomatoes, seeded and diced
¾ cup red pepper, cored with ribs taken out and diced to ¼ inch
8 cured black olives, pitted and diced
½ cup roasted pine nuts
5 sun-dried tomatoes, cut into slices
1 tablespoon capers, drained
1 teaspoon lemon zest, minced
½ cup fresh basil, roughly chopped
4 radishes, sliced in matchstick pieces
3 cups arugula leaves
Sea salt to taste
10 grinds fresh black pepper

**For the dressing**

1 tablespoon balsamic vinegar
1 tablespoon fresh lemon juice
6 tablespoons extra virgin olive oil
8 grinds freshly ground black pepper
Salt to taste
Pinch of sugar

**Difficulty level: Easy**

**Wine pairing:** Sancerre, a vermentino from Liguria, or a Verdejo

### Step 1
Put all the dressing ingredients in a jar and shake until well combined.

### For the chicken
**Step 1**

Combine the breadcrumbs with the lemon zest. Salt and pepper the chicken breast on both sides. Add the breadcrumbs to a plate. In a shallow bowl, beat the eggs and white wine together. Dip the chicken breasts into the egg, letting the excess drip back into the bowl. Place the breast on top of the breadcrumbs, and with a tablespoon, spoon the breadcrumbs on top (this method keeps your hands clean). Transfer to a sheet pan, cover with plastic wrap, and chill for at least 2 hours or overnight.

**Step 2**

Take the chicken breasts out of the refrigerator and let them come to room temperature. Heat a large sauté pan over medium heat and add the olive oil and the butter. When the oil is hot and the butter has melted, add the chicken breasts and sauté until golden brown, about 5 minutes. Flip to cook the other side. If the chicken is not done, put in a preheated 350-degree oven and bake until a thermometer reads 145 degrees.

**Step 3**

In a medium bowl, combine all salad ingredients (except the arugula) and toss. Add the dressing and toss to coat all. Fold in the arugula. Add salt and pepper. Taste and adjust if needed.

Place the chicken breast on a plate and top with the salad.

# CHICKEN BREAST FRANÇOISE PAUL BOUCSE

| Prep time | Actual time | Yields |
|---|---|---|
| 5 min. | 15 min. | 1 |

### Step 1
Preheat oven to 450 degrees.
Put asparagus on a plate and cover with a paper towel. Microwave for 3 minutes. Take out and season with salt and white pepper to taste. Add 1 tablespoon of butter. Set aside until you are ready to serve.

### Step 2
Season breast with salt and pepper, then lightly dust with flour. Heat 4 tablespoons of butter in a sauté pan until it is bubbling. Add the breast and baste with the butter. Lay a piece of parchment paper on top and cover it with a lid. Place in the oven and cook for 5 to 10 minutes until done. Put a toothpick in the center; if it goes through and feels tender, you are done. Alternatively, use a thermometer to register 140 degrees.

### Step 3
Put asparagus spears on a plate and lay the breast on top. Heat the same sauté pan on medium heat and add the cream or crème fraîche. Sauté, stirring until it thickens slightly, and add salt, pepper, and a dash of nutmeg. Swirl in 1 tablespoon of butter until well-incorporated. If using crème fraîche, gently warm it in a microwave on low setting for 30 seconds before adding to the saute pan to avoid separation.
Pour the sauce over the chicken breast and serve.

### Ingredients
- ½ pound asparagus
- 5 tablespoons unsalted butter, plus 1 tablespoon for the asparagus
- Sea salt
- 10 grinds freshly ground white pepper
- Dash nutmeg
- ¼ cup flour
- 1 chicken boneless, skinless breast
- ¼ cup cream or crème fraîche

**Difficulty level: Easy**

**Wine pairing:** A California new world sparkling wine, white Burgundy, or Sancerre

Paul Bocuse, the much-heralded French chef based in Lyon created this recipe. In 1989, he was proclaimed *Chef of the Century* and is referred to in many circles as the *Pope of Gastronomy*. One of my clients procured this recipe from the man himself. This easy yet satisfying meal is my standard go-to when I'm alone and craving something delicious. If your asparagus happens to be on the thicker side, a recommended fix is peeling it before cooking. This enhances its tenderness, ensuring a more enjoyable dining experience. This recipe is tailored for a single serving, but you can easily scale up the portion size by multiplying the ingredients based on the number of people you aim to serve.

By following the footsteps of Paul Bocuse, you not only honor his culinary legacy, but also treat yourself to a delightful meal that is much more satisfying than peeling back the foil on a frozen TV dinner—wink, wink, remember those?

# PAN ROASTED CHICKEN WITH SAGE VERMOUTH SAUCE

**Prep time**
15 min. plus brine time

**Actual time**
40 min.

**Serves**
4

### Ingredients

4 bone-in, skin-on chicken breasts (try to get even sized breasts so they cook evenly. Alternatively, you can buy a whole chicken and butcher it yourself, making stock out of the left over chicken pieces)

Kosher salt and freshly ground pepper, for seasoning the breast

1 tablespoon olive oil

### Sauce

1 large shallots, finely minced

1 cup chicken broth, ideally homemade

½ cup dry vermouth

6 to 8 sage leaves torn in half (you may want more depending on the size of the leaves)

3 tablespoons unsalted butter, cut into 4 pieces, plus 1 tablespoons for sautéing

15 grinds freshly ground white pepper

Salt to taste

### Brine

1 tablespoon salt

Enough water to cover the breasts

**Difficulty level: Easy**

**Wine pairing:**
Vermouth (such as Cocchi Vermouth di Torino), atna blanco, or chardonnay

### Step 1

In a large bowl, add 1 tablespoon kosher salt and chicken breasts. Add enough water to cover the breasts. Brine for at least 1 hour or up to 4 hours at room temperature. If brining overnight, place in the refrigerator.

### Step 2

Preheat oven to 450 degrees.

Take the chicken pieces out of the brine and pat dry. They must be quite dry to get a good sear on your breasts.

### Step 3

Heat the 1 tablespoon unsalted butter in a medium skillet until hot (but not yet smoking). Add breasts skin side down and cook until golden brown, about 5 minutes. Flip over and cook the other side until golden. Put into the oven and cook for about 10 minutes or until the temperature reads 145 degrees. Remove the breasts from the pan and place on a plate, cover with tin foil, and set aside while you make your sauce.

### Step 4

Pour out most of the fat, leaving 1 tablespoon in the pan. Add the minced shallots and sauté until softened, but not brown. Add the chicken stock and vermouth and cook over medium-high heat until it has reduced to about ¾ of a cup. Add 1 tablespoon of butter and swirl in a circular motion until melted. Repeat with the remaining butter. Add the sage leaves, salt, and pepper. Taste and add more seasoning if needed. The sauce should have a nice gloss to it and be slightly thick.

You can garnish with fried sage leaves. Place the breasts on a serving plate and generously pour sauce over.

148

This recipe offers a foolproof method for cooking chicken breasts that results in moist and tender meat. Brining is a crucial step, as it helps to lock in moisture and enhance the overall juiciness of the chicken. Additionally, leaving the skin on during the cooking process adds an extra layer of flavor, sealing in the juices. It can easily be removed before serving for those who prefer skinless chicken.

Pan roasting the chicken breasts not only ensures even cooking but also creates caramelized drippings, or fond, in the skillet. The fond is a valuable base for creating a rich and flavorful sauce to accompany the chicken. With this recipe, you have the creative freedom to experiment with different wines and herbs, allowing you to customize the sauce according to your preferences and imagination. The technique for making the sauce will remain consistent regardless of the specific ingredients chosen.

# PROVENÇAL CHICKEN

| Prep time | Actual time | Serves |
|---|---|---|
| 15 min. | 1 hr. 10 min. | 4 |

### Ingredients

8 bone-in, skin-on chicken thighs
2 teaspoons kosher salt
1 teaspoon freshly ground black pepper
½ - ¾ cup all-purpose flour
3 tablespoons olive oil
2 tablespoons herbs de Provence
1 lemon, sliced thin
8-10 cloves garlic, peeled
4-6 medium-size shallots, peeled and cut into ¼ inch slices
½ cup dry vermouth
4 sprigs of thyme, for serving
½ to 1 cup chicken stock

**Difficulty Level: Easy**

**Wine pairing:** Bandol or chenin blanc, Provençal rosé, or a Vermentino

### Step 1
Preheat oven to 400 degrees.

Season the chicken with salt and pepper. Put the flour in a shallow pan, and lightly dredge the chicken in it, shaking the pieces to remove excess flour.

### Step 2
Swirl the oil in a large roasting pan and place the floured chicken in it. Season the chicken with the herbs de Provence. Arrange the lemons, garlic cloves, and shallots around the chicken. Then add vermouth to the pan.

### Step 3
Put the pan in the oven and roast for 25 to 30 minutes. Baste with the pan juices. Add chicken stock and continue roasting for an additional 15 to 20 minutes, or until the chicken is very crisp and registers 145 degrees internal heat.

### Step 4
Take the pan out of the oven and transfer chicken thighs to a serving plate. Put the pan back in the oven and bake until the remaining ingredients are soft, about 10 to 15 minutes.
To serve, place chicken thighs on a warmed platter, pour pan sauce over the chicken, and garnish with thyme.

Spending one's life in the kitchen, we learn about our own flavor profiles and combinations that we most enjoy. Herbs de Provence has proven to be my favorite herb blend. Whenever I find a recipe that features this wonderful bouquet of aromatic herbs, I give it a try. With a little effort and time, you can find your favorite herbs and truly embrace the love of cooking. I found this recipe years ago, put my own twist to it, and made a succulent and easy recipe I could enjoy on nights when I had already spent all day in the kitchen working. Truly a throw in the oven recipe that creates a satisfying end to a long day.

Black limes used in this next recipe can usually be sourced online or from international markets that carry a diverse range of ingredients. Finding them may require some effort, but the taste they bring to this dish is well worth it. If you're up for an adventurous culinary experience, I encourage you to give this dish a try and savor the unique flavor of the black lime.

The uniqueness of this dish stems in part from the use of black limes, which have distinct and captivating characteristics.

Black limes are a specific type of lime that undergo a preservation process involving blanching in a salty brine, followed by drying in the sun until both the flesh and peel turn black and hard. This drying method intensifies the lime's natural flavors and oils into a robust and powerful ingredient. The profile of the black lime is a combination of sourness, slight sweetness, and bitterness, with a pronounced citrus aroma. When incorporated into cooking, they contribute a remarkable depth and complexity to dishes, particularly this one. Often, they are employed in stews, soups, and other dishes where their unique characteristics can shine.

# PERSIAN BLACK LIME CHICKEN

| Prep time | Actual time | Serves |
|---|---|---|
| 30 min. | 1 hr 45 min., plus marinating time | 4-6 |

### Ingredients
**For the marinade**

2 black limes, plus 1 crushed and seeds discarded

1 tablespoon minced fresh ginger

1 tablespoon fennel seeds

1 tablespoon Aleppo pepper

1 teaspoon ground turmeric

4 cloves garlic, crushed

4 black cardamom pods, crushed, seeds removed, and shells discarded (or, regular cardamon works well)

1 large pinch saffron

¼ cup extra virgin olive oil

3 ½ pounds chicken thighs, skin-on, bone-in

½ to 1 teaspoon kosher salt

**For baking**

2 tablespoons vegetable oil

3 medium onions, roughly chopped

4 cups chicken stock

½ cup dried apricots, chopped

1 tablespoon tamarind paste

1 tablespoon fresh lemon juice

¼ cup parsley, finely chopped

3 tablespoons mint, finely chopped

Salt

15 grinds freshly ground black pepper

Steamed smoked basmati rice

**Difficulty Level: Moderate**

**Wine pairing:** a California chardonnay, German riesling, or a French pinot noir.

### Step 1
In a mortar, combine the 1 crushed lime with the ginger, fennel seeds, Aleppo pepper, turmeric, garlic, cardamom seeds, and saffron; grind until fine. If you do not have a mortar, you can use a spice grinder or coffee grinder. Gradually add the olive oil. Scrape into a large, resealable plastic bag. Add the chicken, turn to coat all sides. Seal and refrigerate overnight.

### Step 2
Preheat oven to 350 degrees.
Remove the chicken from the marinade and season with kosher salt. In a large, enameled cast iron skillet, heat the vegetable oil until it is shimmering. Add half the chicken and sauté over medium heat, turning once, until browned, about 6 minutes. Transfer the chicken to a plate and repeat with the remaining chicken.

### Step 3
Pour off all but 2 tablespoons of the fat from the skillet. Add the onions and sauté over medium heat, stirring occasionally, until softened and browned, about 8 minutes. Add the stock, apricots, tamarind, and the 2 whole black limes and bring to a boil. Return the chicken to the skillet, cover, and braise in the oven for about 50 minutes, turning once, until the chicken is tender. It should be 145 degrees. Transfer the chicken to the serving platter and tent with foil to keep warm.

### Step 4
Discard the whole black limes and simmer the sauce over medium high heat until reduced by ⅓, about 7 to 10 minutes. Stir in the lemon juice, parsley, and mint, and season to taste with salt and black pepper.
Serve with rice.

This dish came into my culinary wheelhouse while working with one of my clients, who had many recipes she had collected in spiral notebooks over the years. One of my jobs was to make copies of her recipes that she could keep for her numerous homes, and she wanted one for each kitchen she used. This was back in the day when computers were not as prevalent, so my task was to copy each one and insert it into a plastic sleeve in a notebook. She insisted that I follow every recipe exactly as it was written, which was something I was not used to doing at the time. Looking back on this experience, it taught me a lot about discipline and the importance of getting a technique down pat so you can best understand how to make adaptations. Now when I read a recipe, I can quickly tell if it will work or not. Later, after I started experimenting with her recipes and had her try them, she enjoyed my tweaks and changes, and I was freed from following her recipes exactly. This is an elegant fall dish that is sure to bring comfort with each bite.

# STUFFED POUSSIN WITH ROASTED GRAPE CLUSTER

**Prep time** 30 min. | **Cooking time** 1 hour | **Serves** 4

### Ingredients
4 whole poussins, I order mine from D'artagnan

### Stuffing
6 chicken livers, trimmed and chopped
1 tablespoon minced chives
1 tablespoon minced shallots
1 tablespoon minced tarragon
3 tablespoons unsalted butter
⅔ cup fresh breadcrumbs, not dried
4 poussin
8 slices of bacon, cut in half
Salt to taste
10 grinds freshly ground black pepper
8 bunches of red grapes

### For the sauce
3 tablespoons unsalted butter
½ medium red onion, chopped
3 cups red grapes
7 grinds of white pepper

### Cornstarch slurry
1 teaspoon of cornstarch
1 tablespoon water
2 tablespoons butter

**Difficulty level:** Moderate

**Wine pairing:** Mâcon, nouveau beaujolais, a white Jura, a good dry sherry from Monteagudo, or pouilly fuissé

### Step 1
Preheat oven to 400 degrees.

Bring 6-8 cups of water to boil in a medium saucepan. Add bacon and blanch for 8 minutes. Drain in a colander and set aside.

### Step 2
**Make stuffing**

In a medium-sized skillet, melt the butter over medium heat until it is almost brown. Add chicken livers, shallots, chives, and tarragon. Cook until the chicken livers are browned on the outside and pink on the inside, turning once. Remove from heat and add the breadcrumbs. Season with salt and fresh ground pepper. Taste and adjust if needed. Set aside while you begin to prepare the sauce.

### Step 3
**For the sauce**

In a medium saucepan over medium heat, melt the butter. Add the grapes and onion. Lower heat and simmer covered for about 20 minutes until the grape's skins have burst open. Transfer to a food processor and purée until smooth. Strain the pulp and juice through a sieve into a small saucepan. Reserve half for basting the poussin and use the other half for step 5.

### Step 4
Stuff the belly of the poussin with stuffing and arrange them breast side up in a baking dish large enough to hold them and 2 clusters of grapes for each poussin. Top with two slices of bacon crosswise on each poussin. Roast in the oven for 20 minutes, basting twice with the grape sauce. You want them to be 145 degrees.

Take out of the oven and remove the poussin to a serving platter. Tent with foil to keep warm. Remove bacon and add to the roasting pan. Continue to roast the grapes and bacon for 5 more minutes.

### Step 5
To finish the sauce, pour in the juices from the roasting pan into a small saucepan, along with the grape puree you set aside in step 3. Over medium heat, reduce the sauce by one third. Make a slurry by combining 1 teaspoon cornstarch with 1 tablespoon of water. Add slurry to sauce and whisk until thicken, about two minutes. Slowly whisk in 2 tablespoons of butter. Cook until thick and glossy, taste and adjust if needed.

To serve, pour sauce over the bird and garnish with roasted grape clusters.

# ROASTED CHICKEN WITH FOIE GRAS BUTTER

**Prep time**
5 hrs. with marinade
10 min. for preparing chicken

**Cooking time**
30 min. to 1 hr.

**Total time:**
7 hrs.
start first thing in the morning

**Serves**
4-6

### Ingredients

One whole chicken

Tarragon

Parsely

7 tablespoons butter, room temperature, air chilled if possible

3 ½ ounces of foie gras room temperature (I order from D'Artagnan. It comes in small pieces wrapped in individual packets)

2 tablespoons cognac or armagnac

Kosher salt

15 grinds freshly white ground pepper, some for the butter and some for the chicken

Juice from half a lemon

Shio Koji marinade, to cover chicken (recipe on page 295)

**Difficulty Level: Moderate**

**Wine pairing:** pinot noir, gamay, chardonnay

### Step 1

Make the foie gras butter.

Mix all ingredients (except for the chicken and lemon) with a wooden spoon, then put in a small food processor and process until well incorporated. Run through a drum sieve. Add salt and pepper to taste.

Using plastic wrap, roll the butter into a log shape and refrigerate or freeze.

### Step 2

To prepare the chicken, put it in a pan or on a sheet pan. Spread the Shio Koji marinade all over the chicken, top and bottom. To marinade, let rest at room temperature for 4 to 5 hours.

### Step 3

Preheat oven to 375 degrees.

Rinse off the marinade and pat chicken dry with paper towels. Part the skin from your chicken, both breast side and underside. Take out the foie gras butter from the refrigerator and cut into slices about ¼ inch thick. Put under the skin of the chicken on both sides. Generously salt and pepper the outside skin and stuff the cavity with whatever herbs you have on hand.

### Step 4

Lay chicken in the Romertopf. Squeeze the juice of the lemon over the chicken. Cover and bake for about 1 to 1 ½ hours. The bird is done when the juices run clear and the thigh easily pulls away, or when your thermometer (placed in the thickest part of the thigh) reads 145 degrees.

Let rest at least 15 minutes and then carve. Serve with the drippings left in the pan.

Happy accidents or maybe just serendipity; sometimes it just happens. This chicken dish is an example of divine intervention from the kitchen gods that can happen when you most need it. It was looking to be a long day. I was having some dear, long-time friends over for dinner, and simultaneously shutting down my condo for months. I had no time for shopping and needed something that did not require my time and attention. There was a whole frozen chicken and some foie gras. The kitchen powers-that-be smiled on me that day. It is *by far* one of the best chickens I have ever roasted!

It is a simple dish made even easier by the tools you employ. I encourage you to use a **Romertopf clay baker,** one of my prized tools. Foie gras butter with it's velvety finish, freezes well so you can have it on hand for steak or sauces such as an **Allemande** or à **Périgueux**. Serve this outstanding dish with a hearty bread and salad, and you are set for a wonderful evening of delicious food.

Fried chicken is a timeless favorite that can invoke powerful memories of shared summer delight. For me, this recipe takes me back to family picnics on the beach in California. The smell of salt in the air and a cool breeze coming off the ocean still lingers on my skin. My mother would fry the chicken in her cast iron skillet, the very same skillet I use today.

OBSERVATIONS FOR GARNISH PG 300 FROM NANETTE — APPX A · APPX A

Cornbread ———————————————————— pg. 234
Old-Fashioned Fried Chicken ——————————— pg. 162
Old-Fashioned Coleslaw ——————————————— pg. 50
Southern Grits ———————————————————— pg. 164

# OLD-FASHIONED FRIED CHICKEN

| Prep time | Actual time | Serves |
|---|---|---|
| 30 min. | 2 days for brining and marinating, plus 1 to 1 ½ hours for cooking | 4 |

### Ingredients
**For brine**
3 pounds cut up, bone-in chicken, or single parts such as thighs and breasts
2 quarts of cold water
⅓ cup kosher salt

**For marinade**
1 quart buttermilk
2 tablespoons paprika
2 tablespoons freshly ground black pepper
2 teaspoons garlic powder
2 teaspoons dried oregano

**For frying mixture**
1 ½ cup all-purpose flour
1 ½ teaspoons sea salt
1 teaspoon fresh ground white pepper
¼ cup cornstarch
2 tablespoons potato flour
1 pound lard (you can use grapeseed, peanut, or avocado oil if you prefer)
¼ pound butter

**Difficulty level: Moderate**

### Step 1
Rinse chicken pieces under cold running water. In a large bowl, combine the kosher salt and water. Stir to dissolve the salt. Add the chicken pieces to this brine and let sit in the water for at least 4 hours or overnight.

### Step 2
Remove the chicken from the brine and discard the water.
Pour the buttermilk into a large bowl, whisk in the paprika, garlic powder, pepper, and oregano. Add the chicken. Marinade the chicken for at least 4 hours or overnight.

### Step 3
Remove the chicken pieces from the buttermilk. Place chicken pieces on a wire rack to drain.

### Step 4
In a large bowl, whisk together flour, sea salt, pepper, cornstarch, and the potato flour until well blended. One-by-one, dredge the chicken pieces in the flour mixture, shaking off any excess. Lay each coated piece on a wire rack.

### Step 5
In a large cast iron or heavy, deep sauté pan, melt lard or oil. Add the butter. When the oil is at 370 degrees add the chicken pieces in a single layer. You do not want to crowd them. The pieces should be half submerged in the oil or lard so that it bubbles up around the chicken. Cook each piece for 10 to 12 minutes on each side until nicely browned and crisp. Total cooking time will be about 25 minutes. You may need to adjust the flame on the stove to keep your temperature even. The chicken will be done when an instant-read thermometer (placed in the center of a piece) reads 145 degrees and the juices run clear. You will need to do at least two batches.

Remove the cooked chicken to a cooling rack with paper towels underneath.

You can serve it hot or at room temperature. If serving warm, place the chicken in a 200 degree oven until you're ready to serve.

I like to serve it with Southern Grits, shown on the next page.

This recipe also reflects the ways in which my work as a private chef has been inspired by my family's traditions, and how, in turn, I've been able to share them with staff from all over the world. I've been fortunate enough to be able to pass on my love for this recipe, allowing others to make new memories with them. The act of sharing transcends borders and brings people together through the love of food. The recipe becomes a conduit for new memories and connections, allowing others to experience the joy and flavors that have been passed down through generations.

# SOUTHERN GRITS

**Prep time**
15 min.

**Actual time**
40 min.

**Serves**
6

### Ingredients
1 cup stone-ground yellow or white grits

4 ½ cups chicken stock

1 tablespoon unsalted butter, plus 4 tablespoons cut into cubes

2 to 3 teaspoons sea salt

¾ pound spicy sausage, such as Andouille,, cooked and sliced into ¼ inch rounds

2 pounds shiitake mushrooms, stems removed and wiped with a damp paper towel to clean

¼ cup extra virgin olive oil, plus 1 tablespoon for sautéing sausage

Sea salt to taste

10 grinds freshly ground black pepper

2 cloves garlic, peeled and minced

2 shallots, peeled and minced

¾ cup freshly grated parmesan cheese, divided (half for cooking and half for topping the grits)

**Difficulty level: Difficult**

**Wine pairing:**
A real Champagne, a Vouvray, a light body zinfandel, or a gamay.

### Step 1
In a heavy, deep saucepan, mix the grits and 4 cups of the stock. Bring to a simmer, stirring continuously. Cover and cook at a simmer over low heat for 25 to 30 minutes, or until creamy, stirring occasionally. Keep warm.

### Step 2
In a medium-sized sauté pan, add 1 tablespoon olive oil, heating over medium-heat until almost smoking. Add sausage and sauté, stirring occasionally until brown, about 8 minutes.
Set aside.

### Step 3
Slice the mushrooms ¼ inch thick. Heat a cast iron or stainless-steel sauté pan over medium heat until very hot. Add enough olive oil to make a ¼ inch layer. Add the mushrooms and sauté, stirring for 30 seconds. Season with salt and pepper while they are cooking. Add the butter, garlic, and shallots, and keep stirring so they do not burn. After 1 minute, add the rest of the stock to the mushroom mixture and simmer, stirring occasionally until mushrooms are tender. Stir in the grits, sausage, shiitake, and half of the Parmesan cheese, until combined.

### Step 4
To serve, put a large spoonful of grits in the center of a plate, top with the remaining Parmesan and two pieces of chicken.

Being a professional chef often comes with the joy of forming meaningful connections and camaraderie with fellow chefs.

These connections ignite our shared passion for delightful experiences through delicious food.

It is through one of these connections that I came across this exceptional recipe. While searching for a recipe for duck à l'orange that exceeded my expectations of this classic dish, my friend shared chef Loic Jaffres' iteration that did just that. This preparation delivers an outstanding result of incredibly tender duck and a sauce that perfectly enhances the meat's juiciness without overpowering it with excessive sweetness. The beauty of this recipe lies in the balance of flavors, which consistently shine with every preparation.

When I prepare this dish, I am reminded of the power that sharing knowledge, recipes, and experiences has in bringing smiles to people's faces, and I am overwhelmed with gratitude for a life in the world of food.

# DUCK A L'ORANGE

| Prep time | Actual time | Serves |
|---|---|---|
| 15 min. | 2 hrs., 30 min. | 2-4 |

### Ingredients
1 quart orange juice, preferably freshly squeezed

6 ounces bitter marmalade

6 ounces sweet marmalade

½ cup maple syrup

1 Peking duck, 5 to 6 pounds, giblets removed, and the wing tips turned under

Kosher salt

15 grinds of freshly ground white pepper

1 large onion, thinly sliced

2 tablespoons all-purpose flour

1 orange, washed, with ends discarded, and cut into thin slices

½ cup Cointreau or triple sec, plus ¼ cup for sauce

**Difficulty: Moderate**

**Wine pairing**
Brute rosé, a full-bodied Côtes de Rhône, Languedoc-Roussillon, or a Gigondas from the Southern Rhone region

**For slurry**
1 tablespoon cornstarch to 2 tablespoons water

### Step 1
Combine orange juice, marmalade, and maple syrup in a large bowl deep enough to hold the duck. Add the duck, cover, and refrigerate for 8 hours or overnight, turning a few times.

### Step 2
Preheat oven to 375 degrees.
Remove duck from the marinade and reserve the marinade. Season the bird inside and out with salt and pepper. Place the duck breast side up on a roasting pan rack and transfer to the preheated oven. After 10 minutes, turn down the heat to 350 degrees and roast for 1 hour and 30 minutes.

### Step 3
Halfway through roasting, carefully remove 2 tablespoons of fat. A baster or spoon will work. Add to a large saucepan. Place over medium heat, add the onion, and sauté until tender and light golden brown, about 5 to 6 minutes. Sprinkle in the 2 tablespoons of flour and cook for 1 to 2 minutes, stirring occasionally. Be sure to stir up any browned pieces, also known as *fond*. Pour in the marinade and bring to a boil over high heat. Turn down the heat to medium and reduce the sauce until thickened, about 20 to 25 minutes. Transfer to a food processor and pulse until purée is smooth. Pour through a strainer into the saucepan. Add slurry and simmer, stirring occasionally until thickened. Keep on low heat until ready to serve.

### Step 4
Once the duck has roasted for 1 hour and 30 minutes, remove the pan from the oven and turn the heat down to 325 degrees. The temperature should read 180 at the thickest part of the thigh. Transfer duck to a serving platter and cover lightly with tin foil. Discard all but a little of the fat from the roasting pan onto a separate sheet pan, coating the bottom. Lay the orange slices on top. Return to the oven and roast until the pieces begin to brown, about 10 minutes. Remove the orange slices and set aside for serving.

**To serve**
### Step 5
Once the duck has rested for 15 minutes, cut the duck in half using poultry shears or a sharp knife. Remove the backbone by cutting along one side and then the other side. Cut along the breastbone. Cut each half into leg and breast sections. Place on a plate and top with the orange slices.
Cover with sauce.

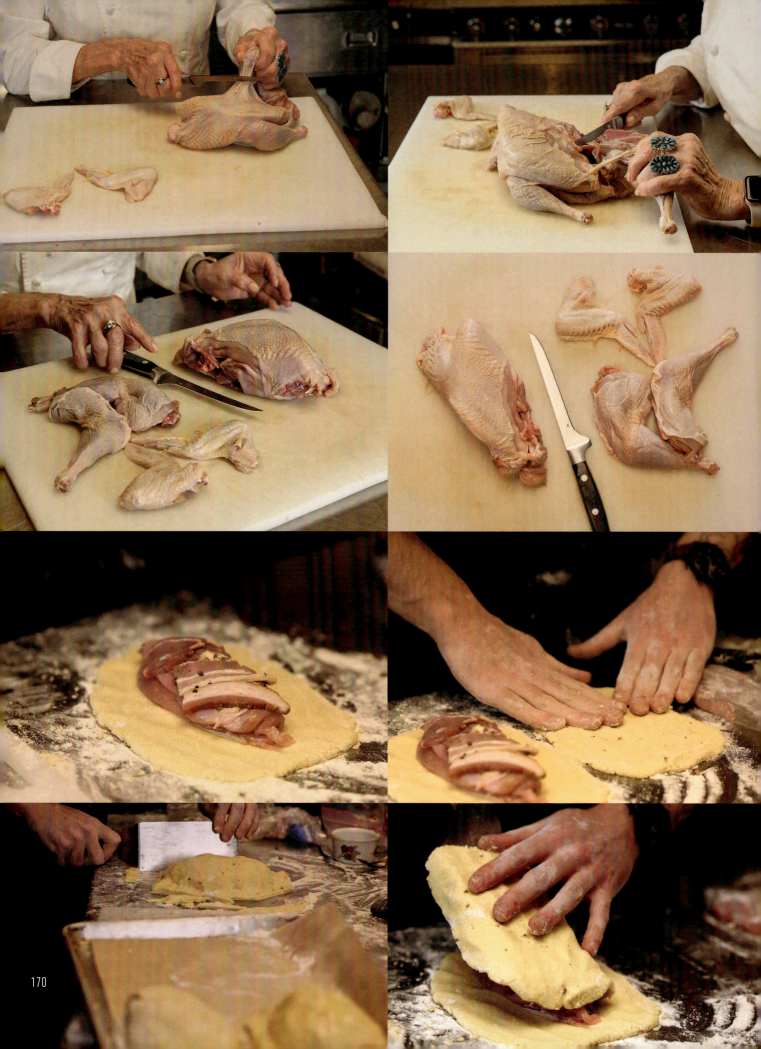

Pheasant is another fantastic but underutilized bird of the culinary world, and I have enjoyed countless recipes with it as the focal point. This unusual dish is my preferred method for preparation. As pheasant is not inherently fatty, the salt crust in this recipe helps to retain moisture, keeping the meat tender and juicy. Additionally, the delicate flavor of the white peppercorn sauce complements the natural sweetness of the pheasant, elevating its taste profile. Although this recipe requires some effort, it is a testament to the adage that great things often demand time and dedication.

The process of creating the dough for the salt crust reminds me of childhood memories of playing with Play-doh, adding an element of nostalgia and enjoyment to the cooking experience. Also, be sure to save the legs to make the recipe for Pheasant Legs in Morel and Chestnut Sauce, page 174.

Indulge in this culinary adventure.

# PHEASANT IN SALT CRUST WITH WHITE PEPPERCORN SAUCE

**Prep time**
45 min.

**Actual time**
1 hr., 30 min.

**Serves**
2

### Ingredients
**For the dough**

1 ½ to 2 cups kosher salt, plus some for seasoning the pheasant

2 ½ cup all-purpose flour, plus a little for flouring your work surface

3 eggs beaten for the crust, plus 1 egg white beaten with 1 teaspoon water for sealing the crust

⅔ cup water (more if your crust is dry)

**For the pheasant**

1 pheasant
4 thick slices of good bacon
10 juniper berries
10 grinds freshly ground white pepper

**For the sauce**

3 tablespoons extra virgin olive oil
1 carrot, finely chopped
2 stalks of celery, finely chopped
1 medium onion, finely chopped
1 leek, finely diced
2 bay leaves
2 ½ tablespoons white peppercorns
1 cup chicken stock
¼ cup brandy or cognac
1 cup heavy cream
Kosher salt to taste

**Difficulty Level: Difficult**

**Wine pairing:** A Rhone chardonnay, a dry Champagne, or a Côte Rôtie

### Step 1
Preheat oven to 425 degrees.

In a large mixing bowl, combine the flour and salt. Make a well in the center and add the 3 beaten eggs. Mix with your fingertips until the eggs are absorbed. Sprinkle ⅓ cup water at time over the mixture, working it into the dough until it is firm yet pliable. You can also do this in an electric stand mixer. Wrap the dough in plastic wrap and set aside while you prepare the pheasant.

### Step 2
**To prepare the pheasant**

If possible, have a butcher separate the legs from the breast. Otherwise, do the following to separate the legs from the breast yourself:

Starting with the bird breast side up, remove the wings and set aside for the sauce. Snap the joint at the torso and cut with a boning knife. Set aside. Grab the legs and rotate away from the breast in a downward motion to separate the thigh and hip joint. Look for the gap between the hip and thigh. At that point, cut parallel to the pheasant breast. Use your boning knife at the joint to cut the leg away from the breast. Repeat on the other side. See photos page 174 for a clear example. Now you have a breast with bone in.

### Step 3
Cut the bacon in half. With the breast side up, season them with freshly ground white pepper. You do not want to add salt because the salt dough will season it. Push the juniper berries into the breast. Lay the bacon slices over the breast to cover.

### Step 4
On a lightly floured surface, cut dough in half and roll out two separate 9 inch disks about ¼ inch thick. Lay the pheasant breast in the middle of the dough with breast side down. Make an egg wash. Whisk one egg with 1 tablespoon of water until well combined. Brush the edges of the dough with the wash. Place the second disk on top of the pheasant. Wrap the dough to cover the breast and form a package, crimping to seal. Brush with the remaining egg wash. Set aside for 30 minutes.

### Step 5
**To prepare the sauce**

Heat 2 tablespoons of olive oil in a large, deep sauté pan over medium heat. Add the pheasant wings, carrot, leeks, celery, onion, and bay leaves. Sauté until the vegetables have softened.

**Step 6**

Crush the peppercorns by sealing in a plastic bag and pounding with a hammer or crush using a mortar and pestle. You want them crushed but not too fine. You can also use a spice grinder, keep in mind you do not want them finely processed.

**Step 7**

In a small sauté pan, cook the peppercorns over medium heat until you smell the wonderful fragrant scent of pepper. About 1 to 2 minutes. Take off the heat and add the peppercorns to the vegetable mixture. Add brandy and sauté for 1 to 2 minutes. Add the chicken stock. Bring to a boil and turn down the heat to simmer for about 20 minutes. Add the cream and continue simmering until the sauce has thickened, about 10 minutes. Strain into a small saucepan and season with salt to taste. Set aside until ready to serve.

**Step 8**

Place the dough package on a parchment lined baking sheet and put into the preheated oven. Bake for 15 minutes, rotate, and bake for another 20 minutes. A thermostat stuck into the center of the breast should read 125 degrees. More cooking time may be required to reach this temperature.

Remove the package from the oven. Set aside while you warm the sauce.

With scissors, cut around the sides of the package and lift off the top of the crust. Remove the pheasant breast. Peel off the bacon and discard the dough.

With a boning knife, remove the breast meat from the bone. Slice at an angle and arrange on a plate.

When you are ready to serve, heat the sauce over medium low heat and add 1 tablespoon cold, unsalted butter, swirling until butter has melted. Taste and adjust seasoning if needed. Pour the sauce over the pheasant and serve.

# BRAISED PHEASANT LEGS WITH DRIED MORELS AND CHESTNUTS

| Prep time | Actual time | Serves |
|---|---|---|
| 45 min. | 1 hr., 30 min. | 2 |

### Step 1
Preheat oven to 325 degrees.

To rehydrate the morels, place in a small bowl and cover with water. Microwave for 2 minutes. After they have steeped for a few minutes, remove the morels from the water, set aside and strain the cooking liquid into the stock.

### Step 2
Salt and pepper the legs and dredge in flour to cover. Set aside.

### Step 3
Heat a large braising pan with oil and butter over medium heat until it begins to sizzle. Brown the legs until deeply brown all over. Remove the legs to a plate. Add the shallots, garlic, and sage. Sauté for 2 minutes.

### Step 4
Add the brandy to the pan, turn up the heat, and cook for a minute or until almost evaporated. Add the legs, stock, morels, and sage. Add salt and pepper to taste. Bring to a boil. Cover the pan with a lid and cook in a preheated oven for 1 hour and 30 minutes or until the meat falls away from the bone.

### Step 5
Remove the legs to a cutting board and cool long enough for you to handle them. Remove the pin bones from the lower portion of each leg. Most of the bones will pull out, but there will be one stubborn, large bone, which you can break off with a pliers or just leave for guests to remove.

### Step 6
Bring the liquid left in the pan to a boil and reduce until thickened. Add the chestnuts and cream. Cook for 5 minutes, taste, and adjust salt and pepper if needed. If you'd like, swirl in 1 tablespoon of butter for a richer flavor.

To serve on plates, add a portion of your starch of choice. Lay the pheasant meat (removed from bones) to the side and pour over the sauce.

**Ingredients**

4 pheasant legs
2 ounces dried morels
Kosher salt to taste
10 grinds freshly ground white pepper
1 tablespoon unsalted butter
1 tablespoon vegetable oil
¾ cup flour
½ cup brandy or cognac
4 cups chicken stock, preferably homemade
½ cup minced shallots
4 to 5 fresh sage leaves, minced
1 clove garlic, minced
1 cup cooked chestnuts
½ cup heavy cream

**Difficulty level:** Moderate

**Wine pairing:** A nice California chardonnay from the Robert Young Winery. If you want to pair it with red wine, use a red Burgundy from Beaune or a pinot noir

# ALWAYS TASTE. TASTE, AND TASTE, AND TASTE!
### —NANETTE

This recipe is a warming, delicious dish which uses the leftover legs of the pheasant from the Salt Crusted Pheasant Breast, on page 174. Repurposing the leftover pheasant legs not only avoids food waste but also transforms them into a standout dish that can be enjoyed with family and friends throughout the year. Mashed potatoes provide a classic and creamy foundation that complements the richness of the pheasant legs and robust flavors of the morels and chestnuts. Wild rice, with its nutty and slightly chewy texture, adds an earthy component that pairs well with the dish. Creamy polenta brings a smooth and comforting element that balances the flavors and completes the meal. Served with any of these starchy bases, this splendid winter dish is sure to delight and satisfy.

# PEPPERCORN MARINATED QUAIL WITH CRANBERRY, CHERRY AND TOMATO RELISH

**Prep time**
25 min.

**Actual time**
45 min.
2 days for marinating

**Serves**
4

### Ingredients

8 quail or Cornish game hens
1 cup Madeira, port or sherry
1 ½ teaspoons kosher salt
3 tablespoons mixed peppercorns (pink, Sichuan, and green—
1 tablespoon of each)
¼ cup honey
3 tablespoons apple cider vinegar

**Difficulty level: Moderate**

**Step 1**
Rinse and pat-dry the quail.

**Step 2**
Marinate the quail for 4 hours or overnight in the Madeira, or whatever you are using.

**Step 3**
Heat a small skillet over medium heat and add salt and peppercorns. Roast the mixture, shaking the pan until the peppercorns become fragrant and the salt just begins to color, about 2 minutes. Transfer the mixture to a mortar and pestle or a spice grinder and grind to a coarse texture.

**Step 4**
Rub the quail generously inside and out with the peppercorn mixture. Refrigerate for 4 hours or overnight.

**Step 5**
When ready to cook the quail, prepare a grill or preheat an oven to 425 degrees. While the grill or oven is heating up, prepare your relish, page 158.

**Step 6**
Whisk together the honey and vinegar.

**Grilling method:** Have coals at medium heat. Place the quail breast side down on the grill and brush them generously with the honey vinegar mixture, turning once in 3 to 4 minutes. Baste with the sauce. Grill until juices run clear, about 6 to 8 minutes. If you are using Cornish game hens, cooking time will be longer. Use a thermometer to ensure a proper temperature of 145 degrees.

**Roasting method:** On a roasting pan fitted with a wire rack, place quail breast side down and brush generously with the honey vinegar mixture. Roast, turning the quail every 5 minutes. Baste with the sauce until they are nicely browned and their juices run clear. Remove from the oven.

Allow the quail to rest for 5 minutes. Place on a platter or individual plates and serve with the relish. If you are using a Cornish game hens, split the birds down the middle and remove the backbone.

Serve with relish.

This recipe features the often overlooked, yet delectable member of the poultry family, quail. The marinade process consists of two steps, serving both to impart a rich depth of flavor and to tenderize the meat. Whether you choose to grill or use a roasting pan, this recipe is sure to satisfy. Accompanying this superb dish is a relish that adds the perfect touch of tartness. The relish beautifully balances the earthy flavors of three different types of peppercorns, creating a distinctive blend. It is important to note that the relish should be prepared on the same day as grilling to ensure freshness and maintain its vibrant taste.

# CRANBERRY, CHERRY AND TOMATO RELISH

**Prep time** 15 min.

**Actual time** 55 min.

**Serves** 4

**Relish ingredients**
1 cup dried cranberries
¾ cup dried cherries
½ cup sun-dried tomatoes
¾ cup apple cider vinegar
¼ cup water
1 tablespoon olive oil
3 shallots, minced
1 granny smith apple, peeled, cored, and diced to ¼ inch
½ cup fresh raspberries
2 teaspoons orange zest
½ teaspoon kosher salt

**Step 1**
In a medium bowl, combine the dried cranberries, cherries, tomatoes, apple cider vinegar, and ¼ hot water cup water. Set aside for 30 minutes.

**Step 2**
Heat a large saucepan over medium heat and add oil. Add the shallots and salt, stir, and cook until they are tender, about 3 minutes. Do not let them brown.

**Step 3**
Add the dried fruit mixture, apple, raspberries, and orange zest. Sauté, stirring occasionally, for about 10 minutes. Taste and adjust seasoning. You might need a touch of sweetness such as honey or maple syrup to balance the tartness of the relish.

**Wine pairing:** A French pinot noir, dry rosé, or a chillable red, such as Cerasuolo d'Abruzzo.

OBSERVATIONS FOR SEAFOOD PG 301 FROM NANETTE
APPX A  APPX A

When hot summer days roll around, I often find myself craving a delicious and easy dish that not only satisfies my taste buds but also delights my *eyes*. The contrasting combination of the scallops' succulent sweetness, the tartness of grapefruit, and the crispness of onion is very refreshing. One trick I've learned while preparing this dish is to add a touch of sugar to the salt and pepper mixture used to coat the scallops. This simple addition helps to caramelize them, resulting in a beautiful golden sear that enhances both the taste and visual appeal of the dish.

The versatility of this recipe is another aspect I love. It can be served as an appetizer to impress your guests, or as a main course for a light and refreshing summer meal. The next time you're looking for a dish that captures the essence of summer, I highly recommend trying this scallop recipe. Its delightful combination of flavors, stunning presentation, and ease of preparation make it a perfect choice for those hot days when you want to enjoy a delicious meal without spending too much time cooking.

# SCALLOPS WITH GRAPEFRUIT AND ONION SALAD

**Prep time** 15 min.

**Actual time** 25 min.

**Serves** 4 as a main course

### Step 1
Using a very sharp knife, peel the grapefruit, removing all the bitter white pith. Carefully cut in between the membranes to release the grapefruit segments into a bowl. Discard all but 1 tablespoon of juice. Stir in the onions and parsley. Add salt and fresh white pepper to taste. Set aside while preparing the scallops.

### Step 2
Pat the sea scallops dry; they must be very dry to sear well. Season with a sprinkling of salt, sugar, and pepper on both sides.

### Step 3
In a non-stick skillet, heat 1 tablespoon of oil until it is shimmering. Sear the scallops over medium-high heat, until golden brown on each side (about 4 minutes per side). If they are sticking to the pan, they are not ready to flip; give them a few more seconds. You want them slightly raw in the center, since they will continue to cook while resting. Reserve the pan juices for serving.

### Step 4
Spoon the grapefruit salad on your serving plate. Top with 4 scallops and drizzle with olive oil and the remaining pan juices.

### Ingredients
**For the salad**

4 ruby red grapefruits

3 tablespoons pickled cocktail onions, cut in half (Crosse & Blackwell is what I use for the best results)

2 tablespoons minced flat-leaf Italian parsley

1 tablespoon minced fresh mint (optional)

8 grinds freshly ground white pepper

Pinch kosher salt

**For the scallops**

16 sea scallops

1 tablespoon sea salt

freshly ground white pepper

sugar, for coating the scallops

1 tablespoon olive oil, plus a little for drizzling to finish

**Difficulty level: Easy**

**Wine pairing:** sparkling rosé, Sancerre, or sémillon

183

# CRAB CAKES AND TARTAR SAUCE

**Prep time**
30 min.

**Actual time**
1 hr., plus time to chill

**Serves**
6 (2 cakes per serving)

### Ingredients

- 3 eggs
- 3 tablespoons heavy cream
- 1 tablespoon Dijon mustard
- 1 teaspoon Worcestershire
- 1 ½ teaspoons Old Bay seasoning
- ⅛ teaspoon cayenne
- 10 grinds freshly ground white pepper
- 3 tablespoons minced scallions
- 2 tablespoons minced fresh parsley, for cakes
- ½ cup mayonnaise
- 2 pounds lump crab meat, picked over for shell and cartilage
- 3 tablespoons crushed soda crackers
- 1 cup fine fresh, white breadcrumbs (preferrably sourdough)
- 9 tablespoons unsalted butter
- 6 tablespoons olive oil
- ½ cup finely chopped parsley, for tartar sauce

### Tartar sauce

- 2 tablespoons white wine vinegar
- 1 tablespoon Dijon mustard
- ¼ teaspoon sea salt
- 10 grinds freshly ground white pepper
- A few drops of Tabasco
- 1 cup mayonnaise
- ⅓ cup onion or shallots, finely minced
- ¼ to ⅓ cup finely minced dill pickles
- ¼ cup finely minced parsley
- 1 tablespoon finely minced chives
- 2 tablespoons minced capers

**Difficulty level: Moderate**

### For crab cakes
**Step 1**

In a large mixing bowl, whisk the eggs. Add the cream, mustard, Worcestershire, Old Bay seasoning, cayenne, and pepper (to taste), and continue whisking until well incorporated. Add the scallions, parsley, and mayonnaise and mix well. Gently fold in the crab and the soda crackers, taking care to break up the crab meat as little as possible. Using your hands, form the mixture into 8 cakes of equal size. To do this, place breadcrumbs in the palm of your right hand, add half a cup of the crab meat mixture with your left hand, add more breadcrumbs on top and gently form a patty. Place on a parchment-lined baking sheet, cover with plastic wrap, and refrigerate for at least 1 hour before cooking. While the cakes are cooling, make the tartar sauce.

### For the tartar sauce
**Step 1**

In a medium size mixing bowl, whisk together the vinegar, mustard, salt, pepper, and Tabasco (to taste). Add the mayonnaise, onion, pickles, parsley, chives, and capers, and mix until all the ingredients are well incorporated. Taste and adjust if needed. Cover with plastic wrap and chill until ready to serve.

**Step 2**

Preheat oven to 300 degrees.

In a large sauté pan over medium heat, heat 3 tablespoons of butter and 2 tablespoons of oil. Add 4 cakes and cook on each side for about 5 minutes until golden brown. Transfer to a sheet pan and place in the oven to keep warm while the second and third batches are sautéing.

Serve with parsley sprinkled over the cakes and the tartar sauce in a small dish on each plate.

### Wine pairing:

Pinot blanc; these whites from the Alsace region in France, California, or Oregon have flavors that range from apples to pears to peaches to citrus. They're generally not overly acidic and have a lovely, soft texture that's great with crab cakes.

The culinary world offers a wide array of crab cake recipes, but it is essential to find a recipe that truly highlights the star ingredient—the crab meat. Unfortunately, some recipes tend to overpower the delicate flavor of the crab with excessive fillers and seasonings. However, after extensive experimentation, I crafted a recipe that strikes a perfect balance, allowing the crab meat to shine while enhancing its natural sweetness with just the right amount of seasoning.

Embracing simplicity, the focus lies on a delicate harmony between seasoning and the essence of the crab. Each ingredient is thoughtfully chosen to complement, rather than overpower. Additionally, making the tartar sauce from scratch is well worth the effort.

# SHRIMP THAI CURRY

**Prep time** 15 min. | **Actual time** 30 min. | **Serves** 4

### Ingredients
- 2 tablespoons oil (I use avocado oil)
- ¾ cup minced shallots
- 1 red pepper, sliced thin
- 1 yellow pepper, sliced thin
- 3 medium carrots, peeled and cut into matchstick pieces
- 2 teaspoons minced fresh garlic
- 2 to 3 tablespoons Thai green or red curry paste, depending on how hot you like your curry to be
- 2 tablespoons fish sauce
- 2 teaspoons brown sugar or palm sugar
- 1 can (14 ounces) coconut milk
- 1 pound medium shrimp, peeled and deveined
- 3 kaffir lime leaves
- 3 tablespoons minced Thai basil
- 3 tablespoons minced cilantro
- Lime wedges for garnish

**Difficulty level: Easy**

**Wine pairing:**

A dry riesling or a good prosecco

### Step 1
In a large wok or sauté pan, heat oil over medium heat until hot. Add the shallots and a pinch of salt, and sauté them until softened, about 5 minutes. Add the garlic and stir until fragrant. Add the carrots and peppers, and stir fry until they are soft. Add the curry paste and stir until fragrant—about 30 seconds to a minute. Stir in the lime leaves, fish sauce, and sugar.

### Step 2
Add the coconut milk and bring to a boil; turn heat down and simmer until slightly thickened, about 2 minutes. Add the shrimp and sauté, stirring until pink and just cooked through, about 3 to 5 minutes. Remove the lime leaves. Stir in the cilantro and basil. Squeeze fresh lime juice over the curry and serve with basmati rice.

## Thai Red Curry Paste
### Ingredients
- 12 dry Thai chili peppers, or other small red peppers, seeded and soaked in warm water for 30 minutes
- 1 tablespoon coriander seeds
- ½ teaspoon black peppercorns
- ½ cup chopped shallots
- ¼ cup chopped garlic
- 3 stalks lemongrass, tough outer leaves and tops removed and tender stalks minced
- 3 tablespoons peeled and chopped fresh ginger or galangal
- 2 tablespoons chopped cilantro stems
- 2 teaspoons chopped lime zest, preferably kaffir limes
- 1 teaspoon shrimp paste

### Step 1
In a skillet, dry roast the coriander and peppercorns over low heat until fragrant, about 3 minutes. Remove and let cool. Grind in a spice grinder or with a mortar and pestle.

### Step 2
Return the pan to medium heat. Add the shallots and garlic and cook, stirring until starting to brown, about 3 minutes. Remove from the heat and let cool.

### Step 3
Drain the chilies, reserving the liquid, and roughly chop. In a blender or food processor, combine all the ingredients with about ¼ cup of reserved water and process until desired consistency. If too thick add more water. Taste and adjust.

One of the beauties of curries is their flexibility, so feel free to incorporate your favorite vegetables if they're not listed in the ingredients. That way, you can truly make it your own and experiment with different flavors and textures.

While the use of Thai basil is traditional in this curry, don't worry if you can't find it. Regular basil can be a suitable substitute. If you're up for it, use the homemade red curry paste. However, if you're short on time or prefer convenience, store-bought curry paste works perfectly fine and will still yield a delicious curry.

Curries are all about getting the basics right, and once you've mastered them, you can easily adapt them to whatever ingredients you have available in your fridge. So, don't hesitate to dive in, unleash your creativity, and enjoy the journey of creating mouthwatering curries that reflect your unique taste.

# CHILI-RUBBED PRAWNS WITH BARBEQUE HOLLANDAISE SAUCE

| Prep time | Actual time | Serves |
|---|---|---|
| 40 min. | 30 min. | 4 |

### Ingredients

1 pound peeled, deveined jumbo shrimp

2 cups applewood chips, soaked in water for 1 hour

### For the chili rub

3 tablespoons brown sugar

5 teaspoons chili powder

4 teaspoons kosher salt

¼ teaspoon chipotle or Aleppo powder

1 ½ teaspoons ancho chili powder

1 ½ teaspoons Spanish paprika

¾ teaspoon dry mustard

### For the BBQ hollandaise

3 large egg yolks

3 tablespoons water

1 tablespoon lime or lemon juice

½ teaspoon hot pepper sauce

1 to 2 teaspoons prepared BBQ sauce (your choice)

1 ½ to 2 sticks of unsalted butter, melted

**Difficulty level: Moderate**

**Wine pairing:**
White Burgundy or a German dry riesling

### Step 1

Mix the ingredients for the rub. You will not need all of it for the shrimp. Set any extra aside for other uses. Toss the shrimp in ½ cup of the rub until well coated. Let rest while you prepare the hollandaise sauce.

### Step 2
**To make the hollandaise sauce**

In a medium metal bowl, whisk together the egg yolks, water, lemon juice, and hot sauce. Heat water in a saucepan until barely simmering. Rest the metal bowl on top of the saucepan. Keep it at a slow simmer while making the sauce. Do not let the bowl touch the water. Alternatively, if you have a double boiler, you can use that. Whisk the egg mixture until light and fluffy, about 3 to 5 minutes. In a slow, steady stream, whisk in the melted butter. Continue to whisk until it is thick and smooth. Whisk in the BBQ sauce. Taste and adjust if needed. You want a BBQ taste but not enough to be overpowering.

### Step 3

Line a heavy, large skillet (one with a fitted lid), with foil. Drain the wood chips. Scatter the chips over the bottom of the skillet. Cover the top of the skillet with foil, wrapping tightly to seal. Place the lid on top. Cook over high heat until smoke begins to form, about 5 minutes. Carefully remove the lid and the top layer of foil. Place the shrimp in a single layer on a rack that fits in the skillet. Cover tightly with the foil and replace the lid. Smoke the shrimp for about 5 to 10 minutes or until done. Carefully remove the lid and place shrimp on a plate or platter.

To serve, spoon the hollandaise sauce over the shrimp.

Having a pantry stocked with key ingredients like this chili rub allows for countless culinary possibilities and experimentation. It's satisfying to know that I always have a reliable seasoning to enhance the flavors of various proteins. The addition of BBQ hollandaise takes the dish to a whole new level, adding a smoky and slightly tangy element that perfectly complements the prawns. Whether you choose to follow the smoking method, grill the prawns, use a Traeger smoker, or even broil them in the oven, the result will be delicious.

OBSERVATIONS FOR SEAFOOD PG 301 FROM NANETTE
APPX A  APPX A

# NEW ORLEANS SHRIMP

**Prep time** 15 min.

**Actual time** 40 min.

**Serves** 4

### Step 1
In a large skillet, preferably cast iron, melt butter and olive oil together until bubbling. Add onion, bay leaves, hot sauce, cumin, and paprika. Bring to a simmer over medium heat. Turn heat down and simmer slowly until the onions are translucent and all the ingredients have mingled together and are fragrant, about 20 minutes.

### Step 2
Add the shrimp and cook on one side until they turn pink. Flip and cook on the other side.
To serve, place shrimp over basmati rice and onion sauce.

### Ingredients
16 large shrimp, peeled and deviened
2 large yellow onions, finely chopped
8 ounces unsalted butter
¼ cup extra virgin olive oil
8 bay leaves
2 tablespoons Louisiana hot sauce
2 tablespoon ground cumin
¼ cup paprika
Sea salt to taste
8 grinds freshly ground white pepper

**Difficulty level: Easy**

**Wine pairing:**
White Côtes du Rhône or a Pouilly-Fuissé.

What I particularly love about this recipe is its simplicity. It is an easy-to-follow dish that doesn't compromise on taste. For those who enjoy a bit of a spicy kick, feel free to add more hot sauce according to personal preference. The next time you're in the mood for a flavorful shrimp dish, consider giving this recipe a try. You'll be pleased with the ease of preparation and the delicious results that are sure to follow. Bon appétit!

When I first started my professional catering journey, a chef friend kindly shared this timeless and savory recipe with me. It has become a staple in my home kitchen, always creating an aromatic and inviting atmosphere for those enjoying it. The key to bringing out the best flavors in this dish is hand-dicing the yellow onion, as it preserves its natural sweetness. However, if time is limited, using a food processor can also yield satisfactory results. To accompany this delightful creation, I prefer serving it with smoked basmati rice.

The smoky undertones perfectly complement the succulent shrimp, creating a rich flavor combination that is difficult to resist. You could also serve it on top of grits.

# ITALIAN BREADED SHRIMP

**Prep time**
15 min.

**Actual time**
25 min., plus marinade time

**Main Course Serves** 4
**Appetizer Serves** 8

### Ingredients

Bamboo skewers, soaked in water
1 lb medium shrimp, deveined
7 tablespoons extra virgin olive oil
$2/3$ cups dry bread crumbs
1 teaspoon finely minced garlic
2 teaspoons finely minced parsley
1 teaspoon dried oregano (preferably Greek if you can find it)
Sea salt and freshly ground white pepper, to taste
Lemon wedges for garnish

**Difficulty level: Easy**

**Wine pairing:** An Orvieto Classico or a Gavi di Gavi

### Step 1

Dry shrimp completely with paper towels. Add the shrimp to a medium size bowl. Add as much olive oil and breadcrumbs in equal parts to coat the shrimp evenly all over. You may not need all of the olive oil indicated in the recipe. Add the garlic, parsley, oregano, salt, and pepper, and toss to coat the shrimp thoroughly. Allow them to sit in the coating for at least 30 minutes or up to 2 hours at room temperature.

### Step 2

When you're ready to cook, thread 3 pieces per skewer. You can, also, lay them individually on a sheet pan. Broil them until golden on one side, then turn to cook on the other side. About 3 minutes on each side.

Serve with lemon wedges.

This dish is one of my go-to Italian recipes that never fails to satisfy my cravings. It's quick and easy, and perfect for those quiet nights after a long workday or as a delightful first course when I have company over. Whenever I prepare this entrée, it brings me comfort and a sense of joy. It's incredibly versatile, and I often serve it on top of angel hair pasta with garlic and oil, creating a delicious combination of flavors, transporting me to relaxing nights in a small Italian village.

It's the perfect dish to share with loved ones or to enjoy on a tranquil evening alone. So, the next time you're in need of a quick and satisfying meal use this foolproof recipe. With every bite, you can savor the essence of Italian cuisine and find comfort in knowing that you're enjoying a homemade dish made with love and care.

Mangia!

# SALMON WITH SCALLIONS GINGER SAUCE

| Prep time | Actual time | Serves |
|---|---|---|
| 10 min. | 20 min. | 2 |

### Step 1
Mix the ginger, scallions, and 1 teaspoon salt in a small bowl and set aside. Sprinkle ½ teaspoon salt and pepper over a portion of the salmon filets.

### Step 2
Bring two cups of water to a simmer over high heat in a sauté pan big enough to hold the salmon. Add the salmon, cover, and turn down the heat to low. Simmer for 3 minutes. Remove from heat and let the salmon rest in the water until the outer layers of the salmon are opaque, about 5 minutes. The temperture should be 120 degrees.

### Step 3
Transfer each salmon filet to a dinner plate. Sprinkle the scallions mixture over filets. Heat the oils into a small saucepan until they start to smoke, about 30 seconds to 1 minute. The oil needs to be very hot, otherwise the scallions mixture doesn't cook properly. Drizzle a little over each filet. Baste with the oil a few times. Serve promptly.

### Ingredients
2 6 oz. salmon filets
4 medium scallions, sliced thinly crosswise
1 tablespoon minced fresh ginger
1 teaspoon salt
10 grinds fresh ground black pepper, or a pinch of long pepper (if you can find it)
1 ½ tablespoons peanut or avocado oil
2 teaspoons sesame oil
2 cups water

**Difficulty level: Easy**

**Wine pairing:**
Chablis, saké, or an Oregon pinot noir

Whenever I'm short on time but still craving a delicious meal, this is a quick and nutritious option. It has become one of my favorite easy salmon recipes, delivering fantastic results with minimal effort. The Chinese poaching technique used in this recipe is truly remarkable. By gently simmering the salmon in water and keeping it submerged while preparing the ginger sauce, ensuring that every bite is tender, succulent, and bursting with deliciousness. I like to serve it with an Asian-style noodle like buckwheat, and a cucumber salad with a good bit of crunch.

The next time you're in the mood for a quick and delightful meal, I highly recommend trying this easy salmon recipe. It's a guaranteed winner in terms of taste and convenience, allowing you to enjoy a fantastic dish without spending too much time in the kitchen.

# SEARED SALMON WITH CORN, SHIITAKE MUSHROOMS
*and Balsamic Beurre Blanc*

**Prep time**
30 min.

**Actual time**
45 min.

**Serves**
4

### Ingredients

½ pound unsalted butter, chilled and cut into 1 inch squares, plus 1 tablespoon for sautéing the vegetables and 3 tablespoons for the corn and shiitake mixture

12 ounces fresh shiitake mushrooms; thinly slice caps and reserve stems for the sauce

¾ cup thinly sliced red onion

1 tablespoon sliced garlic

1 large tomato, coarsely chopped (about 1 cup)

1 teaspoon white peppercorns

1 bay leaf

¼ cup of aged balsamic vinegar, preferably from Modena

½ cup water

¾ teaspoon kosher salt

10 grinds freshly ground black pepper to taste

3 cups corn kernels, cut from the cob (you can use quality frozen corn if fresh corn is not available)

4 6-ounce, center-cut skin on salmon filets

2 tablespoons olive oil

3 tablespoons minced chives

Salt and freshly ground pepper to season salmon

**Difficulty level: Moderate**

**Wine pairing:**
A fruity California pinot noir, a Vouvray, or an Alsatian pinot gris

### Step 1

To make the sauce, melt 1 tablespoon of butter over medium heat in a medium saucepan. Add the mushroom stems, onions, tomato, garlic, peppercorns, and a bay leaf. Sauté and occasionally stir until the vegetables have softened, about 7 minutes.

### Step 2

Add the balsamic vinegar and ½ cup water. Increase heat to medium-high and reduce until the mixture is syrupy.

**Note:** You can make the base hours ahead and set it aside until you are ready to finish the sauce.

### Step 3

Reduce the heat to low and slowly whisk in the ½ pound of chilled butter cut into ½ inch squares, a few pieces at a time. Allow each addition of the butter to melt completely before adding more. The sauce should remain just below a simmer during this whole process, you might have to take it off the heat from time to time to maintain the low simmer. After all the butter has been added, strain the sauce through a fine strainer into a double boiler and set it on low heat to keep warm. Season with salt and pepper.

### Step 3

Preheat oven to 200 degrees.

To cook the corn and mushroom caps, melt 3 tablespoons butter in a large skillet over medium heat. Cook the mushrooms for 4 to 5 minutes until tender; you might need to add a little water if they are sticking to the pan. Stir in the corn and cook for an additional 4 to 5 minutes—season with salt and black pepper to taste. Keep warm in the oven while you prepare the salmon.

### Step 5

Season the salmon with salt and pepper. Heat the olive oil in a large skillet over medium-high heat. Sear the salmon skin side down, until golden, 3 to 5 minutes. Turn over with a spatula and saute for 2 to 5 minutes. Check the temperature in the center. It should be 120 degrees. You may need to put it in the oven for a few minutes until it reaches the proper temperature.

When ready to serve, put a spoonful of the mushroom-corn mixture on a heated plate and top with the salmon filet. Spoon sauce over to cover salmon. Serve Immediately.

My first encounter with this captivating dish was at the renowned Union Square Cafe in New York City. I instantly fell in love with the intriguing combination of flavors—a rich balsamic beurre blanc, delicate sweet corn, the umami of shiitake mushrooms, all complemented by the delightful texture of salmon.

Inspired by that unforgettable restaurant experience, I crafted a version of this dish that is both simple to prepare and produces a result that is nothing short of delicious. The magic of this dish lies in the harmonious interplay of flavors. Every bite offers an explosion of taste and texture. Despite the impressive flavors, it is relatively simple to whip up, making it a fantastic choice when entertaining guests or wanting to treat yourself to a gourmet meal without spending hours in the kitchen. This recipe is certain to become a favorite in your culinary repertoire. Enjoy!

Working as part of a personal staff is often very different from working in a restaurant setting. The responsibilities often extend beyond just serving food and require taking care of guests in a more intimate and personalized manner. I have had the opportunity to experience this firsthand. During one particular occasion, a high-profile guest from France stayed with my client for a continuous 15-day period. Both the butler and I were entrusted with the task of providing breakfast, lunch, and dinner for the guest throughout his stay. As the days went by, we began suggesting that he dine at the exceptional restaurants in the area so that we could have an evening off. **However, to our surprise, he refused our suggestions, stating, "Why go somewhere when the food is so wonderful here?"**

By the fourth day, after an exquisite dinner, the guest insisted that the butler and I indulge in the wine he had left in a bottle from our client's impressive wine cellar. This was an eye-opening experience for me as it was the first time I had the opportunity to taste such fine wine. The experience left a lasting impression on my palate, forever changing my appreciation for the complexities and nuances of wine. I will always be grateful to that seemingly oblivious French guest who kept us busy, but who shared that life-changing wine with us. Among the dishes we prepared during his stay, there was one particular recipe that he requested twice. Being entrusted with the task of satisfying such refined palates and catering to the needs of esteemed guests served as a constant motivation to strive for excellence during my career.

# CHILEAN SEA BASS WITH HONEY SOY GLAZE AND GINGER BUTTER SAUCE

**Prep time** 30 min.

**Actual time** 1 hr.

**Serves** 4

### Ingredients

4, 4-6 ounce Chilean sea bass filets, with skin on

### For the glaze

¼ cup rice vinegar
¼ cup soy sauce
¼ cup honey
1 tablespoon cold water
2 ¼ teaspoons cornstarch

### Ginger butter sauce

1 ½ cups white wine
⅓ cup shallots, minced
2 tablespoons, fresh ginger, minced
1 tablespoon pickled ginger, minced
½ cup cream cheese
2 tablespoons cold, unsalted butter
Salt and freshly ground white pepper

**Difficulty level: Moderate**

**Wine pairing:**
White Rioja, Beaujolais, or saké

### For the Glaze
#### Step 1

Preheat oven to 350 degrees.

Combine vinegar, soy sauce, and honey in a small saucepan over high heat. Mix the water with the cornstarch in a small bowl. Whisk the cornstarch mixture into the soy sauce mixture slowly until it comes to a boil, stirring constantly. Reduce the heat to medium and simmer until the sauce thickens, about 2 minutes. Cool to room temperature.

**While the bass is cooking, make the ginger sauce.**

### For the Bass
#### Step 1

Pour ½ of the glaze into a shallow glass baking dish. Add the fish filets and turn to coat with the glaze. Bake until the fish is opaque in the center, about 18 minutes, and until temperture is at 135. Spoon the remaining glaze over the fish. Turn the broiler on to high and broil until the glaze is bubbling and begins to caramelize, about 2 minutes.

While your filets are baking, prepare the ginger butter sauce.

#### Step 2

Combine wine, shallots, and ginger in a saucepan over medium heat. Boil until the mixture has reduced to 1 cup, about 10 to 15 minutes. Add the cream cheese and simmer over low heat until the mixture is reduced and thickened. Add pickled ginger, salt, and pepper to taste.

#### Step 3

Remove the saucepan from the heat and add the cold butter, 1 piece at a time, whisking until each piece has melted before adding the next

200

# SEAFOOD CRÊPES

| Prep time | Actual time | Serves |
|---|---|---|
| 1 hr. | 1 hr. 30 min., plus chill time | 6 |

### Ingredients for the crêpes
1 cup flour
2/3 cup cold milk
2/3 cup cold water
3 large eggs
1/4 teaspoon kosher salt
3 tablespoons unsalted butter, melted
2 tablespoons minced fresh tarragon

### Crêpe filling
2 tablespoons butter
2 tablespoons olive oil
1 cup fennel, diced in small pieces, 1/2 inch thick
1/2 cup minced shallots
1/2 pound sea scallops
1/2 pound large raw shrimp, cleaned and deveined
1/4 cup vermouth
1/2 cup seafood stock or chicken stock
1 teaspoon fennel seed
1 to 2 tablespoons Pernod or Chartreuse
1/4 to 1/2 cup béchamel sauce

### Béchamel sauce
4 to 5 grates, fresh nutmeg
4 whole cloves
1 small onion, cut into small quarters
2 1/2 cups milk
1 bay leaf
4 tablespoons butter
4 tablespoons flour
1/4 cup cream, optional

### Difficulty level: Difficult
### Wine pairing:
A California chardonnay, a dry riesling, or a Chablis.

### Step 1
**To make the crêpes**

In a blender or food processor, combine all ingredients and process until well combined. Refrigerate for at least 1 hour or overnight. This allows the air bubbles to escape, producing a light, evenly textured crepe.

**To make the béchamel sauce**

Stick the cloves into the onion quarters. Place in a saucepan with the milk and bay leaf. Bring nearly to a boil and simmer gently for 10 minutes. Set aside to cool.

In another medium size saucepan over low heat, melt the butter. Once melted, add the flour and cook, stirring frequently with a wooden spoon. Cook for 2 to 3 minutes. Remove from heat and pour in the milk through a strainer. Place back on heat, stirring with a whisk until thickened, about 2 to 3 minutes. Reduce heat to low and simmer for 20 minutes, stirring often. It should be smooth and glossy. Season with salt, pepper, and nutmeg. Add cream if desired. If you are not using right away, cover with plastic wrap to prevent a crust forming on the top. If it is too thick, add more milk to thin. Sometimes if you let it sit it will not be smooth, if this happens put into a cusinart and pulse until smooth.

**For the filling**

Heat the butter and olive oil over medium heat until it starts to sizzle. Add the fennel, shallots, and a pinch of salt. Sauté until tender, about 5 minutes. Add the vermouth, bring to a boil, and cook until almost dry. Add the fennel seed, stock, scallops, shrimp, and the Pernod. Sauté, stirring occasionally until the shrimp and scallops start to turn color. Season with salt and pepper to taste. Stir in the béchamel sauce.

**Assembly**

Preheat oven to 350 degrees.

In a baking pan, spread a thin coating of the béchamel to cover thinly.

Lay a crêpe on top and spoon about 1/2 cup on the crepe in a diagonal line. Roll up the crepe, seam side down. Repeat until you have 6 crepes. Top with the rest of the béchamel.

Bake for 30 minutes.

202

This recipe holds a special place in my heart as it brings to life the flavors of the old world. When my chef friend Estabon tasted this dish, he exclaimed, "Damn you Nanette, that is amazing!"

Inspired by an old French cookbook, I took the opportunity to update the recipe, giving it a modern touch while still preserving its timeless charm. It has become a favorite among my family, and I love making it on special occasions or whenever I am entertaining. The combination of ingredients and traditional French preparation techniques results in a dish that is both comforting and sophisticated. The familiar aroma that fills the kitchen as I prepare this dish is simply captivating, and it always brings a smile to everyone's face when it sits on the table.

If you're looking to capture the essence of old French cuisine in a modern and delightful way, I highly recommend trying this recipe. It's a surefire way to impress.

# ANGEL HAIR PASTA WITH GARLIC, OLIVE OIL, AND RED PEPPER

**Prep time** 10 min.

**Actual time** 25 min.

**Serves** 4

### Ingredients

¼ pound angel hair pasta
3 tablespoons olive oil
2 tablespoons finely minced garlic
¼ teaspoon red pepper flakes
(This much adds a nice bit of heat. You can use less if it is too much for your palate.)
¼ to ½ teaspoon salt
2 tablespoons cold, unsalted butter
1 tablespoon finely chopped fresh parsley
Freshly grated Parmesan, for garnish

**Difficulty level: Easy**

### Step 1
Fill a large pot with water, add about 2 tablespoons of salt, and bring to a boil.

### Step 2
In a small skillet over low heat, add the olive oil, garlic, pepper flakes, and salt. Slowly cook until you start to smell the garlic. Be careful not to burn it. When the garlic has cooked a bit, add the butter and swirl the pan to incorporate the butter.

### Step 3
Cook the pasta al dente.
Take out about ¼ cup of the water and add it to the sauce.
Drain the pasta, put back into the pan, and add the sauce and parsley. Toss to coat the pasta with the sauce. Taste and adjust if needed.
Serve with freshly grated Parmesan.

We all have days when we could use a comforting dish to lift our spirits. For many of us, no food better fits the bill than pasta. This particular recipe is my ultimate go-to for those moments. Its simplicity and delicacy pairs nicely with other dishes, or can be enjoyed simply on its own.

Whether you're craving something like the tender Braciole on page 126, the refreshing Chicken with Salad on Top on page 144, or the flavorful Chicken Paillard on page 142, this pasta will serve as a perfect accompaniment to enhance the overall dining experience.

# PENNE SAINT MARTIN

| Prep time | Actual time | Serves |
| --- | --- | --- |
| 15 min. | 40 min. | 4-6 |

### Step 1
Heat butter and olive oil in a saucepan over medium heat and add garlic Sauté until golden. Add the shallots, garlic, and sauté until they start to soften, about 5 minutes.

### Step 2
Add the tomatoes, breaking them up with a spoon as they cook. Cook for 10 minutes. Add mushrooms and simmer for 5 minutes. Stir in the rosemary, basil leaves, and peas. Add the cream and simmer for 3 minutes. Season with salt, pepper, and cayenne. Stir in reserved pasta water. Taste and adjust if needed.

To serve, place pasta in a bowl and spoon some sauce on top. Sprinkle with grated Parmesan cheese.

**Ingredients**

2 tablespoons extra virgin olive oil
1 tablespoon unsalted butter
3 cloves garlic, smashed
3 tablespoons shallots, minced
1 32-ounce can of plum tomatoes, preferably San Marzano
⅔ cups small white button mushrooms, quartered
½ tablespoon fresh rosemary leaves
12 fresh basil leaves
⅔ cup shelled peas (I use frozen)
½ cup heavy cream
Kosher salt
15 grinds of freshly ground black pepper
Pinch cayenne
1 pound penne pasta, cooked al dente
¼ to ½ cup grated Parmesan cheese
½ cup reserved pasta water

**Difficulty level: Easy**

**Wine pairing:**

Mourvedre, a mature Verdejo from the Rueda region, Spain, or an Italian Gavi di Gavi

Working as a personal chef doesn't often mean that you are cooking for just one person. Most of the time, you are serving your co-workers as well. It's hard work, being a part of a personal service staff. In the midst of high-pressure situations, such as delivering a highly anticipated dinner party to clients, it is crucial to ensure that the entire staff has a moment to sit, relax, and enjoy a satisfying meal. This recipe was one that would always provide a quick, nourishing bite before returning to long work hours. For me, this easy recipe was my go-to because not only is it convenient, but it delivers unbelievable flavors that will appeal to everyone.

# PENNE PASTA WITH BEETS AND GORGONZOLA

| Prep time | Actual time | Serves |
|---|---|---|
| 30 min. | 1 hr 30 min. | 4-6 |

### Ingredients

4 tablespoons extra virgin olive oil, plus some for frying the sage leaves

½ cup minced red onion

¼ pound pancetta, diced ¼ inch pieces

2 cloves garlic, finely minced

1 ½ to 2 cups heavy cream

10 ounces of creamy gorgonzola cheese (you can substitute a Bleu d'Auvergne French blue cheese)

Sea salt, to taste

10 grinds freshly ground black pepper

3 medium fresh beets

2 tablespoons fresh parsley, minced

1 cup roasted pecans

2 teaspoons fresh sage, minced plus a handful to fry for the garnish

**Difficulty level:** Moderate

**Wine pairing:**

A white Châteauneuf du Pape (one of my favorite white wines) or a Valpolicella ripasso

### Step 1

Preheat oven to 375 degrees.

Peel and cut the beets in half. Put the face side down in a baking dish and add water to come up halfway. Cover with foil and bake in the oven for about 45 minutes or until tender. Take out to cool. When cooled, cut into matchstick pieces (about ¼ inch wide).

### Step 2

Heat a large sauté pan over medium heat and then add olive oil. Add the onion and a pinch of salt and sauté for about 5 minutes over low heat. When they start to soften, add the garlic and pancetta. Cook for about 3 minutes or until the pancetta is fully cooked. Add the cream and bring to a boil. Let simmer until the sauce starts to thicken. Stir in the gorgonzola or blue cheese. It should be the consistency of a custard. Add the beets, parsley, fresh sage, and roasted pecans.

### Step 3

In a small sauté pan, pour in enough olive oil to cover the bottom ¼ inch. Heat over medium heat until hot. Add the sage leaves and cook, turning over once. With a slotted spoon transfer to paper towels to drain. Lightly salt them.

### Step 4

Cook the penne until done. Save about ½ cup of the pasta water to add to the sauce. Drain the pasta.

Transfer the pasta into a large serving bowl. Add the pasta water to the sauce. Add salt and pepper to taste. Pour over the pasta and gently stir to combine.

Serve with fried sage leaves on top.

This pasta dish is a delightful departure from the traditional penne sauces, presenting a unique and unexpected flavor combination. The earthy notes of beets mingle flawlessly with the creamy and tangy gorgonzola, resulting in a truly remarkable taste experience. Additionally, beets provide vibrant color, giving the dish a visually appealing quality that is as enticing as its flavorful. The next time you find yourself craving a pasta dish with a twist, give this non-traditional sauce for penne a try.

The Rotolo Stuffed with Spinach Filling in a Creamy Tomato Sauce is a labor of love, but investing the time and effort required to bring it from the page to the plate is incredibly worthwhile. Not only will it satisfy your friends at gatherings, but it will *also* provide you with a delicious and versatile meal option for various occasions throughout the week.

Potlucks provide a fantastic way to enjoy a casual gathering with friends in a relaxed atmosphere. The opportunity to share and discuss the various dishes prepared by everyone not only fosters a deeper understanding of individual tastes, but also creates a sense of community around food.

One of the key characteristics of this recipe is its ability to be prepared in advance. By allowing you to make it a few days ahead of time, it frees up your schedule on the day of an event, leaving you with more time to socialize and enjoy the company of friends.

If you find a source for premade pasta sheets it will save you time. It also works well as a beginning of the week meal because you can make a double batch—store extra in the refrigerator or freezer—so you have something delicious on hand at a moment's notice. While making your own pasta from scratch is certainly an option, you can *always* save that time and easily source great quality pasta sheets at many local Italian restaurants or delis.

# ROTOLO WITH SPINACH STUFFING AND CREAMY TOMATO SAUCE

| Prep time | Actual tim: | Serves |
|---|---|---|
| 1 hr. 40 min. | 2 hrs. 20 min. | 8-10 |

**Ingredients**
**Pasta dough**
4 ½ cups all-purpose flour
2 teaspoons salt
3 eggs
¼ cup lukewarm water
1 tablespoon olive oil

**To make dough:** Process all ingredients in a food processor until a ball of stiff dough is formed. Turn out onto a floured surface and knead until smooth. Cover the dough and let it rest for 30 minutes.

**Filling**
2 pounds spinach
2 pounds fresh ricotta
3 eggs, slightly beaten, plus one beaten egg for sealing the pasta
1 ½ teaspoons grated nutmeg
½ teaspoon salt
½ teaspoon white pepper
1 cup grated fresh Parmesan cheese
Cheesecloth and string

**Creamy tomato sauce**
½ cup butter
1 onion, minced
10 large fresh tomatoes, peeled, seeded, and chopped (or canned tomatoes) *See process on page 20.*
1 tablespoon fresh sage, minced
1 teaspoon kosher salt
Pinch sugar
½ teaspoon freshly ground white pepper, to taste
1 cup heavy cream

**Difficulty level: Difficult**

**For the creamy tomato sauce**
**Step 1**
Melt butter in a skillet pan (preferably, cast iron) over medium heat. Sauté onions for 5 minutes until soft and translucent. Add the tomatoes, sage, sugar, salt, and pepper. Cover and simmer over low heat until tomatoes are soft, but not disintegrated - you will want some chunks (about 25 to 30 minutes). Taste for texture and flavor and adjust salt, pepper, or sugar if needed.

Add mixture and cream to a food processor and process until smooth. Put the mixture back into the saucepan and simmer until it slightly thickens. Set aside.

**For the filling**
**Step 1**
Blanch washed spinach in boiling water for about 5 minutes until it is limp.

Cool and squeeze out all moisture in a colander or cheesecloth. Put into a food processor and process until it is finely chopped. Alternatively, you can use frozen spinach if you like.

**Step 2**
Mix the spinach, ricotta, eggs, nutmeg, salt, and pepper in a large bowl. Mix in the Parmesan cheese.

**Step 3**
Roll out ½ of the pasta dough onto a floured surface until it is very thin, approximately 1/16 of an inch. Spread half of the ricotta filling evenly over the top of the dough, leaving 1 inch uncovered on all sides. Brush the uncovered inch of dough with the beaten egg. Gently roll up like a jelly roll. Now transfer your roll to a piece of double cheesecloth that is bigger than the pasta sheet so you have enough space at each end to tie. Repeat with the other half of the dough and filling. You can make the sheets a smaller size if needed.

Put the cheesecloth roll into salted boiling water for about 15 to 20 minutes until the pasta is cooked. Take out of the water, cool and remove cheese cloth right before cutting. If storing overnight or longer, cover with damp paper towel and wrap in seran wrap so it does not dry out. You can refrigerate overnight or up to 3 days if you wish.

**Step 4**
Preheat the oven to 350 degrees. Bring pasta roll to room temperature and slice into ½ to ¾ inch slices.

In a baking dish, spoon sauce into the pan. You will want about ½ inch of sauce on the bottom. Lay your sliced rounds diagonally on top of the sauce and sprinkle with grated parmesan. Bake in the oven for about 30 minutes. Serve.

# CHEESE SOUFFLÉ

| Prep time | Actual time | Serves |
|---|---|---|
| 20 min. | 55 min. | 4 |

### Ingredients
Finely grated Parmesan cheese (to coat the soufflé dish)
3 tablespoons unsalted butter
3 tablespoons flour
1 cup whole milk
¼ teaspoon grated nutmeg
Pinch cayenne pepper
1 teaspoon kosher salt
4 egg yolks
5 egg whites
1 ½ cups Gruyère cheese, 1 ¼ cups for soufflé and ¼ cup to sprinkle on top

**Difficulty level:** Moderate

**Wine pairing:** Pouilly Fuissé, Chablis, or a white Burgundy

### Step 1
Preheat oven to 400 degrees.
Butter a soufflé mold, add parmesan cheese, and tilt the dish to coat sides and bottom.

### Step 2
Warm milk in a microwave or in a saucepan and bring it just to a boil. Meanwhile, melt butter in a small saucepan over medium heat. Add flour and whisk until mixture begins to foam and loses its raw taste, about 3 minutes. Remove the saucepan from heat and let it stand for one minute until bubbles die down. Place sauce back on heat.

### Step 3
Pour the hot milk all at once, whisking constantly until very thick, 2 to 3 minutes.

### Step 4
Remove from heat, whisk in nutmeg, cayenne, and salt. Add egg yolks one at a time until each one is thoroughly incorporated into the sauce. Fold in 1 ¼ cups Gruyère.

### Step 5
Scrape the soufflé base into a bowl and let it cool to lukewarm. You can make this up to 2 hours ahead.

### Step 6
Using an electric mixer, beat the egg whites in a large bowl until stiff but not dry. Fold in ¼ mixture into the soufflé base to lighten it. Fold in the remaining egg whites gently. Pour mixture into your soufflé dish and sprinkle the remaining ¼ cup Gruyère on top. Place the dish in the middle of the oven and turn down the heat to 375 degrees. Bake for 25 to 30 minutes or until it has puffed up and cooked through. Serve immediately.

Often, words like *soufflé* and *poach* can initially seem intimidating to home chefs. However, once you understand that these terms are simply concepts to learn, like any other cooking technique, they become much more approachable. In truth, they are not nearly as difficult to master as they may appear. In the case of soufflés, they may sound like a daunting culinary task, but I assure you that they are an excellent example of how something that seems challenging can be conquered with ease.

Embracing new challenges in the kitchen allows you to grow as a chef and expand your culinary repertoire. Mistakes along the way are not failures; instead, they provide valuable opportunities to learn, perfect your skills, and enhance your understanding of different cooking techniques. Remember, your kitchen is a place of exploration and experimentation. It's a canvas for you to unleash your creativity and refine your cooking abilities.

# LISA'S STUFFED PORTOBELLO MUSHROOMS

**Prep time** 45 min.

**Actual time** 1 hr. and 10 min.

**Serves** 8

### Ingredients
**For the mushrooms**

8 portobello mushrooms

2 ½ pounds button mushrooms

4 tablespoons unsalted butter

Salt

15 grinds freshly ground white pepper

1 teaspoon garlic salt

1 teaspoon dried Italian herbs

4 ounces cream cheese, room temperature

½ cup panko breadcrumbs, divided into two ¼ cups

2 cups grated Gruyère cheese

¼ cup sweet vermouth or sherry

¼ cup water

**Spinach filling**

2 large bunches of spinach, washed and large stems removed

2 teaspoons kosher salt

3 tablespoons unsalted butter

3 tablespoons flour

1 cup milk

2 ounces cream cheese

½ teaspoon sea salt

10 grinds freshly ground white pepper

1 to 2 ripe tomatoes, minced for garnish

**Difficulty level: Difficult**
**Wine pairing:** mourvèdre, zinfandel or cabernet franc

### Step 1
Preheat oven to 350 degrees.

Bring a large stock pot filled with water and 2 teaspoons of salt to a boil. When the water is boiling, add the spinach and cook until wilted, about 3 to 5 minutes. Strain into a colander, pressing down on the spinach to drain out excess water. Once it cools, place in a food processor and pulse until finely minced. Transfer to a bowl and set aside.

### Step 2
**Mushroom stuffing**

Remove the stems from the portobellos. Set aside.

In a food processor, process the button mushrooms and the stems from the portobellos until very finely minced. You will need to do 2 batches. Transfer to a bowl.

### Step 3
In a large sauté pan, heat the 4 tablespoons of butter until it bubbles. Add the mushrooms and 1 teaspoon salt, and sauté over medium heat, stirring until they start to release their liquid. Add the Italian seasoning and garlic salt. Boil off the liquid until almost dry. Add the cream cheese, a few tablespoons at a time, stirring into the mushrooms. Add pepper and more salt to taste, if needed. Add ¼ cup of the panko breadcrumbs and stir in until well combined.

### Step 4
**Spinach filling**

In a large sauté pan, melt 3 tablespoons of butter over medium heat until it is bubbling. Stir in flour and cook for 2 minutes while continuously stirring. Bring the milk to a boil in a microwave for about 2 minutes. Add the boiling milk to your butter and flour mixture all at once, stirring with a whisk until it thickens, making a roux. Add a dash of nutmeg, salt, and pepper. Add the spinach and stir into the roux. Sauté a few minutes until it thickens. Add cream cheese, stirring until it is well combined. Stir in the remaining ¼ cup panko until incorporated.

### Step 5
**Assembling the mushrooms**

Put the mushrooms on a sheet pan and bake for 8 to 10 minutes until they start to soften. Remove from the oven. Keeping the mushrooms on the pan, use a spoon to fill the mushrooms with a layer of spinach filling. It should be even with the top of the mushroom. Mound the mushroom filling on top of the spinach. Sprinkle the Gruyère cheese on top of the mushrooms. Pour the sweet vermouth and water into the pan and bake another 15 to 20 minutes until the cheese has melted.

To serve, transfer mushrooms to a serving platter. Pour the juices over the mushrooms and top with the minced tomato.

Gathering around a table full of food is one of the most inclusive acts we can do with family, friends, and strangers soon-to-be-friends. However, catering to the dietary preferences or restrictions of everyone present can sometimes pose a challenge. Lisa, a member of my extended family, is a lifelong vegetarian, so I created this recipe with her in mind. Considering the diverse needs of those you're cooking for, you're opening up opportunities for everyone to share a meal together, regardless of their dietary choices. The star of this recipe is the rich portobello mushroom, which offers a dense structure and a satisfying texture that can please both vegetarians and meat lovers alike.

Indian-Spiced Cauliflower — pg. 224
Jerusalem Artichoke and Vegetable Tagine — pg. 220
Basmati Rice

Throughout many regions of the world, vegetarian dishes are a common staple in various ethnic cuisines. One cuisine that stands out for its amazing fusion of aromas and spices are Indian dishes. The way the various spices come together creates a truly magical culinary experience that is hard to find elsewhere. In my role as a private chef, I often received requests to incorporate specific themes into menus for big parties. One time, a very talented chef friend of mine asked for my help in preparing an Indian-themed menu for a special gathering.

I fell in love with this recipe of his in particular, which has become one of my all-time favorite vegetarian side dishes.

# JERUSALEM ARTICHOKE AND VEGETABLE TAGINE

**Prep time** 25 min.

**Actual time** 1 hr.

**Serves** 4-6

### Ingredients for the harissa sauce

½ cup extra virgin olive oil
½ to 1 teaspoon cayenne pepper
1 tablespoon ground cumin
2 to 3 tablespoons tomato paste
¼ cup fresh lime juice
½ teaspoons salt

### Ingredients for tagine

1 pound peeled Jerusalem artichokes* or potatoes
2 teaspoons salt for boiling water
2 tablespoons extra virgin olive oil
1 large sweet onion, cut into 1 inch pieces
1 red bell pepper, 1 inch pieces
1 yellow pepper, 1 inch pieces
2 tablespoons harissa sauce
1 teaspoons saffron threads, steeped in hot water to cover
1 ½ cups cooked chickpeas (I cook dried chickpeas, but you can used canned)
¾ cup pitted Kalamata olives, halved
2 tablespoons finely chopped lemon confit see page
1 to 2 cups vegetable or chicken stock
3 tablespoons chopped cilantro

**Difficulty level: Easy**

**Wine pairing:** Grenache, white graves, or Gigondas

### For the harissa sauce

**Step 1**

In a food processor, mix all harissa ingredients together until well combined. Taste and adjust if needed. If it's too hot, you can add more lime; if more heat is needed, add additional cayenne. Set aside.

### For the vegetable tagine

**Step 1**

Peel the Jerusalem artichokes; they are rather knotty so do the best you can. Cut into 1 inch pieces. If using potatoes, peel and cut into 1 inch pieces.

**Step 2**

Fill a large saucepan ¾ full of water, add salt, and bring to a boil. Add the Jerusalem artichokes or potatoes, place over high heat, and bring back to a boil. Lower heat and simmer for about 10 minutes until they just begin to soften. Drain and set aside.

**Step 3**

In a large skillet, or tagine, heat olive oil over medium heat and add onions, peppers, and the harissa sauce. Sauté, stirring for about 3 minutes. Stir the saffron that has steeped in the water to the vegetables. Add the Jerusalem artichokes, chickpeas, olives, lemon confit, and broth. Lower the heat and cover to simmer for 10 minutes or until the Jerusalem artichokes are tender. Season with salt and black pepper to taste.

Serve with rice or couscous. Pass the harissa sauce.

*Peel the Jerusalem artichokes as best you can by cutting into 1 inch pieces. They are knobby so just clean, and peel as you go.*

One of the joys of being curious about food is discovering new techniques and interesting tools used all over the world. For me, the tagine pot is a fantastic example of this exploration and curiosity. The conical shape creates a unique environment inside the vessel where the moisture from the food travels up the sides and back down to continually baste the dish. Recipes prepared in a tagine are exceptionally flavorful and moist. This dish is one I prepare often for my vegetarian friends. Layered within this dish is a combination of Moroccan flavors. The nuttiness of the Jerusalem artichokes, the sweetness of the onion and peppers with the heat of the harissa to create a flavorful dish.

# FAVORiTE SIDE DiSHES

Vegetables, Risotto, and Breads

The recipe begins by simmering a head of cauliflower in turmeric-infused water. This not only imparts a beautiful golden hue to the vegetable, but also adds subtle earthy flavors that enhance its overall complexity. It's a mesmerizing process to watch as the cauliflower transforms in color and becomes tender.

Whether you're planning an Indian-themed party or simply want to indulge in a fantastic vegetarian side dish, I highly recommend trying this cauliflower recipe. Immerse yourself in the alchemy of Indian spices and prepare to be amazed by the aromatic and visually stunning dish that emerges from your oven. Enjoy!

# INDIAN-SPICED CAULIFLOWER

**Prep time** 25 min. | **Actual time** 1 hr., 40 min. | **Serves** 4-6

### Ingredients

**For poaching the cauliflower**
1 tablespoon ground turmeric
1 tablespoon salt
1 3-pound cauliflower

**For coating**
2 tablespoons chickpea flour
1 cup plain whole fat yogurt
2 tablespoons ginger paste
2 tablespoon garlic paste
1 tablespoon olive oil, divided

**For stuffing**
1 tablespoon olive oil
¼ cup roasted cashews, coarsely chopped
⅓ cup finely chopped green beans
1 small carrot, finely chopped
½ teaspoon garam masala
½ teaspoon ground cumin
⅛ teaspoon cayenne pepper
¼ teaspoon ground fenugreek
1 cup cottage cheese
¼ cup shredded cheddar cheese
1 tablespoons dried currants
15 grinds freshly ground black pepper

**Difficulty level: Difficult**
**Wine pairing:**
An off-dry riesling from Oregon or a sparkling wine

### Step 1
Preheat oven to 425 degrees.
Fill a pot large enough to hold the cauliflower with water and bring to a boil. Stir in the turmeric and salt. Add the cauliflower and partially cover it with a lid. Cook until barely tender, about 15 minutes. Be careful not to overcook it. You want to be able to pull the florets apart when it has cooled. Transfer the cauliflower to a large colander and let it cool. You can also refrigerate it overnight.

### Step 2
In a small skillet, toast the chickpea flour over moderate heat, stirring until golden brown, about 2 minutes. Scrape the flour into a medium bowl and let cool. Whisk in the yogurt, ginger paste, garlic paste, and 1 tablespoon olive oil. Season with salt.

### Step 3
In a small skillet, heat 1 tablespoon olive oil over medium heat and add the carrots and green beans. Sauté over low heat until crisp and tender, about 5 minutes. Add the garam masala, cumin, cayenne, and fenugreek. Sauté, stirring until fragrant, about 1 minute. Scrape the mixture into a medium bowl to cool. When it is cool, add the cottage cheese, cheddar, currants, and cashews. Season with salt and freshly ground pepper.

### Step 4
Carefully stuff the cauliflower by packing a small spoonful of the vegetable mixture in between the florets with your fingers toward the center of the cauliflower, or by using a pastry bag as mentioned in the notes. Put the cauliflower on a parchment-lined baking sheet. Coat all over with the chickpea yogurt mixture. Bake for about 1 hour or until lightly brown. Let cool for about 8 to 10 minutes before serving.

What I've found to work wonderfully is to stuff the cauliflower using a pastry bag and pipe it into every nook and cranny. This technique shown here offers more control and ease ensuring each bite produces an explosion of flavors, with the creamy yogurt and crispy chickpea crust perfectly complementing the tender cauliflower and richly spiced stuffing.

# CAULIFLOWER STEAKS WITH CAPER PANCETTA SAUCE

| Prep time | Actual time | Serves |
| --- | --- | --- |
| 15 min. | 45 min. | 4 |

Salt to taste. Preheat oven to 350 degrees.

**Step 1**

Drain the capers through a sieve. Set aside.

**Step 2**

In a 12-inch dry skillet, cook the pancetta over medium heat, occasionally stirring until crisp, about 10 minutes. Transfer with a slotted spoon to paper towels to drain. Pour off the fat and wipe the skillet clean with a paper towel.

**Step 3**

In a small bowl, stir together the lemon juice and raisins.

**Step 4**

Trim the cauliflower stalk flush with the base of the crown, discarding the stalk, then trim off any leaves. Put cauliflower crown, stalk side down, on a cutting board. Cut a 1-inch slice from 2 opposite sides of the crown and discard, then cut the crown lengthwise into 4 steaks, about 1 ¼ inch wide. Salt and pepper on each side.

**Step 5**

In a large skillet, heat 2 tablespoon olive oil and 2 tablespoon butter over medium heat, swirling the oils occasionally, until the butter starts to brown. Add the steaks and cook until golden on one side. Flip over and cook on the other side until golden, about 4 to 5 minutes on each side. You might need to do two batches; it depends on the size of your skillet and your steaks. Transfer the oven-safe skillet to the middle of the oven to roast cauliflower until tender, about 8 to 10 minutes.

**Step 6**

While the cauliflower roasts, bring the 2 tablespoons of water to a boil in a small saucepan over medium heat. Stir in the pancetta, capers, raisins, and lemon juice. Add the remaining ½ stick of cold cubed butter, stirring after each addition until incorporated. Remove from heat and season with freshly ground white pepper. Taste and adjust if needed.

Remove the cauliflower from the oven.

To serve, carefully place on a platter with a spatula and pour sauce over the steaks.

## Ingredients

- ½ cup capers, drained
- 5 ounces of pancetta, diced into ¼ inch pieces
- ½ cup golden raisins
- 3 tablespoons fresh lemon juice
- 1 head cauliflower, about (1 ¾ pound)
- 10 grinds freshly ground white pepper
- 2 tablespoons extra virgin olive oil
- ⅞ stick (7 tablespoons) cold, unsalted butter, cut into cubes 1 inch
- ½ teaspoon sugar
- 2 tablespoons water

**Difficulty level: Moderate**

I had the pleasure of preparing this recipe as part of a menu for a feast I cooked for my friends. As we gathered around, it became clear that this dish was the undeniable favorite.

One valuable tip to consider is to use caution with the amount of pancetta you include. The salt levels can differ among brands. Start with less and add more if needed.

When selecting the cauliflower, I highly recommend choosing one with a dense crown. This allows the cauliflower steaks to hold together beautifully, contributing to an impressive presentation. Keep in mind that even if they don't hold together perfectly, you can rest assured that the taste remains exceptional.

What makes this recipe work is the versatility of the sauce. While it pairs wonderfully with the cauliflower steaks, it also complements grilled shrimp or any filet wonderfully. It's a fantastic opportunity to explore different flavor combinations and elevate other dishes in your culinary repertoire.

This side is a perfect addition to any Asian-styled dinner. It pairs particularly well with the Miso Glazed Chilean Sea Bass or the Salmon with Scallions Ginger Sauce, on pages 199 and 194.

The beauty of this side dish lies in its simplicity. Requiring minimal effort to prepare, it will allow you time to focus on the main courses. The combination of flavors and textures adds depth and interest to each bite as you savor this delightful side dish alongside the main courses.

# GLAZED MISO EGGPLANT

| **Prep time** | **Actual time** | **Serves** |
|---|---|---|
| 10 min. | 40 min. | 6 |

### Ingredients
3 eggplants
2 tablespoons sesame oil

### For the glaze
2 teaspoons honey
7 ounces sweet white miso
2 teaspoons grated fresh ginger
2 tablespoons rice vinegar
2 tablespoons soy sauce
2 to 3 teaspoons sambal

**Difficulty level: Easy**

**Step 1**
Heat oven to 425 degrees.
Cut each eggplant in half and score the flesh in a crisscross pattern about ½ inch deep.

**Step 2**
Sprinkle the eggplant with salt. Pour the oil into a flat pan large enough to hold the eggplant. Roll the eggplant in the oil to coat and turn, so the flesh side is down. Roast in the oven for 25 minutes or until they are completely soft.

**Step 3**
Place the glaze ingredients in a medium size bowl and whisk until well incorporated.

**Step 4**
Remove the eggplant from the oven and turn the oven to low broil.

**Step 5**
Turn the eggplant so the flesh side is up and spread the glaze over the surface to cover.
Broil for about 5 minutes until the glaze is bubbling. Keep an eye on them so they do not burn.

# SWEET POTATOES IN ORANGE SHELLS

| Prep time | Actual time | Serves |
|---|---|---|
| 10 min. | 40 min. | 6 |

### Ingredients

3 pounds sweet potatoes

2 eggs

¾ to 1 cup brown sugar

¼ cup unsalted butter, melted

½ to 1 teaspoon cinnamon

1 teaspoon salt

15 grinds freshly ground white pepper

1 cup finely ground pecans, plus a few for garnish

½ to 1 cup fresh orange juice

8 large oranges

Optional garnishes: miniature marshmallows, chopped pecans, or drizzle of honey

**Difficulty level: Moderate**

### Step 1
Preheat oven to 375 degrees.

Rub the sweet potatoes with oil, prick them with a fork, and put them on a sheet pan. Roast until soft, about an hour. Let them cool. When cool, remove the skin, put it in a large bowl, and mash.

### Step 2
Cut the tops off of the oranges and juice them. Set aside. Remove the pulp from the oranges. Set aside.

### Step 3
Combine the sweet potatoes, eggs, melted butter, brown sugar, cinnamon, salt, and pecans in a food processor. Pulse until blended, taste and adjust if needed. Add the orange juice slowly until it reaches a nice consistency. Do not overprocess and make too thin, as you will be filling the orange shells with this mixture. You can pipe the mixture into the shells or spoon it in. Refrigerate until ready to bake.

### Step 4
Preheat oven to 375 degrees.

Place the filled orange shells on a baking sheet and bake for 20 to 30 minutes.

If you are using any of the additional garnish as mentioned in the ingredients, after the initial bake time, take the filled shells out of the oven and add them before returning to the oven a few minutes until melted or browned.

Serve and enjoy.

Citrus season during the holidays is truly a delightful time, and this particular dish perfectly captures the vibrant flavors of citrus. The ease of preparing this recipe in advance truly comes in handy during the busy holiday preparations. It provides an opportunity for the sweet potato and citrus flavors to meld, creating a truly harmonious combination. A drizzle of honey, sprinkle of toasted nuts, or tiny marshmallows can add a touch of sweetness and crunch, enhancing the overall texture and taste profile. In addition to the delectable flavors, the presentation of this dish is equally remarkable. The natural beauty of the oranges, combined with the contrasting hues of the sweet potato, creates an appealing visual display that is sure to impress your guests.

When I was in Paris a few years ago, I had the pleasure to visit Joël Rubuchon's Restaurant, L'Atelier De Joël Robuchon when he was still the head chef overseeing the kitchen. As to be expected, the meal was a delicious experience, most notably his famous potato puree. I was inspired to create my own version. I call this recipe *Potato Bliss*, as it showcases the sheer heavenly potential of the humble potato. Though it is a rather involved dish to prepare, the end result is unquestionably worth the effort. Commenting on Joël's creation, the food writer Patricia Wells noted, "Ever homey, ever elegant, ever irresistible, this is the dish that helped make Chef Joël Robuchon's reputation. Clever man he is, he realized early on that if you give people potatoes, potatoes, and more potatoes, they will be eternally grateful, forever fulfilled." Prepare yourself for a journey of pure potato indulgence. Let the elegant simplicity of this dish speak for itself.

# BLISS POTATOES

| Prep time | Actual time | Serves |
|---|---|---|
| 30 min. | 1 hr. | 6, depending on serving size |

## Ingredients

2 pounds baking potatoes, such as Idaho or russets, whole

¾ to 1 ¼ cups whole milk

16 tablespoons unsalted butter, chilled and cut into 1 inch cubes

Sea salt

15 grinds freshly ground white pepper

**Difficulty level: Difficult**

### Step 1

Scrub the potatoes. Do not peel them (these are peeled hot). Place them in a large stockpot and add cold water to cover, at least 1 inch of water over the potatoes. Add 1 tablespoon of salt per quart of water. Simmer the potatoes uncovered over medium heat until a knife inserted into a potato comes away easily, 20 to 30 minutes.

Drain the potatoes as soon as they are cooked. If they are allowed to cool in the water, they will not taste right.

### Step 2

In a large saucepan, bring the milk just to a boil and set aside. As soon as the potatoes are cool enough to handle, peel them and pass them through a fine grind of a food mill into a heavy bottomed saucepan set over low heat. With a wooden spoon, stir the potatoes vigorously until they start to dry out. About 3 to 4 minutes.

### Step 3

Now begin adding the cubes of butter little by little until you have added 12 tablespoons, continuing to stir vigorously to incorporate the butter into the potatoes. The mixture should be fluffy and light. Then slowly add ¾ of the hot milk in a thin stream, stirring vigorously until the milk is incorporated. You may need to heat it back up later.

### Step 4

Now pass the mixture through a flat drum sieve, or a sieve into another saucepan, stirring vigorously. If it still seems a bit heavy, add additional milk and butter.

To keep it warm if you are not going to serve it right away, put the saucepan of your Potato Bliss in a larger pot with gently simmering water and cover. Make sure the water in the second pot only comes up an inch on your saucepan of potatoes. Stir it every once in a while, until you serve the puree.

*If you are in a hurry, you can skip step 4, it just won't be as divine.

Risotto is a versatile dish that pairs beautifully with several entrées featured in this book. I recommend pairing are the Pork Tenderloin with Cherry Salsa on page 136. Once you have experienced the flavors of this risotto, you can explore your own creative food pairings.

One aspect I particularly appreciate about this recipe is how it utilizes the oven, offering you the convenience of preparing the rest of the meal without the need for constant stirring. This allows for greater flexibility and multitasking in the kitchen, ensuring that everything comes together seamlessly.

There are varieties of risotto you can choose from. Risotto rice contains the perfect amount of starch to create a dish that has a creamy texture and luxurious sauce. Italy produces wide varieties of rice, which are ideal for making risotto. I always found it confusing which rice to choose. I hope this will help you to understand the proper rice for your risotto.

The highest Italian risotto grade is *superfino*, followed by *fino*, and then *semi-fino*. The three common types of superfino rice are Arborio, Carnaroli, and Vialone Nano. These differ in length and vary in starch content and texture. Most chefs have a preference, so you must experiment and see which type you prefer. For this recipe, I use Carnaroli.

# CILANTRO RISOTTO

**Prep time:** 15 min.
**Actual time:** 45 min.
**Serves** 4 to 6

### Ingredients
1 cup risotto
½ cup shallots
2 tablespoons unsalted butter
1 tablespoon olive oil
1 teaspoon sea salt
⅓ cup chopped cilantro, stems included
¼ teaspoon cayenne pepper
1 to 2 tablespoons minced jalapeno (depending on how hot the peppers are)
2 cups chicken broth

**Difficulty level: Easy**

### Step 1
Preheat oven to 350 degrees.

Heat butter and olive oil over medium heat in a medium saucepan with a lid. When the butter is bubbling, add the shallots and sauté until they are soft, about 5 minutes. Add the jalapenos and stir for a few more minutes. Add salt and the risotto, and stir to coat the rice. Add the cayenne and chicken stock. Bring to a boil, cover with a lid, and put in the oven to bake for 30 minutes.

### Step 2
After 30 minutes, take it out of the oven. Remove the lid, stir in the cilantro, place a dishcloth or paper towels over the saucepan, and replace the lid. Let rest 5 to 8 minutes.

Serve with the entreé of your choice.

# CORNBREAD

| Prep time | Actual time |
|---|---|
| 10 min. | 35 min. |

### Ingredients

½ cup butter (1 stick)

1 ½ cups of buttermilk, sour milk, or yogurt

2 medium eggs

⅓ cup sugar

1 teaspoon baking powder

1 teaspoon baking soda

1 teaspoon salt

1 cup cornmeal

1 cup flour

**Difficulty level: Easy**

### Step 1

Preheat oven to 400 degrees.

Put the butter into a 9 inch cast iron skillet and put in the oven to melt butter and heat the skillet.

### Step 2

In a bowl, mix the flour, cornmeal, baking soda together and set aside.

### Step 3

In a large bowl, combine the buttermilk, eggs, sugar, and salt. Use a whisk to mix thoroughly. Pour in all but a tablespoon of the butter and whisk together. Add the flour mixture and whisk until smooth. Pour into the hot skillet and place in the oven. Bake for 25 minutes. It will be golden brown and the edges will pull away from the skillet.

If you do not have a cast iron skillet you can use a pyrex baking dish.

This can be served with soup, homemade stew, or chili. Enjoy!

As an archivist by nature I have scoured magazines, cookbooks and articles to find the best balance of sweetness to cornmeal for that ol' down home cornbread taste. This recipe is the most delicious one I have found and delivers time and time again.

Delicious additions prior to baking are cheddar cheese, chopped green Chilis, corn kernels, or toasted cumin seeds. For a gluten-free substitution, you can use garbanzo bean flour, or quinoa flour.

# FAVORITE DESSERT

Cakes, Cookies and Tarts

# FRENCH LEMON CAKE

| Prep time | Actual time | Serves |
|---|---|---|
| 15min. | 1 hr. and 10 min. | 8 |

### Ingredients
2 lemons or oranges, peel and juice
1 cup sugar
1 cup (2 sticks) unsalted butter, at room temperature, cut up into chunks
4 eggs, at room temperature
1 ¾ cup flour
2 teaspoons baking powder
1 teaspoon vanilla extract
Pinch salt

### For the glaze
1 cup confectioners' sugar
1 tablespoon limoncello (optional)
Juice of the 2 peeled lemons

**Difficulty level: Easy**

### Step 1
Preheat oven to 325 degrees.
Butter and flour a 6-cup ring mold.

### Step 2
Remove the peel from the lemon or orange using a vegetable peeler and cut into 2-inch pieces.

### Step 3
Sift together the flour and baking powder into a bowl. Set aside.

### Step 4
In a food processor with a metal blade, combine the lemon peel and sugar, and process until the peel is finely chopped, about 60 seconds. Add the butter and process until smooth, about 30 seconds. Add the eggs and vanilla extract, process until smooth, about 30 seconds. Scrape down the sides of the bowl as needed. Add the flour mixture. Pulse on and off only until the flour just incorporates (do not over process it).

### Step 5
Transfer batter into the prepared ring mold; it will be thick. Tap the pan on the counter a few times to get the air bubbles out. Bake in the oven until a toothpick inserted into the center of the cake comes out clean, about 50 to 55 minutes. Let cool slightly.

### Step 6
Mix together the confectioners' sugar, juice of the 2 lemons, and limoncello. Spoon some of the mixture over the cake, repeat as the cake cools.

When cool, serve. This cake keeps well if wrapped in plastic wrap and kept in the refrigerator.

This exquisite cake recipe has been a complete lifesaver throughout my culinary career. In the chaotic realm of professional kitchens, a quick and heavenly dessert is a godsend when under pressure to deliver an impressive experience. Just 15 minutes of effort creates a moist and delicious cake that delights even the most discerning of palettes. For variety, you can use orange instead of lemon, or try a glaze with elderflower syrup. This efficient yet delectable recipe is the perfect end to any meal.

# ROSEMARY OLIVE OIL ORANGE CAKE

| Prep time | Actual time | Serves |
|---|---|---|
| 25 min. | 40 min. | 8 |

### Ingredients
**For the syrup**
- 2 large oranges
- ⅓ cup sugar
- ⅓ cup water
- 2 teaspoons minced fresh rosemary

**For the cake batter**
- ¾ cup extra virgin olive oil
- 1 ¾ cup flour
- 2 large eggs
- 2 heaping tablespoons cornmeal
- 1 ½ teaspoon baking powder
- ½ teaspoon baking soda
- ½ teaspoon kosher salt
- ¼ cup crème fraîche
- 2 teaspoons finely minced rosemary
- 1 ½ teaspoon vanilla extract

**Difficulty level: Easy**

**For the syrup**

**Step 1**

Finely zest the oranges and set aside for the cake batter. Using a knife, shave off the orange skin and the white pith. Hold the shaved oranges over a small bowl and cut between the membranes to release the orange segments into it, all the while letting the juices drop into the bowl.

**Step 2**

In a small saucepan, combine the water, sugar, and rosemary. Bring to a boil, stirring occasionally until sugar dissolves, about 4 minutes. Remove from the heat and stir in the reserved orange juice and segments. Let cool while you prepare the cake.

**For the cake**

**Step 3**

Preheat oven to 325 degrees.

Position a rack in the center of the oven. Lightly grease a 9-inch cake pan with olive oil, cut a piece of parchment paper to fit the bottom of the cake pan, and oil it.

**Step 4**

In a medium bowl, whisk the flour, cornmeal, baking powder, baking soda, and salt. Set aside.

**Step 5**

In a stand mixer with the whisk attachment or in a bowl with a hand held mixer, beat the oil, sugar, eggs, crème fraîche, rosemary, vanilla, and orange zest until well incorporated.

**Step 6**

With the mixer on low speed, add the flour mixture, scraping down the sides of the bowl as needed. Whisk until the batter comes together; it will be thick. Spoon the batter into the prepared cake pan and spread the mixture to even it out. Tap the cake pan on the counter a few times to release any air bubbles. You can add a sprig of rosemary in the center if you wish.

**Step 7**

Bake the cake until it is lightly brown at the edges and a toothpick inserted into the center comes out clean, about 18 minutes. Place on a wire rack and cool until slightly warm. Pour over the syrup (it will be absorbed by the cake).

When ready to serve, take out the rosemary sprig and set it aside. Set a plate on top of the cake and flip it over, remove the parchment paper and replace the rosemary spring on top.

I like to serve this with a whipped cream flavored with a little orange liqueur and powdered sugar.

Nestled in the serene ambiance of Palm Springs, our home is surrounded by an abundance of citrus trees. **During our evening strolls, my partner and I relish in gathering the vibrant oranges, grapefruits, and lemons, along with harvesting from the three fragrant rosemary bushes that greet us at our patio entryway. Inspired by this abundance, I created this dessert recipe that incorporates oranges, and is enhanced by the inclusion of olive oil. The result is a moist, citrus delight.**

While I was thinking of a recipe for a wine tasting, an inspired thought happened: wouldn't it be wonderful to pair chestnuts with red wine. I discovered this very old traditional Italian recipe. Chestnut flour was used to make "poor man's cake" during the 1500's in Tuscany. At the time, chestnut trees were plentiful and harvesting them was accessible to everyone, which is how the moniker came to be.

The sweet nuttiness of the chestnut flour and the earthy tones of the rosemary create a culinary symphony which intertwines harmoniously. I love that a vegan, sugar-free recipe can still provide sweet notes appealing all walks of life.

# CASTAGNACCO CHESTNUT FLOUR CAKE

*With Rosemary and Pine Nuts*

| **Prep time** | **Actual time** | **Serves** |
|---|---|---|
| 10 min. | 40 to 50 min. | 10 to 12 |

### Ingredients

½ pound fresh chestnut flour*

2 to 3 cups water (this will depend on the quality of the flour)

⅓ cup raisins

¼ cup pine nuts

1 tablespoon extra virgin olive oil

3 to 4 sprigs fresh rosemary

1 teaspoon minced rosemary

½ teaspoon salt

1 teaspoon honey

**Difficulty level: Easy**

**Wine pairing:** port wine, or your favorite red wine.

* you can buy chestnut flour at supermarketitaly.com or giannettiartisans.com

### Step 1

Heat the oven to 400 degrees.

Sift the flour into a bowl. Slowly mix in the water. You want the batter to be soft enough to fall from the spoon but not too liquid. I usually use 2 ½ cups of water.

### Step 2

Add the raisins, pine nuts, olive oil, minced rosemary, and honey. Pour the batter into a quiche pan with a removable bottom. Put rosemary sprigs on top. Bake for 30 to 40 minutes until it has little cracks all over. Take out and cool. Sprinkle sea salt to taste.

Trial and error is an important teacher in your development as a chef. This recipe is a prime example of my own experience with the great equalizer that is failure. After multiple unfortunate attempts, I persisted and came up with this wonderful recipe, which my friend dubbed *the million-dollar bite*. The original recipe comes from one of the most cherished and referenced books in my library, *Hows and Whys of French Cooking* by Alma Lach.

This cake brings a certain depth to the classic chocolate cake and my hope is that you enjoy it in all its decadence.

# NANETTE'S CREAMY CHOCOLATE CAKE

**Prep time**
20 min.

**Actual time**
38 min.

**Serves**
10-12

### Ingredients
**For the cake**

¼ pound unsalted butter, plus 2 tablespoons

¼ pound semisweet chocolate

1 tablespoons cognac

1 tablespoon almond flour or ground almonds

1 tablespoon flour

1 tablespoon cocoa powder

8 tablespoons sugar, divided into 4 tablespoons

4 egg whites

4 egg yolks

¼ teaspoon kosher salt

½ teaspoon vanilla extract

**For the glaze**

2 tablespoons butter

1 tablespoon Kirsch

1 tablespoon cognac

1 tablespoon water

3 tablespoons white corn syrup

1 teaspoon instant espresso powder

Pinch sea salt

4 ounces bittersweet chocolate

**Difficulty level: Difficult**

### Step 1
Preheat oven to 425 degrees.

Butter a 9-inch springform pan. Cut a piece of parchment paper to fit the bottom. Place in the bottom of the pan. Butter the parchment, mix equal parts sugar and cocoa powder, and coat the pan by tilting and rotating it until the mixture is evenly spread to cover the surface of the pan. Tap out the excess.

### Step 2
Put the butter on a plate and cut into 4 pieces. Put the chocolate and butter in a glass bowl and microwave for 40 seconds. Stir in a circular motion. Repeat until your chocolate has melted and is smooth.

### Step 3
Combine the almond flour, flour, cocoa, and 4 tablespoons of sugar in a small bowl. Stir into the chocolate mixture.

### Step 4
In a stand mixer, or with a handheld mixer, beat the egg yolks with the salt until light and thick. Slowly add the chocolate mixture and beat so the mixture blends and does not separate. Beat in the vanilla and cognac.

### Step 5
With a hand-held mixer, beat the egg whites until they start to stiffen. Gradually add the 4 tablespoons of sugar and beat until stiff.

### Step 6
Mix the beaten egg whites into the chocolate batter at the lowest speed of a stand mixture until incorporated. Scrape down the sides with a spatula a few times.

### Step 7
Pour into the prepared cake pan. Tap on the counter to remove air bubbles. Bake for just 18 minutes. No longer! The cake will firm as it cools. Place the cake on a cooling rack until it has cooled. Remove from the pan and glaze with the following chocolate glaze.

**Chocolate glaze**

**Step 1**

Bring the liquids, instant espresso, and salt to a boil in a small saucepan. Boil for 2 minutes. Add the chocolate, cover the pan, turn heat off, and let it rest for 5 minutes.

**Step 2**

Stir the chocolate in one direction from the center until cooled and thickened.

**Step 3**

Put the cake on a cardboard round to fit. Transfer to a wire rack. Put a cookie sheet under it to catch the glaze. Pour all the glaze on the cake. Then push the glaze over the sides with a spatula to cover the cake completely. Work quickly, or the glaze will thicken and become difficult to spread.

The cake will sink in the middle which is normal, so you have to help the glaze down over the sides.

I like to decorate this with little bits of gold leaf. This cake freezes well. You can take it out of the freezer and heat it in the microwave for a few seconds. You will get a different taste—cold on the inside and warm on the outside

# FINANCERS

| Prep time | Actual time | Serves |
|---|---|---|
| 20 min. | 40 min., plus 3 hours resting time | 6 little loafs (or bars of baked gold) |

### Step 1
Generously butter a 6 cake silicone mold and refrigerate until ready to bake.

### Step 2
In a small saucepan over medium heat, melt butter, occasionally swirling, until butter starts to brown, about 5 minutes. Take off heat and set aside. Watch carefully so that you don't let it burn.

### Step 3
Place the almond flour into a medium size bowl. Sift the powdered sugar, flour, cake flour, salt, and baking powder over the almond flour. Stir to combine with a fork.

### Step 4
In a separate bowl, whisk together the egg whites until lightly beaten. Slowly add to the flour mixture, stirring just to combine. Do not over-mix or the cakes will be tough.

### Step 5
Whisk the vanilla into the melted butter. Through a strainer, in a steady stream, slowly whisk the butter mixture into the batter until incorporated. Spoon into molds to fill halfwayway. Refrigerate for at least 2 hours or overnight.

### Step 6
Preheat oven to 375 degrees. Bake for 18 to 20 minutes or until they are browned and springy to the touch. Place on a wire rack for 5 minutes, unmold, and dust with powdered sugar.

**Ingredients**
9 tablespoons unsalted butter, plus melted butter for the molds
1 ¼ cup powdered sugar
¾ cup almond flour
¼ cup all-purpose flour
1 tablespoon, plus 2 teaspoons cake flour
Pinch salt
1 teaspoons baking powder
4 egg whites, at room temperature
1 teaspoon vanilla extract

**Difficulty level: Difficult**

With their versatility and heavenly taste, financiers truly represent the possibilities of French pastry making. These little cakes were developed by Lasne whose bakery was located in the Parisian financial district. As such, the rectangular molds used to create this dessert leads to a finished product resembling a bar of gold.

Financiers are a splendid choice to accompany a warm cup of tea for a relaxing afternoon snack. They can also be dressed up with a scoop of ice cream, allowing the contrasting temperatures and flavors to create a delightful combination. Another great way to enjoy financiers is to pair them with a freshly brewed cup of coffee in the morning, as their buttery richness provides an indulgent start to the day.

# CHRISTMAS FRUIT CAKE
*(you will actually like)*

**Prep time**
1 hr., 30 min.

**Actual time**
1 day for marinating the fruit, 3 days to baste

**Serves**
6 cakes

### Ingredients
4 cups water

1 cup of each of the following dried fruits:

Dried apricots, chopped

Dried cherries

Currants

Dried cranberries

Dark raisins

Golden raisins

Prunes, chopped

1 pound pitted, dried dates, chopped

3 cups all-purpose flour

1 teaspoon salt

1 teaspoon baking soda

1 teaspoon baking powder

2 sticks unsalted butter, at room temperature

3 cups sugar

6 eggs

1 cup sour cream

¼ cup orange liqueur or brandy (for the fruit)

½ to 1 cup brandy (to pour over the loaves)

1 tablespoon vanilla extract

1 cup nuts of choice (pistachios, walnuts, or pecans)

Zest of one orange

**Difficulty level: Moderate**

### Step 1
In a large saucepan over medium heat, bring the water to a boil. Add the apricots, cherries, currants, cranberries, both of the raisins, and prunes, and simmer for 10 minutes, stirring occasionally. Remove pan from the heat and stir in the dates. Stir in brandy or orange liqueur.

Set aside and let cool until the fruit has completely cooled and plumped, about 2 hours (or you can leave it covered in a cool place overnight).

### Step 2
Heat oven to 350 degrees. Butter the loaf pans.

### Step 3
Combine the flour, salt, baking powder, and baking soda in a medium bowl and set aside.

In an electric stand mixer on medium speed, beat the butter until light and fluffy, and gradually add the sugar. Continue beating until the mixture is creamed. Add the eggs, one at a time, beating after adding each egg until well incorporated. Add the liqueur and vanilla.

Beat for 2 minutes, then lower speed to low. Slowly add half of the flour to the mixture, then add the rest of the flour, along with the sour cream, beating until just blended. Continue mixing for 2 minutes. Fold in the fruits, nuts, and orange zest.

### Step 4
Pour the mixture into the buttered loaf pans filling to ¾ full. I use 4 by 9 inch pans. Bake for about 45 minutes or until the top of each loaf is firm to the touch. Remove from the oven and pour over the rest of the liqueur, a few tablespoons for each cake.

Repeat marinating with ½ cup of brandy for the next three days.

Enjoy, or give away!

Through cherished memories, a time-honored tradition emerges: crafting fruitcakes each Christmas season. My culinary exploration has encompassed countless recipes, from classic candied fruit to decadent chocolate variations. Among them, one recipe reigns supreme that truly keeps on giving. Year after year, I lovingly create these fruitcakes as gifts for beloved friends and family. **Now, I extend this treasured recipe to *you*. A recipe that produces a moist and flavorful holiday companion that certainly has never ended up as a doorstop by valentines day.**

# OAK'S WHITE BARK COOKIES

**Prep time**
5 min.

**Actual time**
20 min.

**Serves**
30

### Ingredients
2 pounds white chocolate (I use Valrhona)
2 cups Kellog's Rice Krispies
2 cups mini marshmallows
2 cups Skippy Chunky peanut butter
1 cup dry roasted peanuts

**Difficulty level: Easy**

### Step 1
Stovetop version: Put the white chocolate in a double boiler with the water barely simmering. Stir occasionally until it has melted. Stir in the peanut butter until smooth.

Microwave version: Put chocolate in a glass bowl and microwave for 30 seconds; stir another 30 seconds until melted and smooth (I prefer this method, as it is easier to control; white chocolate is very delicate and burns easily).

### Step 2
In a large bowl, combine Rice Krispies, marshmallows, and peanuts. Slowly stir in the melted chocolate mixture until well incorporated.

### Step 3
Line baking sheets with parchment paper. Drop golf ball-size dollops of the cookie mixture onto the parchment. You can put them fairly close together. Chill in the refrigerator until they are set.

These freeze well.

This multi-generational recipe holds a special place in my heart. My mother lovingly taught me how to make these delightful cookies, usually during the magical Christmas season. Over the years, they have become a tradition of my family and one of my son's most looked forward to holiday treats. Which is why they are named after him.

When making these quick, no-bake cookies, it is important to use high-quality white chocolate, as lower quality options often substitute vegetable oil for cocoa butter. Genuine white chocolate tends to have a yellowish hue instead of a pure white shade due to the presence of real ivory-colored cocoa butter. Because of this, it's important to avoid mixing two different brands of white chocolate, as they may have varying melting properties.

OBSERVATIONS FOR BAKING PG 298 FROM NANETTE
APPX A
APPX A

# PECAN LEMON SHORTBREAD

**Prep time** 10 min.

**Actual time** 35 min.

**Serves** 2 dozen cookies

### Step 1
Preheat oven to 350 degrees.

In a food processor fitted with the metal blade, combine the flour, sugar, cornstarch, lemon zest, and vanilla extract. Pulse briefly until well incorporated. Add the butter and vanilla extract. Using a rapid on/off pulse, process until the mixture resembles a fine meal. Add the pecans and process until mixture forms a dough.

### Step 2
Transfer the mixture to a large sheet of waxed paper and gather to form a flat disk. Top with another sheet of waxed paper. Roll out the dough to ¼ inch thick. Using a cookie cutter of your choice, cut out the cookies. Gather up the scraps, roll out again and cut additional cookies.

### Step 3
Lay the cookies on a sheet pan lined with parchment paper. Bake until just beginning to lightly brown, about 20 minutes. Transfer cookies to a cooling rack and let cool.

You may sprinkle them with sugar before baking, or when they are out of the oven and cool. You can also make a paste with powdered sugar and a little limoncello and spread on top. Grate a little lemon zest on top.

Once cool, they can be kept in an airtight container for up to a week.

## Ingredients
- 1 ½ cup all-purpose flour
- ½ cup sugar
- ¼ cup cornstarch
- 1 tablespoon plus 1 teaspoon grated lemon zest
- ¼ teaspoon salt
- ¾ cup unsalted butter, chilled and cut into ½ inch pieces
- 1 teaspoon vanilla extract
- 1 cup pecans

**Difficulty level: Easy**

Creating delectable sweets on the fly was a common request that would often be handed to me at a moment's notice when I worked as a private chef. Traditional shortbread has the potential to be overly simple and dry. However, this iteration with rich pecans and bright lemon zest creates a delicate and pretty cookie. Pairing them with raspberry or vanilla ice cream, or even a lemon gelato, takes this easy recipe to the next level.

259

# WALNUT SHORTBREAD COOKIES

**Prep time**
25 min.

**Actual time**
1 hr., 10 min.

**Serves**
4 dozen cookies

### Ingredients
4 cups walnut pieces
1 cup (2 sticks) unsalted butter, softened to room temperature
¾ cup brown sugar
¾ cup confectioners' sugar
2 teaspoons vanilla extract
Sugar (to sprinkle on cookies before baking)
2 cups all-purpose flour
½ teaspoon salt

**Difficulty level: Moderate**

### Step 1
Preheat oven to 350 degrees.

Spread walnut pieces on baking sheets and roast in the oven for about 10 minutes, or until they are golden brown and you start to smell the fragrant aroma. Let cool.

### Step 2
In a food processor, add walnuts and finely chop. Be careful to not overdo it or they will start to turn to nut butter.

### Step 3
Reduce oven temperature to 325 degrees.

In an electric stand mixer, cream the butter, brown sugar, and confectioners' sugar until smooth, creamy, and pale. This will take some time. You will need to scrape the mixture from the sides of the bowl from time to time. Beat in the vanilla extract.

### Step 4
In a separate bowl, mix together the flour, salt, and ground nuts. Add the dry ingredients to the butter mixture and beat until it forms a soft dough.

Wrap the dough tightly in plastic wrap and chill until firm enough to handle, at least 30 minutes, or overnight.

### Step 5
Line 2 sheet pans with parchment paper.

Divide the dough into 2 pieces. Rolling one piece at a time, flour your work surface and roll to ½ an inch thick. You can either use a cookie cutter or make 2 ½ inch long by 1 inch wide pieces. Pat the remaining dough back into a rectangle and continue to cut out cookies. Repeat this process with the second piece of dough until all the dough has been used.

Place cookies on a sheet pan, allowing some room for them to expand. Sprinkle cookies with sugar. Bake for 15 to 25 minutes until they are a golden brown. Remove cookies to a wire rack to cool.

I like to melt bittersweet chocolate and drizzle it over the cookies.

When cooled, they can be stored in an airtight container for up to a week.

There's nothing quite like a scrumptious cookie to convey heartfelt appreciation, especially during the holiday season when we all long for that extra connection. It's a time when we can remind our loved ones that their dedication and hard work has not gone unnoticed. As a token of respect to my dear friends and treasured colleagues who have filled my life with their presence, I take great delight in baking these irresistibly delicious walnut cookies as my way of saying "thank you." They carry the warmth of gratitude for the ease and joy others bring to my life throughout the year and beyond.

# SAFFRON SHORTBREAD

**Prep time**
15 min.

**Actual time**
35 min.

**Serves**
9 – 12 shortbreads

### Ingredients
½ teaspoon saffron threads
2 cups all-purpose flour
1 teaspoon baking powder
¼ teaspoon salt
⅔ cup sugar
2 sticks unsalted butter, cold, cut up into 1-inch cubes
2 teaspoons orange flower water

**Difficulty level: Easy**

### Step 1
Preheat oven to 325 degrees.
Set a small wire rack over a small saucepan of boiling water. Put the saffron into a small saucer and steam it for 2 to 3 minutes, or until it is brittle.

### Step 2
Mix the saffron, flour, baking powder, salt, and sugar in a food processor and pulse until well combined. Add the butter cubes and pulse until it resembles coarse cornmeal. Sprinkle the dough with the orange flower water and pulse to blend.

### Step 3
Remove the dough and pat it into an ungreased, 8-inch square baking pan. Bake until golden, about 20 minutes. Remove from the oven and cut into squares while it is still warm in the baking pan. Cool on a wire rack.

Saffron is an incredible spice that enchants dishes with its scent, flavor and vibrant color. The reason for its high price point is because it is sourced from *Crocus Sativus*; the vivid crimson stigma and styles, called *threads*, are gently collected by hand and dried. A substantial amount of threads is required to yield just one ounce. These delightful cookies make a wonderful finale to any Indian meal, perfectly showcasing the allure of saffron's flavors.

OBSERVATIONS FOR SAFFRON
APPX A
PG 300
APPX A
FROM NANETTE

# COWBOY COOKIES

| **Prep time** | **Actual time** | **Serves** |
|---|---|---|
| 20 min. | 40 min. | 72 cookies |

### Step 1
Preheat oven to 350 degrees.
Whisk together the flour, baking powder, baking soda, cinnamon, and salt in a bowl.

### Step 2
In a stand mixer, beat the butter on medium speed until smooth and creamy. Depending on the temperature of the butter, it will take about 3 to 6 minutes. Gradually beat in sugars and look for a fluffy texture. Add eggs one at a time, beating well after each egg. Beat in the vanilla extract. Stir in the flour mixture until combined. Turn mixer to low and slowly add the chocolate chip, rolled oats, coconut, and pecans.

### Step 3
Line two baking sheets with parchment paper, and with a large tablespoon, drop cookies on the pan, leaving enough space between the cookies for them to expand (about 1 ½ inch). Bake for 17 to 19 minutes, until the edges are lightly browned.
Rotate the pans halfway through the cooking. Remove cookies to a wire rack. Serve with milk or coffee.

**Ingredients**
3 cups flour
1 tablespoon baking flour
1 tablespoon baking powder
1 tablespoon baking soda
1 tablespoon ground cinnamon
1 teaspoon kosher salt
1 ½ cups unsalted butter, at room temperature
1 ½ cups sugar
1 ½ cups light brown sugar
3 large eggs
1 tablespoon vanilla extract
3 cups semisweet chocolate chips
3 cups old-fashioned rolled oats
2 cups sweetened coconut flakes
2 cups chopped pecans

**Difficulty level: Moderate**

264

I love searching for recipes in various places: magazines, cookbooks, online, and those shared by my friends and family. Unexpectedly, in one such pursuit, I stumbled upon this recipe in an old magazine featuring an expose on Laura Bush. *What captivated me was its delightful combination of nuts, chocolate, coconut, oats, and a hint of cinnamon*—a true delight for cookie lovers!

Finding ways for individuals with ingredient sensitivities to enjoy specific dishes can be challenging, but the effort is undoubtedly rewarding and appreciated. Those who have gluten intolerance will adore these chocolate walnut cookies. I initially discovered this recipe at Payard, a renowned New York bakery and restaurant named after the esteemed French pastry chef, François Payard. The ambiance at Payard was delightfully warm and inviting, reminiscent of these fantastic cookies. Regrettably, the establishment is no longer open, but this treasured recipe continues to thrive in its memory.

# FLOURLESS CHOCOLATE COOKIES

| Prep time | Actual time | Serves |
|---|---|---|
| 20 min. | 45 min. | 15-18 cookies |

### Ingredients

2 ¾ cups walnuts

3 cups confectioners' sugar

½ cup plus 3 tablespoons Dutch processed cocoa powder (I use Valrhona)

¼ teaspoon sea salt

4 large egg whites, at room temperature

1 tablespoon vanilla extract

**Difficulty level: Easy**

### Step 1

Preheat oven to 350 degrees.

Spread the walnuts on a baking sheet and toast in the oven for 9 to 10 minutes, or until they are golden brown; you will probably smell the wonderful nutty fragrance when they are ready. Transfer them to a cutting board and coarsely chop them when they are cool.

### Step 2

Position two racks in the upper and lower sections of your oven. Turn down the temperature to 320 degrees. Line baking sheets with parchment paper.

### Step 3

In an electric stand mixer bowl, add the powdered sugar, cocoa powder, and salt, and mix on low speed. Add the walnuts. Increase the speed to medium and add the egg whites and vanilla extract. Beat the batter until it is moistened. Do not overbeat, or the batter will stiffen, about 30 seconds.

### Step 4

Place a heaping spoonful of batter onto the parchment-lined sheet pans to form large cookies—about 6 per tray. Bake for 14 to 16 minutes, until they are glossy and slightly cracked. Shift the pans from front to back and top to bottom halfway through the baking to ensure even baking. Cool on a wire rack. You can store them in an airtight container for up to 3 days.

267

# MOCHA COOKIES

| Prep time | Actual time | Serves |
|---|---|---|
| 20 min. | 1 hr. | 36 cookies |

### Ingredients

4 ounces of Baker's unsweetened chocolate, chopped

3 cups semisweet chocolate chips, divided into 1 ½ cups (be sure to purchase real chocolate semi-sweet chocolate chips. Most inexpensive brands are full of chemicals, which alter the flavor and texture)

1 stick unsalted butter

½ cup all-purpose flour

½ teaspoon baking powder

½ teaspoon kosher salt

4 large eggs, at room temperature

1 ½ cup sugar

1 ½ tablespoons instant espresso powder

2 teaspoons vanilla extract

**Difficulty level: Moderate**

### Step 1

Preheat oven to 350 degrees.

Combine the unsweetened chocolate, 1 ½ cups of chocolate chips, and butter in a plastic or glass bowl. Place in the microwave and cook for 30 seconds. Stir and repeat this process until the chocolate and butter have completely melted. You can also do this in a double boiler. However, I find the microwave so much easier.

### Step 2

In a small bowl, stir together the flour, baking powder, and salt. Set aside.

In a bowl, beat the eggs and sugar using a handheld beater or a stand mixer until the mixture is thick and pale, about 8 minutes. Beat in the espresso powder and vanilla. With a rubber spatula, fold in the chocolate mixture into the egg mixture. Fold in the flour mixture. Stir in the remaining 1 ½ cups of chocolate chips. Let the batter rest for 15 minutes.

### Step 3

Drop a heaping spoonful of batter onto a parchment-lined baking sheet. Bake in the oven on the middle rack for 8 to 10 minutes. Rotate halfway through the baking. They should be puffed, shiny, and cracked on top. Transfer to a cooling rack.

The softness inside these cookies resembles a truffle when you bite into it. These also freeze incredibly well; I love eating these either fresh out of the oven or right out of the freezer. The cold creates an entirely different texture and taste that is just delightful.

When I lived in New York, my apartment was right next door to FDNY Rescue #1 in Hell's Kitchen. I knew most of the brave and hardworking people of that station house by name, and will always have a place in my heart for our first responders and their immense sacrifice. As a chef, I found my own way to show appreciation by bringing them whatever I could, whenever possible. However, my most frequent offering would be cookies. Sometimes, when they would see me coming, and would shout, "Here comes the cookie lady!" To be recognized as a part of the neighborhood by the guardians who I admired so much was a true testament to how the simple act of sharing a plate of cookies can form meaningful and lasting memories within a community.

# BITTERSWEET CHOCOLATE TART

**Prep time**
25 min.

**Actual time**
1 hr. and 30 min.

**Serves**
Serves 6 with one 9-inch tart

### Ingredients
¾ cup heavy cream
⅓ cup whole milk
7 ounces bittersweet chocolate
1 egg, lightly beaten

### Shortbread Crust
*This recipe makes enough for 1, 8 inch tart shell.*

1 cup all purpose flour
⅓ cup confectioners sugar (powdered sugar)
⅛ teaspoon kosher salt
1 teaspoon vanilla extract
4 ounces unsalted butter, chilled and cut into small cubes

**Difficulty level: Moderate**

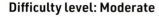

**For the shortbread pastry shell**

**Step 1**

In a food processor, place flour, sugar, salt in a bowl and pulse to combine.

Add the cold butter and vanilla and pulse until mixture starts to come together and forms a clumps, about 1 1/2 to 2 minutes.

**Step 2**

Lightly butter or spray with a nonstick spray a tart pan with a removable bottom. This prevents the crust from sticking.

Transfer the pastry to the prepared pan and using your fingertips evenly press the pastry onto the bottom and up the sides of the tart pan. Take your time with this and try to make it even as possible. You can use the back of a spoon to even it out. Gently pierce the bottom with the tines of a fork. Cover and place in a freezer to chill for 15 minutes.

**Step 3**

Preheat oven to 425 degrees.

When the 15 minutes is up place the tart pan on a larger baking sheet. Line with parchment paper and pie weights or beans to bake blind. Bake for 13 to 15 minutes or until it starts to turn golden.

Take out of oven and cool on a wire rack. When cool, remove pie weights, and add the chocolate filling.

**For the filling**

**Step 1**

Preheat oven to 375 degrees. In a small saucepan, combine the cream and bring to a simmer over medium heat. Remove from heat, add the chocolate, and stir until thoroughly melted, about 2 minutes.

**Step 2**

When it is cool, whisk in the beaten egg until thoroughly blended. Pour it into the cooled pastry shell. Bake it for 12 to 15 minutes until it is set.

Transfer to a wire rack to cool. It may be served warm or at room temperature.

My chef friend, Trudy, gave me this fantastic recipe. She and her husband Steve are the most talented, thoughtful, and creative chefs I have had the pleasure to work with. We first met when we were all working as private chefs in New York City. When you're a private chef, you mostly work alone except when you're having a large dinner party and bringing in help for the day. We formed a lasting bond as we helped each other deliver sensational food for our clients. Occasionally, we would all have a night off together which gave us a chance to go out to one of the many exceptional restaurants in New York, curiously seeking out inspiration, laughter, and comradery. All we did was talk about food! It was always a delightful time and bittersweet as it ended but it that still influences my creativity to this day.

**This delectable tart offers a luscious, chocolate indulgence.** By preparing the pastry tart in advance, this uncomplicated recipe yields a sophisticated result, perfect for an elegant finish to any memorable evening.

When the crisp Autumn air starts to chill the bones, we all need a little extra something to warm the soul. This classic French apple tart is like a reliable friend who you can always count on to lift the spirits.

I have made this recipe hundreds of times and it never fails to deliver. The thinly sliced apple melts into a buttery expression of autumn that is heightened by a hint of cinnamon and finished with an apricot jam glaze, creating a simple yet scrumptious bite.

**YOU'VE GOT TO READ THE RECIPE!**
**READ THE RECIPE NOT ONCE, TWO TIMES**
**BEFORE MAKING YOUR MASTERPIECE... ALWAYS!**
—NANETTE

# FRENCH APPLE TART

| Prep time | Actual time | Serves |
|---|---|---|
| 35 min. | 1 hr. and 15 min. | 6-8 |

### Ingredients

1 tart dough (see page 17), at room temperature

2 teaspoons cinnamon (added when making the pastry)

6 Golden Delicious apples; you can use another apple if you wish such as Pink Lady, Macintosh, or Fuji

⅓ cup sugar

½ stick (¼ cup) unsalted butter, cut into small slivers and chilled

½ cup apricot jam

Tart pan

### Whipped Cream for tart

1 cup whipping cream

2 tablespoons powdered sugar

½ to 1 teaspoon cinnamon

1 to 2 tablespoons Calvados brandy

**Difficulty level: Easy**

### Step 1

Preheat oven to 400 degrees.

Roll out the room-temperature pastry dough to about ⅛ to thickness, fold into threes, move to a tart pan and unfold. Press the dough firmly into the pan and cut off any excess with a floured rolling pin. Prick the bottom of the shell with a fork and chill for 1 hour.

Cut a piece of parchment to fit over the dough. Cover dough with it and fill with pie weights (you can also use rice or beans). Bake for 15 minutes, then remove the parchment and pie weights. Bake for another 10 minutes, or until lightly browned.

### Step 2

Increase oven temperature to 450 degrees.

Core apples (I like to use an apple corer). Cut apples in half, and using a mandoline, slice very thinly. Arrange the slices in the shell overlapping one another. Add one layer of apples, sprinkle half the sugar and cold butter cubes, then repeat with another layer in that order. Bake for 45 minutes, until the crust and apples are browned.

### Step 3

Remove the tart from the oven and transfer to a cooling rack. Melt the apricot jam in a small saucepan over moderate heat until it liquifies. Strain through a fine sieve and brush it on the apples. Let sit until the tart is lukewarm and serve.

I like to serve it with a dollop of flavored whipped cream (recipe follows).

### Make the Whipped Cream
### Step 1

Using a hand mixer, whip cream until it has stiff peaks. Add cinnamon, sugar, Calvados and whip until blended.

274

Early summer brings an abundance of luscious treats, and one of my favorites is rhubarb. I prepare this recipe every year, aiming to strike the perfect balance between sweetness and tartness. The inspritaion for this recipe, courtesy of Alice Waters, the esteemed farm-to-table restaurateur and chef of Chez Panisse, stands out as the best among many that I have tried.

The defining quality of a galette—also known as a *crostata* if you have Italian inclinations—is its free-form shape, baked without the confinement of a pie pan or tart ring. While the dough requires some effort, the result is truly worth it. I enjoy serving it with raspberry sorbet or ice cream, as the sublime combination of tangy raspberry and rhubarb, aside warm and cold temperatures, creates a landscape of sensation that embodies the color of 9pm sunsets, wonder of fireflies, and the jubilate delight of empty plates.

# RHUBARB GALETTE

| Prep time | Actual time | Serves |
|---|---|---|
| 35 min. | 1 hr. 20 min., plus chill time | 6 |

**Galette dough**

*This recipe is enough for 2 galettes. I freeze one, so I have it on hand when needed.*

2 cups unbleached flour

1 teaspoon sugar

¼ teaspoon salt

12 tablespoons unsalted butter (1 ½ sticks), chilled and cut into ½ inch pieces

7 to 9 tablespoons ice water

**Filling**

1 ½ pound rhubarb

2 cup sugar, plus 2 tablespoons for the outside of the dough

½ cup flour

¼ cup almond flour

¼ cup graham crackers, or amaretto cookies, coarsely ground

1 tablespoon heavy cream

3 tablespoons unsalted butter

**Difficulty level: Difficult**

**For the dough**

**Step 1**

Combine the flour, sugar, and salt in a large mixing bowl. Cut 4 tablespoons of butter into the flour mixture with a pastry blender, mixing until the dough resembles coarse cornmeal (butter dispersed throughout the flour in tiny pieces makes the dough tender). Cut in the remaining 8 tablespoons of butter with the pastry blender until the biggest pieces of butter are the size of large peas. These bigger pieces of butter in the dough make it flaky.

**Step 2**

Dribble 7 tablespoons of ice water into the flour mixture in several stages, tossing and mixing between additions until the dough holds together. Toss the mixture with your hands, letting it fall through your fingers; do not pinch or squeeze the dough together, or you will overwork it, which will make the dough tough. Keep tossing the mixture until it starts to pull together; it will look rather ropey, with some dry patches. If it seems like there are more dry patches than ropey parts, add another tablespoon of water and toss the mixture until it comes together.

**Step 3**

Divide the dough in half, firmly press each half into a ball, and wrap tightly in plastic wrap, pressing down to flatten each ball into a 4-inch disk. Refrigerate for at least 30 minutes before rolling out. It will freeze for several weeks.

**Step 4**

When you're ready to roll out the dough, take one disk. Let it soften slightly so that it is malleable but still cold. Unwrap the dough and press the edges so that there are no cracks. On a lightly floured surface, roll the disk into a 14-inch circle, about ⅛ inch thick. Brush off any excess flour from both sides with a dry pastry brush.

**Step 5**

Transfer the dough to a parchment-lined baking sheet and refrigerate at least 30 minutes before using.

## For the filling
### Step 1
Preheat oven to 400 degrees.

Line a baking sheet with parchment paper. Trim and discard every bit of leaves from the rhubarb, and cut off the tough part at the end of the rhubarb. Cut into ½ inch cubes. In a large mixing bowl, toss the rhubarb with 1 ¾ cup of sugar and the flours. Chill the mixture for 30 min.s to allow the flours to be absorbed.

### Step 2
Take out the rolled dough and place it on the parchment-lined sheet pan and sprinkle the graham cracker crumbs over the dough, leaving a two-inch border. Pile the rhubarb mixture high on top (it will reduce down when cooking).

### Step 3
To form the galette, rotate the dough, fold over the 2-inch border to expose the dough, and pull up and over on itself at regular intervals, crimping and pushing it up against the circle of fruit. Make sure there are no holes where the juices can leak out. Brush the border with the cream and sprinkle with the 2 tablespoons of sugar. Dot the top with the butter.

### Step 4
Place sheet pan in the center of the oven, rotating every 15 minutes to ensure even baking on all sides. Gently push down the rhubarb in the center with a spatula to flatten it. Bake for 45 minutes. Let cool.

To serve, place on a serving platter.

# OAK'S CHOCOLATE MOUSSE

**Prep time**
15 min.

**Actual time**
15 min., plus several hours to chill

**Serves**
6

### Step 1
In a small saucepan, bring sugar and water to a boil until sugar has dissolved. Set aside.

### Step 2
In a food processor with a metal blade, add the eggs, chocolate bits, coffee, and salt. Process several seconds until combined. With the machine running, pour syrup carefully through the feed tube and process until smooth, about 20 to 30 seconds more. Add liquor and pulse a few times.

### Step 3
In a small bowl, add cream and beat with a handheld mixer until stiff. Place the whipped cream on the chocolate mixture and pulse the processor on and off until the cream disappears. Transfer the mixture to individual dessert bowls or one serving bowl, and place in the refrigerator to chill for at least 4 hours. I like to pour it into old coupe glasses.

### For whipped cream garnish
In a small mixing bowl, combine heavy cream and sugar. With a handheld mixer, beat until almost stiff; about 3 to 4 minutes. Add liquor and beat until stiff.

To serve, remove from the refrigerator and add a spoonful of whipped cream on top.

### Ingredients
½ cup heavy cream, chilled
½ cup sugar
¼ cup water
2 eggs
6 ounces semisweet chocolate, chopped (I use two different brands, 3 ounces of each. You can also use milk chocolate instead)
½ teaspoon instant coffee
Pinch salt
2 tablespoons Grand Marnier; feel free to use any other liqueur such as Kahlua or Framboise

### For the garnish of whipped cream
½ cup heavy cream, chilled
1 to 2 tablespoons powdered sugar
1 to 2 tablespoons of the same liqueur used for the mousse, to taste

**Difficulty level: Easy**

The satisfaction I derive from preparing food for my son is truly indescribable. He serves as my best critic, my pillar of purpose, and an all-around wonderful support in my life. I came up with this recipe when he was just a kid banging pots and pans on the kitchen floor of our tiny apartment in Santa Fe. The happy look on his face whenever he takes his first bite lights up my entire world. Even when he travels and spots chocolate mousse on a menu, he always orders it, but never fails to mention that mine is his favorite.

I formulated this recipe while juggling the many demands of single parenthood, and sought to create a dessert that is quick and easy to make. It's worth noting that the taste may vary depending on the type of chocolate and liqueur you choose to incorporate. Moreover, the entire preparation is done in a food processor, ensuring hassle-free cleanup.

# MY FAVORITE CHOCOLATE TRUFFLES

| Prep time | Actual time | Serves |
| --- | --- | --- |
| 10 min. | 2 hr., 30 min. | 30 - 35 |

### Ingredients
10 ounces bittersweet chocolate; 5 ounces of one brand and 5 ounces of another brand
3 tablespoons unsalted butter
1 tablespoon light corn syrup
¼ cup Grand Marnier
1 tablespoon grated orange rind
Cocoa powder for rolling the truffles

**Difficulty level: Easy**

### Step 1
In a medium glass bowl, combine the chocolate and butter, and place it in the microwave. Microwave for 30 seconds, remove, and stir. Repeat this process until thoroughly melted and smooth, about 4 times.

### Step 2
In a small saucepan over medium heat, add the corn syrup and heat until simmering. Remove from the heat, pour over the melted chocolate mixture, and let stand for 2 minutes.

### Step 3
Using a rubber spatula, stir gently, starting in the middle of the bowl and working in a concentric circle; stir until the chocolate is smooth and creamy. Gently stir in the Grand Marnier and orange rind until incorporated. Pour this into an 8X8 glass baking dish, and refrigerate for 2 hours or overnight. If you leave it overnight, take it out and let it soften until it is easy to scoop.

### Step 4
Place a melon baller in a glass of hot water. Then, scoop into the chocolate to form a ball and place on a parchment-lined baking sheet. Return melon baller to hot water and repeat until all the chocolate is formed. Chill for 30 minutes.

Add cocoa powder or whatever you are rolling them into in a small bowl. Roll the truffle in the cocoa, put it back on the baking sheet, and chill.

Serve.

The addition of Grand Marnier lends a delightful hint of orange, though you can also try different liqueurs like Framboise (raspberry) or Kahlua (coffee) for alternative flavors. As for the coating, some delicious options are to roll the truffles in coconut, ground nuts, or cocoa nibs. Some chefs prefer to use a pastry bag and pipe the truffle mixture onto a baking sheet, but I find that method results in significant loss of the truffle mixture. Therefore, I personally prefer the melon ball scoop method.

I have experimented with various truffle recipes over the years, but I always gravitate back to this particular one because it effortlessly produces these delicious morsels. They are the perfect treat to give as gifts to family and friends. Years ago, I took a class at the famous La Maison du Chocolat in New York City. One of the vital lessons I learned there was to always use two different kinds of chocolate in a recipe, as they add rich complexity to the finished product.

# RICOTTA DOUGHNUTS WITH CHOCOLATE SAUCE

**Prep time**
20 min.

**Actual time**
45 min., plus time to drain the ricotta

**Serves**
4-6

### Ingredients
**For the ricotta**
yields 1 ½ cups

4 cups whole milk

2 cups heavy cream

1 teaspoon kosher salt

3 tablespoons high-quality white wine

¼ teaspoon citric acid

**For the chocolate sauce**

1 ½ cup water

1 cup sugar

1 ⅓ cup Dutch process cocoa powder

½ teaspoon kosher salt

½ teaspoons cinnamon

2 teaspoon vanilla extract

**For the doughnuts**

1 cup fresh ricotta

2 large eggs

½ tablespoon Kirschwasser or liquor of choice

½ to 1 cup all-purpose flour

1 ½ teaspoons baking powder

Oil for frying (I like to use avocado or grapeseed oil)

**For dusting the doughnuts**

1 cup sugar

2 teaspoon ground cinnamon

**Difficulty level: Moderate**

### For the ricotta
**Step 1**

Set a large sieve over a deep bowl. Dampen 4 layers of cheesecloth with water and line the sieve with the damp cheesecloth.

Pour the milk and cream into a stainless steel or enameled saucepan. Stir in the salt and citric acid. Bring to a full boil over medium heat, stirring occasionally. Add white wine and continue to stir until curds begin to form. Take off heat, allowing the mixture to stand for 10 to 30 minutes or until it curdles.

**Step 2**

Pour the mixture into the cheesecloth-lined sieve and allow it to drain into the bowl separating the curds from the whey; the longer you let it drain, the thicker it will become. I like it to be on the thicker side, so I usually let it drain overnight.

Transfer the ricotta to a bowl and use it immediately, or cover it with plastic wrap and refrigerate. It will keep for five days.

### For the chocolate sauce
**Step 1**

In a medium saucepan, boil the water and sugar over medium heat, occasionally whisking, for 5 minutes. Whisk in the cocoa powder, salt, and cinnamon. Reduce heat to low and simmer until sauce thickens, about 3 minutes. Remove from heat and stir in the vanilla extract.

### For the doughnuts
**Step 1**

In a bowl, whisk together the ricotta, eggs, and Kirschwasser. Sift the flour, baking powder, and salt in another bowl. In a small mixing bowl, combine the cinnamon and sugar set aside.

**Step 2**

Add ricotta mixture to flour mixture and stir until well combined. Batter can be made ahead of time, covered with plastic wrap until ready to fry.

**Step 3**

Fill a heavy-bottom saucepan (I use a 6 inch) ¾ full with oil. Heat over medium heat until the thermometer reads 350 degrees. Using 2 spoons, drop a rounded spoonful of the batter into the hot oil. Fry in small batches to help maintain a steady temperature. Fry the doughnuts until they are golden on all sides, flipping once, about 5 minutes. Remove from oil to a baking sheet lined with paper towels to drain. While they are hot, roll in the cinnamon sugar.

Transfer to a serving dish and serve with the chocolate sauce.

Many homechefs may initially feel intimidated by the prospect of making homemade ricotta or managing the deep frying aspect of this recipe. I'm here to tell you that diving into these processes with confidence are both well worth the effort, and will only add to your repertoire of skills in the kitchen. Once you get the chemistry down, you will find that making ricotta yourself is actually quite easy and very enjoyable. The key here is in the consistency; you want a finished product that is firm and not too wet. However, if you're in a pinch or prefer to save yourself the time, store-bought works just fine. Either way, prepare yourself for deep fried delight!

Many years ago, I started making this recipe on Valentine's Day as you hope to share love as cooking has always been my favorite expression of the heart .for whomever I was cooking for at the time. It is a revered traditional French recipe, which produces a light, delicious treat seldom experienced these days. The heart shaped mold provides an endearing presentation that creates lasting memories. The Flourless Chocolate Cookies on page 266 compliments this heavenly dessert exquisitely and guarantees enjoyment for all who taste it.

# CŒUR A LA CREME

| Prep time | Actual time | Serves |
|---|---|---|
| 15 min. | 4 hrs. or overnight, plus 15 min. | 4 |

### Ingredients

4 10x10 inch squares of cheesecloth

1 8-ounce package of cream cheese, at room temperature

1 cup crème fraîche (you can use sour cream or yogurt, but it won't be as unique or distinct)

4 tablespoons powdered sugar

1 teaspoon fresh lemon juice

1 teaspoon vanilla extract

Pinch sea salt

### For the berries

2 cups berries of choice

2 to 3 tablespoons powdered sugar

1 to 2 tablespoons Chambord liqueur

### Coulis

1 pint fresh red raspberries

3 tablespoons sugar (approximately), or more to taste

**Difficulty level: Easy**

### Step 1
Rinse cheesecloth under water; squeeze until just damp. Line each mold with one square of cheesecloth.

### Step 2
In a large bowl, using a stand mixer or a hand held mixer, beat the cream cheese, crème fraîche, 4 tablespoons powdered sugar, lemon juice, vanilla, and pinch of salt until smooth. Scrape down the sides from time to time. Taste, and if the mixture isn't sweet enough, add another tablespoon of powdered sugar.

### Step 3
Divide the mixture between the molds. Fold cheesecloth over the top.

Place the molds on a plate or in a shallow baking dish. Cover with plastic wrap. Chill in a refrigerator for at least 4 hours or overnight.

### For the berries
Stir the powdered sugar and Chambord into the berries and let marinade for at least an hour before serving. When ready to serve, unwrap the molds and invert onto your serving plate. Spoon the berries and juice around the hearts. For an added layer of enjoyment, serve with a raspberry coulis.

### For the Coulis
Put berries and sugar into a food processor or a blender and pulse until pureed. Taste and add more sugar if needed. Strain through a sieve to remove the seeds, and chill until you are ready to serve.

I crafted this delightful dessert specifically for a Japanese-themed dinner, aiming to capture the essence of the region's flavors and textures. The result is a blend of the delicate and earthy notes of matcha, the indulgent allure of hot fudge, and the delicious crunch provided by the pistachio and sesame brittle.

To create this multi-layer experience, start by preparing the hot fudge sauce. You can store it for up to a month and enjoy it on various treats. Consider gifting some of this fantastic sauce to your friends. Enjoy every spoonful and savor the flavors and textures that make this sundae truly exceptional.

# MATCHA ICE CREAM SUNDAES WITH CHOCOLATE
*and Sesame Brittle*

| Prep time | Actual time | Serves |
|---|---|---|
| 30 min. | 1 hr., plus refrigeration time | 6 |

### Ingredients

1 tablespoon matcha powder; depending on the strength of the powder, you might need a touch more (taste and adjust to your palette)

1 cup whole milk

2 cups heavy cream

2 eggs

¾ cup sugar

### Hot fudge sauce

2 cups heavy cream

4 tablespoons unsalted butter

½ cup light brown sugar

¾ cup granulated sugar

½ teaspoon fine sea salt

2 ounces bittersweet chocolate, broken into small pieces

1 ¼ cup sifted high-fat Dutch processed cocoa (sift before you measure); I like Valrhona or Droste brands

1 teaspoon vanilla extract or cognac

**Difficulty level: Moderate**

### Step 1
In a measuring cup, add the matcha powder and 1 tablespoon milk, and stir until well incorporated. Whisk in the rest of the milk.

### Step 2
In a small bowl, whisk the eggs and sugar until blended.

### Step 3
In a medium-sized saucepan, combine the cream and the matcha milk mixture. If you still have lumps of matcha that have not dissolved yet, you can run it through a fine strainer into your measuring cup to better incorporate. Over medium heat, bring mixture to a boil. Remove from heat and slowly add a ½ cup of the mixture into the egg sugar mixture, whisking until blended. Add this back into the saucepan with the matcha mixture. Stir over medium heat until it reaches 170 degrees. Remove from heat and strain into a bowl to cool to room temperature. Refrigerate overnight.

Pour the matcha mixture into an ice cream maker and freeze according to the manufacturer's directions.

### Hot fudge sauce
### Step 1
In a medium saucepan, combine cream, butter, sugars, and salt. Bring to a simmer over medium low heat and simmer for 45 seconds. Add the chocolate and whisk to dissolve. Remove from the heat and add cocoa. Whisk until it is smooth and no lumps remain.

### Step 2
Return the pan to the heat and simmer sauce until it becomes glossy, whisking constantly. Remove from the heat and add the vanilla or cognac.
Do not boil.

### To serve
Decide what serving dish you wish to serve in. I use a pretty old-fashioned champagne glass (a coupe, not a flute), as it is easy to pick up in one's hand. Scoop a nice size serving of ice cream into the dish, top with a ladle of the hot fudge sauce, and top with a piece of the brittle.

# SESAME PISTACHIO BRITTLE

**Prep time** 30 min.
**Actual time** 1 hr.
**Serves** 6

### Step 1
Prepare a baking sheet by lining with parchment paper and lightly buttering it.
Add the sugar to a medium, heavy-bottomed saucepan, and cook over medium heat, watching it carefully. When it begins to liquefy and darken at the edges, use a heatproof spatula to stir it very gently, encouraging the liquefied sugar around the edges to moisten and melt the sugar crystals in the center.

### Step 2
Gently stir in all the sugar until it is melted and the caramel begins to smoke. Once it has a deep, golden color, remove it from the heat and immediately stir in the nuts, seeds, and 5 spice. Scrape the mixture onto the prepared baking sheet and spread it with a spatula into an even layer. Let cool completely. Once cooled, chop the brittle into bite-size pieces with a chef's knife. Store in an airtight container until ready to use.

## Ingredients
- ¼ cup plus 2 tablespoons shelled pistachios
- 3 tablespoons black sesame seeds
- ½ cup sugar
- 1 teaspoon 5 spice seasoning

**Difficulty level: Moderate**

As you continue your journey of a life in food, may you, my dear reader, continue to come back to this book as a source of inspiration and curiosity. Never forget to create your own favorite recipes along the way and share them with the ones you love.

— Nanette

# FAVORITE SAUCES

Sauces and Marinades

# PICKLED CHERRIES

**Actual time:** 20 min.
**Difficulty level:** Easy

## Ingredients
¾ pound cherries, stemmed and pitted (I recommend a cherry pitter; they work so well and save time)
2 sprigs fresh tarragon
3 tablespoons balsamic vinegar
¼ cup sugar
½ cup water
12 black peppercorns
½ stick cinnamon

When cherries are in season, I always make sure to have a fresh supply of these vibrant fruits on hand in my refrigerator. Their juicy and sweet flavor adds a burst of summer flavor to various dishes. They are particularly delicious when incorporated into fresh salads, providing a fruity element to a normally savory dish. Additionally, cherries make a perfect accompaniment as a topping for sautéed duck breast. With their versatility, cherries lend themselves well to many other culinary creations, making them a foundational ingredient that can be used in a myriad of ways.

### Step 1
Take the pit out of the cherries. Put the cherries and tarragon in a glass jar big enough to hold the cherries and liquid.

### Step 2
In a small saucepan, add the vinegars, sugar, peppercorns, cinnamon stick, and water. Over medium-high heat, bring the mixture to a boil until the sugar dissolves. Turn off heat and let cool slightly, about 5 minutes. Pour over the cherries in the jar. Put on the cap. This will keep for one month in the refrigerator.

# LEMON CONFIT

**Prep time:** 15 min.
**Actual time:** 3 days
**Difficulty level:** Easy

## Ingredients
12 lemons (I use Meyer lemons when I can find them)
6 garlic cloves, peeled and minced
5 shallots, peeled and minced
⅔ cup kosher salt
⅓ cup sugar
Extra virgin olive oil

### Step 1
Heat a large pot filled with water. When it has come to a boil, carefully add the lemons and blanch for 1 minute. Strain the lemons into a colander to drain. Dry them on a towel. When they are cooled, remove the ends, slice very thinly, and discard the seeds. Put into a bowl and set aside.

### Step 2
In a small bowl, stir together the garlic and shallots.
In a separate small bowl, stir together the salt and sugar.
In a large mason jar with a wide mouth, or any straight sided jar with a tight fitting lid, arrange a layer of the lemons in the bottom. Sprinkle the lemons first with a layer of the shallots mixture, then with the salt mixture. Repeat, layering all of the lemon slices. The last layer should be with the salt on top. Cover with the lid. Refrigerate the confit for 3 days, shaking it well every day. After 3 days, add enough olive oil to cover the lemons.
When you have used all the lemons, you can use the flavored oil for cooking or in salad dressings.

### Suggestions for using the lemons
Finely mince the drained lemons and add to crème fraîche to place on top of smoked salmon or caviar. Add minced lemons to a hollandaise for asparagus. You can also add to Moroccan tagines.

# SHIO KOJI MARINADE

**Prep time:** 5 min.
**Actual time:** 10 days
**Difficulty level: Easy**

### Ingredients
1 20 ounce container of Cold Mountain Koji
3 ⅓ cups warm water
10 tablespoons kosher salt

### Step 1
Empty the container of dried koji into a large bowl. Add the salt and warm water. Stir until the salt has dissolved.

Put into a flat-bottom, tight-sealing container for fermentation. During the fermentation, carbon dioxide gas will be produced, so keep the lid on a little loose. Place it in an area where the temperature is constant.

During the fermentation, stir the mixture once every day. Fermentation will be from 7 to 10 days. This mix is done when you see a slight thickness when you stir. It will have a nice fragrance when done.

### Marinating
The rule of thumb is to weigh whatever is being marinated. You will want 10 percent of the koji for your marinade. More than that and the marinade will be too salty. After you have marinaded your item, rinse off the koji and dry.

### For vegetables:
Marinate ½ a day in the refrigerator.

### Meats and poultry:
Marinate 1 hour to half a day in the refrigerator.
If it is a large piece of meat, for instance, a standing rib roast, marinade it overnight.

# HOMEMADE MAYONNAISE

**Prep time:** 5 min.
**Actual time:** 10 days
**Difficulty level: Easy**

### Ingredients
3 egg yolks
2 tablespoons vinegar
½ teaspoon salt
⅛ teaspoon white pepper
¾ cup grape seed oil
¾ cup olive oil
Juice of ½ lemon
1 tablespoon hot water

### Oil options:
Grapeseed, Walnut, Safflower, Truffle, Peanut

### Vinegar options:
Raspberry, Red wine, Balsamic, White wine, Champagne
**Difficulty level: Easy**

### Step 1
Have all the ingredients at room temperature. For a better mayonnaise, remove the white, hard piece from the core of the egg that clings to the yolk. In a food processor or a handheld electric mixer, beat the yolks together, then add the vinegar, salt, and pepper.

### Step 2
Slowly add the oil by drops (until your mayonnaise begins to thicken), then add the oil in a very fine, steady stream. After half of the oil has been added, beat until it thickens. Add the rest of the oil in a steady stream until it is all incorporated. It will be thick now. Add the lemon juice to taste. Beat in the hot water, which keeps it from separating.

### Variations: Oils
- You can use different oils and vinegars, which will impart their taste to the mayonnaise.
- My favorite combination is 1 cup grape seed or avocado oil and ½ cup extra virgin olive oil. I found using all olive oil was too strong of a taste.
- You can also add herbs, such as tarragon, dill, or mint.
- I liked one I made with avocado oil, walnut oil, and raspberry vinegar (this one is very good on smoked duck). Try your own combinations and see which ones you like.
- You can also add herbs, such as tarragon, dill, or mint. I liked one I made with avocado oil, walnut oil, and raspberry vinegar (this one is very good on smoked duck).

# ALL PURPOSE BUTTER FOR STUFFING UNDER POULTRY SKIN

**Actual time:** 10 min.
Makes enough for two chickens or one large turkey.

### Ingredients

3 ½ sticks unsalted butter, at room temperature
Juice and grated zest of two lemons
3 cloves garlic, finely minced
2 tablespoons extra virgin olive oil
One lemon to squeeze over the bird before roasting
A handful of herbs such as tarragon or thyme, optional

**Difficulty level: Easy**

### Steps 1

In a food processor, combine all the ingredients and pulse until they are well blended. If you are using herbs, you can add them during this step.

Put your chicken on a cutting board. Gently lift and put your hand under the skin so that it is pulled away from the meat. Do this on both sides. Now take some of the butter compound and flatten it out.

### Step 2

Stuff it under the skin all over the breast, legs, and back. Massage the bird until the butter is distributed. Add a little of the butter to the cavity of the bird. Generously salt and pepper both sides of the bird, and squeeze the juice of the lemon over. Now you're ready to roast your bird.

I use this butter when roasting a whole chicken or turkey, as it helps to keep the poultry moist and adds a delightful flavor to the meat. This is a versatile recipe that can be prepared in advance and kept on hand for any time you want to roast a bird for a special occasion or a comforting weeknight dinner. It can be stored in the refrigerator for about two weeks or frozen for future use. With this butter prepped and ready for use, you'll easily be able to prepare a flavorful meal with minimal steps.

I would like to thank all the chefs who influenced me to become a better chef on my journey:

Julie Child, who made me realize I adore French food.

Anthony Boudain, for being so amazing and showing us other foods of the world.

Jacques Pepin, whose cookbooks were always inspiring.

The Roux Brothers, who helped me to uplevel my game in French cooking.

James Beard, whose recipes brought diversity and worked like a charm every time.

Alma May, who taught me a new trick every time I used her book.

Roger's Verge, who made even the simple vegetable a work of art.

Irma S. Romauer, who wrote the only cookbook I would demand if I were to be stranded on a desert island.

Ottolenghi, for helping me to make more interesting and delicious vegetables and healthy alternatives.

Chef Pate, my instructor at the CIA, who believed in me and helped me see myself as a talented chef.

» FOR THE HOME CHEF «

# OBSERVATIONS FROM NANETTE

CHOP · BAKE

IN THE KITCHEN

## FOR BAKING

1. When placing your cookie dough on a parchment-lined baking sheet, place a small amount of dough on the underside of the four corners of the paper to adhere it to the baking sheet to avoid it curling up.

2. Always use room temperature ingredients for a fluffy and consistent batter or dough. If your eggs are right out of the refrigerator, you can cover them in hot water out of the tap for 5 to 10 minutes to bring to room temperature.

3. Depending on the weather and temperature of the butter, it may take up to 10 minutes to beat the butter to a light and fluffy state.

4. Always use unsalted butter in these recipes.

5. Brown sugar can get rather hard, when that happens, place a slice of apple in the bag to maintain moisture or microwave it for a few seconds while turning to rehydrate and soften.

## FOR COOKING

1. Pay attention to what happens when you're cooking. What is working, what is not working?

2. Taste and then taste again; what does the recipe need to make it right?

A pinch of sugar, a pinch of salt, a dash of balsamic vinegar, a touch of lemon juice.

3. You will know when it is right, it has the balance.

## FOR BEEF

1. Always make sure you bring whatever cut you are using to room temperature before cooking.

2. Try to find a local butcher and develop a relationship with them.

3. Season well and season early when applying salt to a cut of beef; this will tenderize the beef through reverse osmosis. At first, the salt will draw out the moisture from the cut of beef, but as it comes to room temperature, that moisture will be absorbed back into the cut along with the salt.

4. Always allow any cut of beef 10 to 15 minutes of rest after cooking and before carving.

## FOR POULTRY

A great way to save money is to purchase a whole chicken and butcher it yourself. This will also give you the bones to use for a richer chicken stock. Save the skin, put it on an sheet pan, and roast at 350 degrees until crispy for a delicious treat (great to sprinkle on top of a salad).

## FOR DUCK BREAST

Chill the duck breast in the freezer for 10 minutes before scoring the skin crosswise to release the fat so it renders while cooking. Do not pierce the skin.

## FOR GOOSE

If you love goose as much as I do, be sure to pour boiling water over the top and bottom of the bird before seasoning. This process opens the pores of the skin to release more of the fat during roasting.

## FOR THE HOME CHEF
# OBSERVATIONS FROM NANETTE
### CHOP · BAKE
### IN THE KITCHEN

## CHOPPING APPLES

**Don't core or peel!** Start by slicing off the top and bottom then slice vertically around the core. Once you have four sections, slice off the skin and cut into desired shape.

## COUNTER HEIGHT

It is very important to treat your body well when in the kitchen; posture is crucial to long-term health, so make sure your counter is positioned to your natural waistline.

## CUTTING BOARD

When positioning your cutting board, place a kitchen towel larger than your cutting board underneath to:

1. Prevent slipping of the board
2. To collect crumbs and other refuse for quicker clean up.

## FOR GARNISH

**Grinds of a pepper mill:** Depending on your grinder, the coarseness of the grind will affect the number of grinds per recipe. I use a very fine pepper grinder that has been in my family for 3 generations. So, if your grinder is producing a coarser grind, adjust to taste. For example, if a recipe reads for 10 grinds, start with 6 and go from there.

In the fried chicken recipe on page 160 recommends using lard. Lard is actually good for you. It has vitamin D and is a monounsaturated fat which the body can easily break down. It also helps maintain healthy cholesterol levels.

## FOR MAYO

When making homemade mayo, you can hold back on the acidity a bit at first and incorporate more acidity into whatever recipe you are making it for, at the time, using either vinegar or lemon juice.

## SAFFRON

1. When cooking with saffron, I usually add more than the recipe calls for. This is because most recipes limit the amount used, as it is rather expensive. Depending on the recipe, a useful tip is to soak the saffron in hot water or warm milk to draw out the flavor, much like steeping a tea.

2. Saffron is a powerful antioxidant, aphrodisiac, and anti-inflammatory spice which has many health benefits.

## FOR SAUCES

1. Always save your rinds from Parmesan cheese to enrich the flavor of any Italian red sauce or white sauce. You can also use rinds to make a delicious broth. It adds an umami flavor to any sauce.

2. **Deglazing or reduction**: Use the back of the spoon to judge the precise thickness of the sauce by running the spoon through the sauce. The way it adheres to the back of the spoon will let you know if the sauce needs to be lightened or thickened. A light sauce will run easily off the back of the spoon, while a demi glace will adhere to the spoon. There are three stages of reductions: slightly syrupy, syrupy, and demi glace (which is rich and thick).

# FOOD IS ALCHEMY.
# IT'S FUN TO OBSERVE.

## LIAISON TECHNIQUES: THE THICKENING OF SAUCES

**Breadcrumbs:** Breadcrumbs are used in rustic, flavorful sauces such as pan sauces from a roast. Crumble into the warm sauce and gently cook for about 20 minutes whisking from time to time until desired thickness is reached.

**Egg Yolks:** Egg yolks are used as a binding agent to produce a velvety texture that is highlighted by a delicate color. In a bowl break up the yolks with room temperature liquid that compliments the recipe such as milk, wine, or stock. Remove sauce from heat and add yolk mixture to sauce stirring with a spoon. Place the sauce over low heat to bring back up to temperature, stirring constantly until it covers the back of a spoon. It is essential that the sauce does not boil, or it will separate. As soon as it has thickened pass through a fine strainer into a clean saucepan and place over low heat to keep warm.

**Corn Starch, Rice flour or Arrowroot:**
A slurry is an efficient and modern way to thicken almost any sauce. In a small bowl, add whatever thickening agent (corn starch, rice flour or arrowroot) to room temperature liquid that compliments the recipe (milk, wine, water) at a ratio of 1 teaspoon thickening agent to 1 tablespoon liquid. Slowly pour into boiling sauce whisking until incorporated, simmer over low heat for about 5 to 10 minutes.

**Heavy Cream:** this thickening agent is usually used for fish poultry and certain soups which creates a rich and smooth finish. Boil the cream for a few minutes then stir into boiling sauce. In France crème fraiche is used, which is slightly acidic so if you use crème fraiche make sure to boil it slightly before adding because the acid will cause the sauce to separate.

*Beurre Manie:* The French word for kneaded butter. It is equal parts softened butter and flour, kneaded together. Bring your sauce or soup to a gentle boil and add the Beurre Manie in small increments to thicken your sauce to the desired thickness.

## SEAFOOD

When pan frying a fillet of fish always uses Wondra Flour by Gold Medal, it has a fine blend of wheat and barley that creates a crispy crust.

**Scallops:** Always purchase dry scallops, this means that the scallops are shucked on the boat as soon as they are caught and placed in dry storage without the use of phosphates.

**Shrimp:** when preparing shrimp always soak shrimp in water with one teaspoon of salt for 30 minutes before cooking.

Much like finding a local butcher a local fishmonger is important to making sure you are getting the highest quality ingredients for you.

**Stocks:** always keep your bones and vegetable scraps for stocks.

## WINE PAIRING

One of the things I have learned is when pairing wine with a dish is to **focus on the sauce not the protein**. Pair the wine to the sauce, not the protein. For example, filet of beef with blue cheese on page 118 and popular logic would say having red wine with beef is not necessarily true. The blue cheese works perfectly with an oaky buttery California style Chardonnay. A perfect pairing accentuates the flavors of both the dish and the wine so both sing in harmony.

# MENUS FOR THE HOME CHEF

## SUMMER DINNER

**TO START**
Smoked Salmon Tartare ........... page 88

**FIRST COURSE**
Watermelon Gazapacho ........... page 34
🍷 A California Cabernet

**ENTRÉE**
Seafood Crêpes
🍷 Chardonnay or Chablis ........... page 206

**DESSERT**
Rhubarb Galette with Whipped Cream ........... page 276

## INDIAN-INSPIRED DINNER

**TO START**
Golden Spiced Chèvre Cheese ........... page 100

**ENTRÉE**
Persian Black Lime Chicken ........... page 156
Tomato and Mango Salad ........... page 52
Rice

**DESSERT**
Rosemary, Olive Oil, and Orange Cake ........... page 244
🍷 Dry Reisling

> A PERFECT PAIRING ACCENTUATES THE FLAVORS OF BOTH THE DISH AND THE WINE SO BOTH SING IN HARMONY.
>
> *— Nanette*

## VEGETARIAN DINNER

**TO START**

Jacqueline's Baked Brie with Curry and Chutney Crackers ..... page 102

**ENTRÉE**

Indian-Spiced Stuffed Cauliflower ..... page 218
Jerusalem Artichoke and Vegetable Tagine Couscous ..... page 200

**DESSERT**

Saffron Shortbread ..... page 262
🍷 Oregon Pinot Noir

## A LOVELY BRUNCH

**BEVERAGE**

Brunch Punch ..... page 109

**ENTRÉE**

Baked Eggs La Querencia ..... page 14
Palo Alto Salad ..... page 46
Blueberry Muffins ..... page 28

## ELEGANT DINNER

**TO START**

Roquefort Grapes with Pistachios ..... page 76

**FIRST COURSE**

Cream of Watercress Soup ..... page 38

**ENTRÉE**

Roasted Pheasant in a Salt Crust with White Peppercorn Sauce ..... page 174

Roasted Cauliflower Steaks Pancetta and Caper Sauce ..... page 226

🍷 Pinot Blanc or Chardonnay

**SALAD COURSE**

Escarole and Gruyère Salad with Walnut Oil Dressing ..... page 47

🍷 California Sparkling Wine

**DESSERT**

Nanette's Creamy Chocolate Cake ..... page 248

## LADIES LUNCH

**FIRST COURSE**

Spring Tonic ..... page 36

**ENTRÉE**

Exotic Chicken Curry Salad ..... page 48

Cream Scones ..... page 30

🍷 Sémillon

**DESSERT**

Flourless Chocolate Cookies ..... page 266

## COCKTAIL PARTY

**COCKTAILS**

🍷 French 75 .................................................. page 108

🍷 California Pinot Noir

**LITTLE BITES**

Caramelized Bacon .................................................. page 98

Reto Cheese Puffs .................................................. page 82

Pickled Celery, Apple, and Celery Root Salad with Endive Leaves .................................................. page 78

Cashew Sesame Chicken .................................................. page 94

Phyllo Triangles with Mousse Royale, Pistachios, and Cremini Mushrooms .................................................. page 84

Corn Cakes with Smoked Black Cod and Lemon Confit Crème Fraîche .................................................. page 86

## MEAT LOVERS DINNER

**FIRST COURSE**

Bitter Greens Salad with Goat Cheese Soufflé .................................................. page 56

🍷 Chardonnay

**ENTRÉE**

Beef Filet with Blue Cheese and Pistachios .................................................. page 118

Potato Bliss .................................................. page 234

🍷 Syrah

**DESSERT**

Bittersweet Chocolate Tart .................................................. page 270

## ITALIAN DINNER

**FIRST COURSE**

Radicchio Salad with Thyme, Chestnuts and Prosciutto ........ page 64

🍷 Tempranillo

**ENTRÉE**

Rotolo Stuffed with Spinach Filling in a Creamy Tomato Sauce ........ page 206

Cauliflower Steaks with Pancetta and Capers ........ page 226

🍷 Dolcetto

**DESSERT**

Ricotta Doughnuts with Chocolate Sauce ........ page 284

*"We may live without poetry, music, and art;
We may live without conscience, and live without heart;
We may live without friends; we may live without books;
But civilized man cannot live without cooks.
But where is the man that can live without dining?"*

*– Edward Robert Bulwer-Lytton*

# LIST OF ONLINE PURVEYORS

### CHEF SHOP
For Koji and other hard-to-find ingredients from around the world.

www.chefshop.com
800.596.0885

### CHESTNUT HILL FARM
Fine pork products. Forest-raised and acorn-fed pork from Orchard Park, NY.

6405 Ward Rd
Orchard Park, NY 14127

www.chestnuthillfarm.org

### D'ARTAGNAN
For pheasant, poussins, quail, foie gras, beef, and pork. They have a wealth of wonderful products.

www.dartagnan.com
877.858.0099

### DUFOUR PASTRY KITCHENS
For puff pastry and premade tart shells. They make such wonderful products, with quality ingredients.

www.dufourpastrykitchens.com
800.741.7787

### EL POTRERO TRADING POST
Chimayó chili, the real deal.

P.O. Box 706
Chimayó, New Mexico

elpotrerotradingpost.com
505.351.4112

### JB PRINCE
For cooking equipment, from knives to the most esoteric needs.

www.jbprince.com
800.473.0577

### LOBEL'S OF NEW YORK
For exceptional beef, meats, and great customer service.

www.lobels.com
563.607.5131

### LA BOîTE
A producer of wonderful spice blends. An excellent source for black limes.

724 11th Avenue
New York, NY 10019

info@laboiteny.com

### PENZEYS SPICES
A quality spice shop with a quick turnover in products, which ensures freshness.

www.penzeys.com
800.741.7787

### SUPERMARKET ITALY
For the chestnut flour I use.

www.supermarketitaly.com

# INDEX

## A

Agave, 98
Aleppo pepper (see peppers)
Aleppo powder (see spices)
Almond (see nuts)
**All Purpose Butter for Stuffing Under Poultry Skin**, 296
Amaretto cookies, 278
**Angel Hair Pasta**, 126, 143, 193, **204**
Apple; Cortland, 60, Fuji, 274, Gala, 60, Golden Delicious, 274, Granny Smith, 179, Macintosh, 274, Northern Sky, 60, Pink Lady, 274
Apricot; jam, 94-95, 272, 274, dried (see dried fruits)
Arugula; 145, baby, 60
Asparagus, 146-147, 294

## B

Bacon; 16, 157, thick-cut, 172-173, applewood smoked, 98-99, drippings, 25
Baking powder; 28, 30, 86, 105, 238, 242, 244, 252, 254, 262, 264, 268, 284, double acting 92-93
Baking soda, 28, 238, 244, 254, 264
**Baked Eggs La Querencia, 14-15**
Batter; 135, 298
  -baking, 28, 93, 242, 244, 247, 250, 252, 267, 268,
  -frying, 80, 86, 284,
BBQ sauce, 124, 188-189
Bechamel sauce, 202
Beans; green 225, garbanzo 45
Beef; 114-115, 298, 301
  -Center-cut beef filet, 116-117, filet of beef, 118, 120, flank steak, 128
  -Beef Stock, 25, 120, homemade beef stock 118 (see also stock)
  -Ground beef, 124
  -Stewing beef, 120
  -Veal shanks & bones, 120
Beet, 40-41, 208
**Bitter Greens Goat Cheese Souffle, 56-59**
**Bittersweet Chocolate Tart, 270**
Black Lime, 153-156
Blender; or food processor, 34, 38, 186, 202, 287
**Bliss Potatoes, 235**
Blue Cheese (see cheese)
Blueberries, 28, 31
**Blueberry Muffins, 28**
**Braised Pheasant Legs with Dried Morels and Chestnuts, 174-175**
**Braciole, 126-129**, 205, 316
Brandy (see liquor)
Bread; 222
  -**Cumin Bread, 91-93**
  -French/Italian, 72, 159
  -White, 36, 82, 112-113
  -Whole wheat, 112-113
Breadcrumbs, 14, 124-125, 145, 192, 301
  -Fresh, 157, 184
  -Italian breadcrumbs, 128-129
  -Panko, 216
Brine, 210, 154, 162,
**Brittle, 288-291**
Broccoli, 69
Brown stock, 120
**Brunch Punch, 109**
*Butter;
  -salted, 14, 17, 20, 40, 42, 80, 84, 120, 145, 209, 158, 162, 202, 238, 250, 252, 298, 301
  -unsalted, 25, 28, 30, 36, 38, 58, 84, 113, 118, 128, 130, 134-135, 136, 140, 146, 210, 157, 164, 172-173, 174, 184, 188, 190, 196, 200, 202, 204, 206, 210, 216, 228, 232, 235, 237, 242, 250, 252, 254, 259, 260, 262, 264, 268, 270, 274, 278, 282, 289, 296
Butter lettuce (see lettuce)
Butternut squash, 45
Beurre Blanc, 196-197

## C

Cabbage, 40, 50-51
Capers, 72, 145, 184, 228
**Caramelized Bacon, 98-99**
Carrots, 186, 225, 40, 50, 120, 128, 172
**Cashew Sesame Chicken, 94-95**
**Castagnaccio Chestnut Flour Cake with Rosemary and Pine Nuts, 246-247**
Castelfranco, 64
Cauliflower, 69, 224-226, 228-229
**Cauliflower Steaks with Caper Pancetta Sauce, 228**
Cayenne pepper (see spices)
Celery, 36, 42, 49, 60, 78, 120, 128, 172
Celery Root, 78
Champagne, 108, 289
Cheese; 239
  -Blue Cheese; 76, 301, Gorgonzola, 76, 118, 208, Bleu d'Auvergne, 78, 208, Saint Agur, 78, 118
  -Colby, 17
  -Cream cheese, 18, 20, 70, 76, 112-113, 200, 216, 287, 287
  -French brie, 102

308

-French chèvre, 100
-French Feta, 34
-Gruyère, 14, 17, 47, 210, 216
-Manchego, 64
-Monterey Jack cheese, 22
-Montrachet, 58
-Parmesan, 14, 20, 124; freshly grated, 36, 58, 82, 209, 164, 204, 206, 210, 300, rind of, 300
-Pecorino romano, 128
-Provolone, 72, 128
-Roquefort cheese, 76

**Cheese Souffle**, *210-215*

Cherries; 236, 294, fresh pitted, 136-137, dried (see dried fruits)

Chicken; 24, 91, 149, 160-161, 164, 205, 296, 298, 300
-Bone-in; 162, bone-in, skin on 210, 158-163
-Breast; boneless 94, boneless and skinless 92-93, 96-97, 142-143, 144-145, 146
-Broth, 40, 42, 210, 237,
-Chicken liver, 157
-Chicken poached, 49
-Chicken stock (see stock) 25, 38, 45, 155, 164, 172-173, 174, 202, 220, 237, 298
-Chicken thighs; skin-on, bone-in 150-151, 155, 158-163
-Whole, 158, 298,

**Chicken Breast Francoise Paul Boucuse**, *146*

**Chicken with Salad on top**, *144-145*

**Chicken Satay**, *96-97*

**Chili-Rubbed Prawns with Barbeque Hollandaise Sauce**, *188*

**Chilean Sea Bass with Soy Glaze and Ginger Beurre Blanc**, *200-201*

**Chimayo Chile Sauce**, *24-25*

Citric acid, 284

Chocolate; 111, 248, 255, 257, 267, 271, 281, 283, 286
-Baker's unsweetened chocolate, 268
-Bittersweet chocolate, 250, 260, 270, 282, 288-289
-Milk, 280
-Semisweet chocolate, 250, 280; chips 264
-White, Valrhona 256-257

Chocolate sauce, 284

**Christmas Fruit Cake**, *254-255*

Chutney; Major Grey, 49, 102-103, 102, 112

**Cilantro Risotto**, *236-237*

Cinnamon (see spices)

Cocoa powder; 250, 282
-Dutch processed; Droste, 284, 289, Valrhona, 267, 284, 289

Coconut flakes, sweetened 264

Coconut milk, 96, 186

Cod, smoked, 86

**Coeur à La Crème**, *287*

Coffee; 253, 264, 282, 316, instant, 280

Cognac (see liquor)

**Cognac Marinated Filet of Beef**, *116-117*

Colby (see cheese)

Cookies, 240, 256-257, 259, 260-261, 264-269, 278, 286

Corn; kernels 86, 196, 239, frozen 196

Cornbread, 161, 238-239

**Corn Cakes with Smoked Black Cod**, *86*

Cornichons, 88

Cornish game hen, 177

Cornmeal, 238, 244, 262, 278

Cornstarch, 94, 140, 157, 162, 169, 200, 259

Cornstarch Slurry, 157

Corn syrup; light 282, white 250

Cortland, apple (see apple)

Couscous, 220

Crackers; 101, graham, 278, Ritz, 134-135, soda, 184

**Crab Cakes with Tartare Sauce**, *184*

Crab meat; lump, 54, king, 70, Dungeness, 70

Cranberries, dried (see dried fruits)

*Cream;
-Heavy, 14, 17, 30, 38, 42, 70, 86, 108, 121, 209, 172, 174, 184, 206, 208, 270, 278, 280, 284, 289, 301
-Sour, 28, 34, 40, 69, 86, 112, 254, 287
-Whipped, 244, 274, 280, 316

Cream cheese (see cheese)

**Cream of Watercress**, *38-39*

**Cream Scones**, *30-31, 316*

Crepes, 202

Cucumber, 34, 88, 113, 135, 195

Cumin (see spices)

Cumin Bread, 91-93

Currants, 30-31, 225, 254

Curry paste, 186-187a

Custard, 208

# D

Dijon mustard (see mustard)

Dill (see herbs)

Dill pickles, 184

Dairy ;
-Butter; salted, unsalted (see butter)

# INDEX

-Buttermilk, 28, 162, 238
-Cheese (see cheese)
-Cottage cheese, 225
-Crème fraiche, 28, 30, 60, 86, 146, 244, 287, 294, 301
-Heavy cream (see cream)
-Milk, 20, 34, 58, 92, 202, 216, 264
-Ricotta, 64, 209, 284-285
-Sour cream, 28, 34, 40, 69, 86, 112, 254, 287
-Sour milk, 238
-Whole milk, 80, 210, 235, 270, 284, 289, 300-301
-Whole milk yogurt, 28
Dates (see dried fruits)
Dough; pasta, 209, pastry 17, 274, 298 *(see also tart shell)
Dredge; 124, 150, 162, 174
Dried Fruits;
-Apricots, 31, 155, 254
-Currents, 254
-Raisins; dark 254, golden 254
-Dates, 254
-Cherries, 31, 179, 254
-Cranberries, 179, 254
-Golden raisins, 228, 254
-Prunes, 254
Duck, Peking 169
Duck a L'orange, 169

## E

Edamame, 69
Eggs, 14-15, 17, 20, 22, 24, 26, 54-55, 86, 93, 108, 145, 209, 172, 184, 202, 232, 238, 242, 244, 254, 264, 268, 280, 284, 289, 298,
Electric mixer; 76, 105, 210, 244, 268, 286, hand, 274, 295, stand, 30, 108, 135, 172, 250, 254, 260,

264, 267,
Endive, Belgian 58
English muffin, 70
Escarole, 47, 58
**Escarole, Gruyere and Walnut, 47**
Espresso powder, instant 250-251, 268
**Exotic Curry Chicken salad, 48**
Extra virgin olive oil (see oil)

## F

Fennel; fresh, 202, seed (see spices)
**Filet of Beef with Blue Cheese, 118,** 301
**Filet of Beef with Green Peppercorn Sauce, 120-121**
Fish sauce, 186
**Financiers, 252-253**
Flank steak (see beef)
Food processor; 22, 72, 76, 113, 232, 262, 270, 296, (see also Blender)
Flour;
-Almond flour, 250, 252, 278
-All-purpose flour, 28, 30, 58, 80, 92, 105, 209, 150, 162, 169, 172, 252, 254, 259-260, 262, 268, 270, 284
-Cake flour, 252
-Chestnut flour, 246-247
-Chickpea flour, 225
-Potato flour, 162
-Rice flour, 301
-Unbleached flour, 278
**Flourless Chocolate Cookies, 267,** 286
Foie gras, 158-159, 307
Freeze; 289, chill, 158, 270, 298, for future use, 29, 128, 208, 251, 256, 268, 278,
**French 75, 108**

**French Apple Tart, 272-275**
French bread, batard, French baguette, (see also bread)
French brie (see cheese)
French chèvre (see cheese)
French feta (see cheese)
**French Lemon Cake, 242**
**French Quiche, 16**
Frisee, 58
Fry; 80, 94, 160, 162, 208, 284-285, 301
Fuji, apple (see apple)

## G

Gala, apple (see apple)
Garbanzo beans (see beans)
Garlic; 101, cloves, 22, 25, 42, 45-46, 70, 72, 94, 96, 100, 116, 124, paste, 225, powder/salt (see spices)
Giblets, 169, 315
Ginger; fresh, 94, 96, 155, paste, 225, pickled, 113, 200,
Glaze; 200, 231, 242, 250, 251, 272,
**Glazed Miso Eggplant, 231**
Golden Delicious, apple (see apple )
Gorgonzola (see cheese)
Graham crackers (see crackers)
Granny Smith, apple (see apple)
Grape; red, 157 green, 49, 76, 102
Grapefruit, ruby red, 10, 180-183, 316
Green beans (see beans)
**Grilled Tenderloin of Pork, 136-137**
Grits, 161, 162, 164-165, 191,
Gruyère (see cheese

310

## H

Harissa Sauce, 220
Hemp hearts, 78
*Herbed Egg Ribbons and Crab*, 54-55
Herbs,
- Basil; dried, 36, fresh leaves, 20, 34, 52, 54, 72, 128, 145, 206 purple, 52, Thai, 186-187
- Bay leaves; 42, 45, 78, 120, 128, 172, 190, 196, 202
- Chervil, 14
- Chives, fresh, 34, 46, 58, 70, 84, 86, 113, 142, 157, 184, 196,
- Cilantro, fresh, 22, 26-27, 92-93, 112, 136, 186, 220, 236-237,
- Dill, fresh, 20, 40, 46, 50, 86, 113, 142, 295
- Herbs de Provence, 142, 150,
- Italian herbs, dried, 216
- Mint, fresh, 34, 92, 155, 182, 295
- Oregano; dried, 25, 45, 128, 162, 192,
- Parsley; 316, fresh; 20, 45-47, 50, 58, 128, 134-135, 142, 155, 192, 204, 208, flat leaf Italian, 54, 182
- Rosemary; dried, fresh, 142,
- Sage; dried, fresh, 142, 208
- Tarragon, fresh, 14, 58, 157,
- Thyme, dried, fresh, 14, 46, 54, 86,

*Herb Chicken Paillard*, 142-143
*Homemade Mayonnaise*, 49, 69-70, 93, **295**, 300,
*Homesick Southwest Breakfast*, 24-27
Honey, 40, 64, 78, 86, 136, 177, 179, 200, 231-232, 247,
Honeydew, 34
Horseradish, white, 60
Hot pepper sauce, 188

## I

*Indian Spiced Cauliflower*, 222
Italian Bread (see bread)
*Italian Breaded Shrimp*, 192

## J

*Jacqueline Baked Brie with Curry and Chutney*, 102
*Jerusalem Artichoke*, 218, 220-221
*Jerusalem Artichoke and Vegetable Tagine*, 220-221

## K

Kaffir Limes, 186
Kale, 45
Ketchup, 124
Kosher salt (see salt)

## L

Lamb; 114, 314-315
- Chops, 130-131,
- Ground, 133-135

*Lamb Meatballs with Tahini*, 132
Leek, 42, 172
Lemon; 11, 150, 245, 296,
- juice, 36-37, 49, 52, 54, 70, 72, 78, 86, 88, 94, 96, 108-109, 113, 120, 134-135, 145, 155, 158, 188, 228, 242, 287, 294-295, 296, 298, 300,
- peel, 108, 142, 145, 242,
- rind, 28, 94, 96, 142,
- wedge, 142, 192,
- zest, 96, 145, 259, 296,

*Lemon Confit*, 86, 220, **294**
*Lemon Confit creme fraiche*, 86
Lemongrass, 186
Lettuce; 316, Boston Bibb, 46, 60, Butter, 46, 49, Escarole, 47, 58, Iceberg, 54
Limoncello (see liquor)
Lime;
- juice, 34, 94, 96, 113, 136, 186, 188, 220
- leaves, 186,
- rind, 94, 96,
- wedge, 34
- zest, 113, 186,

*Lisa's Stuffed Portobello Mushrooms*, 216
*Liquor: 107, 280
- Armagnac 158
- Brandy, Calvados 274
- Bourbon 107, 108
- Chartreuse 109, 202
- Cointreau 169
- Cognac 84, 107, 108, 116-118, 120, 158, 172, 174, 250, 289
- Cynar 109
- Framboise 280, 282
- Gin 108
- Grand Marnier 280, 282
- Irish whiskey 107
- Kahlua 280, 282
- Kirschwasser 250, 284
- Madeira 177
- Orange liqueur 244, 254
- Pernod 202
- Port 36, 177
- Rum 107
- Sherry 157, 177, 216; dry 94
- Triple sec 169
- Vermouth; 202, Dry 210, 150, sweet 216

# INDEX

Louisiana hot sauce, 190
Lychee nuts, 49

## M

Macintosh, apple (see apple)
Major Gray's Chutney (see chutney)
Manchego (see cheese)
Mango, 52, 131, 316
Maple Syrup, 64, 98, 169, 179
Marinate; 64, 69, 70, 94, 100, 116-117, 131, 133, 136, 177, 295,
**Marinated Vegetable Salad**, 70
Marmalade; 169
Marshmallows, 232, 256
**Matcha Ice Cream Sundaes with Chocolate**, 288
Matcha powder, 289
Mayonnaise, 184, (see also **Homemade Mayonnaise**)
Miso, sweet white, 230-231
Milk (see dairy)
**Mocha Cookies**, 268-269
Monterey Jack (see cheese)
Montrachet (see cheese)
Mousse Royale au Sauternes, 84
Mushrooms, 16,
 -Button, white, 206, 216
 -Cremini, 84,
 -Morels, dried, 171, 174
 -Portobello, 216,
 -Shiitake, 164, 196-197,
Mustard; Chinese Hot, Colemans, Dijon, English, dried (see spices)
My Favorite Chocolate Truffles, 282

## N

**Nanette's Creamy Chocolate Cake**, 248
**New Orleans Shrimp**, 190
Northern Sky, apple (see apple)
Nuts, (see also roast)
 -Almond, 250, blanched, 270, slivered, 49
 -Cashew, 94-95, 225
 -Chestnut, 171, 174-175
 -Hazelnut, 136
 -Peanut, 256,
 -Pecan, 76, 98, 102, 113, 208-209, 232, 254, 259, 264,
 -Pine nut, 145, 247
 -Pistachio; chopped, shelled, 76, 254,
 -Walnut, chopped, 47, 254, 260-261, 266-267,
Nutmeg (see spices)

## O

**Oak's Chocolate Mousse**, 280
**Oak's White Bark Cookies**, 256
Olives; cured black, 145, Kalamata, 72, 220, Spanish, 113,
Oil,
 -Avocado, 58, 92, 162, 186, 194, 284, 295
 -Black truffle, 60, 298
 -Extra Virgin Olive, 20, 22, 34, 36, 46, 52, 54, 58, 64, 66, 72, 78, 84, 86, 88, 100, 116, 128, 134, 136, 142, 145, 155, 164, 172, 190, 192, 206, 208, 220, 228, 244, 247, 294, 296,
 -Grapeseed, 92, 134, 162, 284, 295

 -Peanut, 162, 194, 295
 -Safflower, 92, 134, 295
 -Sesame, 96, 194, 231, dark sesame, 96,
 -Walnut, 47, 295,
**Old Fashioned Coleslaw**, 50
**Old-Fashioned Fried Chicken**, 160
Onion; 22, 38, 40, 70, 96, 120, 124, 128, 133, 138, 209, 155, 169, 172, 181, 184, 202
 -Red, 66, 88, 134-135, 140, 157, 196, 208,
 -Spring; (chive) 82
 -Sweet, 220
 -White, 134-135
 -Yellow, 36, 45, 134-135, 190-191
 -Pickled; cocktail onions, 182
**Open Faced Crab Sandwich**, 72
Orange; 54, 66, 232, 243, 244, 282, 316
 -blood, 54
 -cara cara, 66
 -juice, 66, 109, 169, 232, 242, 244
 -peel, 242
 -rind, 282
 -sections/slices/segments 66, 109, 169, 244
 -shells, 232
 -zest, 179, 254, 244, 254
 -blood orange, 54
Orange flower water, 262
Orange liqueur (see liquor)

## P

**Palo Alto Salad**, 46
Pancetta, 208, 228

312

Parchment paper; 54, 84,
 cut to fit, 244, 250,
 cover with, 146,
 line with, 17, 20, 102, 116, 136, 142, 256, 259, 260, 264, 267, 270, 279, 291,
 roll between two sheets of, 270,
Parmesan (see cheese)
Pasta; 208
 -angel hair, 126, 143, 193, 204-205
 -egg, 54-55
 -dough, 209
 -penne, 206, 208
Pastry blender, 278
Pastry Dough (see dough)
*Pan Roasted Chicken with Sage Vermouth Sauce*, **148**
*Pan Roasted Pork Loin with Balsamic Vinegar Onions*, **138**
Peas; shelled 206, frozen 69, 206
Peanut (see nuts)
Peanut butter, Skippy Chunky 256, smooth creamy 96
Pecan (see nuts)
*Pecan Lemon Shortbread*, **258**
Pecorino romano (see cheese)
*Penne Saint Martin*, **206**
*Penne Pasta with Beets and Gorgonzola*, **208**
Pepper (fruit);
 -Bell pepper;
  green, 36, 124,
  red, 45, 54, 86, 145, 186, 220
  yellow, 54, 186, 220,
 -Jalapeño pepper, 22, 136
Pepper; Black, Peppercorn, (see spices)
*Peppercorn Marinated Grilled Quail with Cranberry, Cherry and Tomato*, **176**

*Persian Black Lime Chicken*, **152**
Pheasant, 167-171, 307, 316
*Pheasant in Salt Crust with White Peppercorn Sauce*, **170**
Phyllo pastry dough, 84
*Phyllo Triangles with Goose Liver Mousse and Pistachios*, **84**
Pickle, cornichons 88
*Pickled Cherries*, **294**
*Pickled Celery Apple and Celery Root Salad with Blue Cheese*, **80**
Pie weights; 17, 270, 274
Pink Lady, apple (see apple)
Poach; 195, eggs, 22, 26, cauliflower, 225, chestnuts, 64 chicken, 49, 92-93,
Pork; 114, 138, 236, 307, 315
 -Pork tenderloin 136, 140, 236
*Portuguese Stew*, **44**
Potato; 40, 42, 175, 220, baking 235, sweet 232-233, 316
Provolone (see cheese)
*Provencal Chicken*, **150**
*Provencal Sandwich Loaf*, **74**
Prunes (see dried fruits)

Quail, 177-176, 307
*Quiche*, **16-17**

Radicchio, 58, 62-65, 66, 316
*Radicchio with Chestnuts and Prosciutto*, **64**
*Radicchio, Oranges and Grilled Onion*, **68**

Raisin; dark, golden (see dried fruit)
Raspberry, 179, 259, 277, 282, 287
*Red Wine Biscuits*, **104**
*Retro Cheese Puffs*, **84**
rhubarb, 277-279
Rhubarb Galette, 276
Rice; 200, 220
 -Basmati, 186, 190-191, 218, smoked 155
 -Risotto 137, 222, 236-237
 -Wild 175
Rice Krispies, Kellog's 256
*Ricotta Doughnuts*, **284**
Ricotta, fresh (see dairy)
Rolled oats, old-fashioned, 264
Roast; 178, 295, 301,
 nuts, 49, 52, 66, 76, 94, 102, 113, 118, 136, 145, 208, 225, 256, 260
 meats, 116, 120, 140, 148-151, 150, 157, 158, 169, 177, 296, 298
 seeds/spices, 92, 177, 186,
 vegetables, 72, 228, 231, 232,
*Roasted Chicken with Foie Gras Butter*, **158**
Roasted Red Peppers, jarred 72
Roquefort (see cheese)
*Roquefort and Pistachio Grapes*, **78**
*Rosemary Olive Oil Orange Cake*, **244**
*Rotolo with Spinach Stuffing and Creamy Tomato Sauce*, **206**
*Russian Cabbage Borscht*, **40**

S

*Golden Spiced Chevre Cheese*, **100**
*Saffron Shortbread*, **262**
Saffron threads (see spices)
Sage (see herbs)

313

# INDEX

*Sage Fritters*, 82
Salmon; 88-89, 230
Filets; 194-195,
 -center cut, skin on 196-197
Smoked 86-87, 88-89, 113, 294
Trout 88
*Salmon with Scallion Ginger Sauce*, 194
*Salt;
 -fleur de sel, 34
 -Kosher, 28, 36, 40, 47, 52, 54, 58-59, 60, 64, 92, 100, 112-113, 116, 120, 128, 134-135, 209, 148, 150, 155, 158, 162, 169, 172, 174, 177, 179, 182, 188, 196, 202, 206, 210, 216, 244, 250-251, 264, 268, 284, 294-295
 -Maldon, sea salt flakes 34
 -Sea, 14, 30, 66, 70, 80, 84, 118, 130, 136, 140, 142, 145, 146, 162, 164, 184, 190, 192, 208, 216, 235, 237, 250-251, 267, 287, 289
Sambal Oelek, 96, 231
Sausage; spicy Italian: linguiça, 45, andouille 164
Scallion, 20, 50, 72, 82, 86, 92, 184, 194, 230
*Scallops with Grapefruit and Onion Salad*, 180-183
Sea Bass filets, 200, 230
Sea scallops, 182, 202
*Seafood Crepes*, 202
*Seared Salmon with Corn, Shiitake Mushrooms with Balsamic Beurre Blanc*, 196
Sesame seed, 289, white 94, black 291
Shallots, 58-59, 116, 118, 136, 148, 150, 157, 164, 174, 179, 184, 186, 200, 202, 206, 237, 294,

Shio koji, 136, 295
*Shio Koji Marinade*, 295
Shrimp 191, 229, 301, Jumbo 188, 190, 202, Medium 186, 192
Shrimp paste, 186
*Shrimp Thai Curry*, 186
Simple syrup, 108
*Smalley Family Eggnog*, 106
Smoked Black Cod, 86
Smoked Trout Chowder, 42
*Smoked Trout Salad with Black Truffle Vinaigrette*, 62
Soy sauce 49, 94, 96, 200, 231, low sodium soy sauce, 96
Spice, rub; 102, 130, 177, 188,
*Spices;
 -5 spice seasoning 291
 -Allspice 142
 -Aleppo pepper 155
 -Aleppo powder 188
 -Ancho chili powder 25, 188
 -Caraway, seed 40
 -Cardamom pods, black 155
 -Cayenne, 20, 34, 45, 50, 58, 82, 98, 130, 134, 142, 184, 206, 210, 220, 225, 237,
 -Celery Seeds, 69
 -Crushed red pepper, 34, 100; Red pepper flakes 204
 -Chimayo chile powder, 24-27, 124, 307
 -Chipotle powder, 188
 -Cinnamon 130, 134-135, 232, 264, 272-274, 284; stick 294
 -Cloves; whole 36, 202, ground 130
 -Coriander; ground 92, 130, 134-135, seed 54, 186
 -Cumin 91; ground 22, 25, 92-96, 124, 130, 134-135, 190, 220, 225, seed 92-95, 100, 239

 -Curry powder; 52, 102-103, Madras 49,
 -Fennel Seeds, 78, 155, 202
 -Fenugreek; ground 225
 -Garam masala 225
 -Garlic powder, 36, 162 salt, 216
 -Ginger; ground 130
 -Juniper berry 172
 -Kashmiri red chili powder 134
 -Mustard; dry/ground, 58, 92-93, 188; Chinese Hot, 94; dry English Style, 50, 94
 -Nutmeg; freshly grated 108, 202, 210, 216, ground 17, 20, 58, 146, 209
 -Old Bay seasoning 184
 -Paprika 36, 162, 190, 210; spanish paprika 188
 -Pepper; black 22, 34, 34, 36, 47, 49, 54, 64, 66, 70, 72, 84, 98, 112-113, 116, 118, 120, 124, 128, 146, 158, 169, 174, 196, 202, 206, 208, 220, 228, 296; white 209
 -Peppercorn; 178
 -Black peppercorns 36, 45, 100, 105, 186, 294; freshly ground, 47, 58, 60, 80, 84, 112-113, 116, 118, 120, 128, 130, 134-135, 136, 140, 142, 145, 148, 150, 155, 157, 162, 164, 194, 196, 206, 208, 225, 300
 -Green peppercorns 177, 120
 -Long peppercorns 17, 194
 -Pink peppercorns 177
 -Sichuan peppercorns 177
 -White peppercorns 171-172, 196; freshly ground 14, 20, 34, 38, 40, 42, 50, 54, 64, 66, 70, 78, 82, 112, 145, 146, 157, 162, 169, 172, 174, 181-182, 184, 190, 192, 200, 216, 228, 232, 235, 295,
 -Saffron threads 220, 262-263, 300,

314

100-101, 155
 -Sumac, 133-135
 -Turmeric, ground 225, 130, 134-135, 155

**Spiced Lamb Chops with Cherry Tomatoes**, *130*

**Spicy Zinfandel Meatballs**, *124*

Spinach; 16, 206, 209, 216, baby 22

**Spring Tonic**, *36*

Stock; 10, 40, 136, 301-302
 -Beef, 25, 118, 120, (see also brown stock)
 -Chicken, 38, 45, 298, 148, 150, 155, 164, 172-173, 174, 237
 -Seafood, 202
 -Vegetable, 220

Sugar; 17, 20, 28, 30, 36, 49, 50, 52, 58-60, 66, 78, 86, 92-93, 94, 96, 105, 134-135, 136, 209, 181, 182, 228, 238, 242, 244, 250, 254, 259-260, 262, 264, 268, 274, 278, 280, 284, 289, 291, 294
 -Brown, 98, 124, 186, 188, 232, 260, 298
 -Brown (Light) sugar, 264, 289
 -Confectioners sugar, 260, 267,
 -Granulated, 289
 -Palm sugar, 186
 -Powdered, 108, 242, 244, 270, 274, 280, 287
 -White sugar,

Sunflower seeds, toasted 46

**Stuffed Poussin with Roasted Grape Clusters**, *156*

**Summer Roulade**, *18*

Sweet potato (see potato)

**Sweet Potatoes in Orange Shells**, *232*

# T

Tamarind paste, 155

Tart shell, 17, premade, 307,

**Tea Party Sandwiches**, *112-113*

**Thai Chicken Salad**, *90*

Thai chilies, 92-93, 186,

Thermometer, 118, 120, 145, 146, 158, 177, 284, instant read, 135, 162,

Tabasco, 70

Tortilla; 22, 26

**Tomatillo Shakshuka**, *22-23*

Tomatoes, 18, 52, 216
 -Cherry, 72, 130, 134-135
 -Crushed, can (San Marzano) 36, 45, 128, 209
 -Fresh, 20, 52, 209, 196, 216
 -Heirloom, 145
 -Paste, 45, 124, 220
 -Plum, can (San Marzano) 206
 -Puree, 40
 -Sauce, 25, 128, 206, Creamy 209
 -Sun-dried, 145, 179

**Tomato and Mango Salad**, *52, 131, 316*

Trout; smoked, Salmon (see salmon)

# V

Vinegar; 295, 300
 -Aged balsamic (Modena) 64, 196
 -Apple cider, 40, 50, 177, 179
 -Balsamic, 20, 138-140, 145, 294, 295, 298
 -Champagne, 64, 295
 -Chardonnay, 64
 -Raspberry, 295
 -Red wine, 34, 124, 295
 -Rice, 200, 231
 -Sherry, 34, 47, 58, 64, 66, 78

 -White wine, 46, 60, 184, 295

Vanilla extract, 28, 242, 244, 250, 252, 254, 259, 264, 267, 268, 270, 284, 287

Valrhona (see chocolate)

# W

Walnut (see nuts)

**Walnut Shortbread Cookies**, *260*

Watercress, fresh 38, 60, 72

**Watermelon Gazpacho**, *34*

White bread (see bread)

**Wine** (see in wine list page 316)

Worcestershire Sauce, 70, 88, 184

# WINES

## A
Aglianico, from Southern Italy, 129
Albarino, Portugal, 22
Alvarinho vinho verde, 45
Atna blanco, 152

## B
Bandol, 154
Beaujolais, 17, 20, nouveau, 161, 204
Blend, red; GSM, 124
Bordeaux, 118
Brute Rosé, 173
Burgundy; Beaune, 174, White, 38, 146, 192, 214

## C
Cab Franc, 98, 216
Cabernet; 38, 116,
 -big red Napa 118,
 -Walla Walla 34, 120
Campagna, a red from, 129
Cerasuolo d'Abruzzo, 183
Chablis; 54, 70, 78, 142, 198, 206, 214,
 -French, 94
Champagne, 17, 76, 82, 102, 164,
 -Dry, 176
Chardonnay; 54, 70, 86, 100, 152, 158,
 -Unoaked, 78,
 -California, 42, 159, 206,
 -Caymus, 118,
 -Full bodied, 82
 -Rhone, 176,
 -Robert Young, 60, 174
Châteauneuf du Pape; Red 121, White 121, 212
Chianti, 140
Chenin; blanc 154, South African blanc, 45
Côte de Rhône; Full-bodied 173, White, 194
Cote Rotie, 176

## D
Dolcetto, from Northern Italy, 40, 134

## E

## F

## G
Gamay, 14, 98, 158, 164
Garnacha; Rioja, Spain 136
Gavi di Gavi; Italian, 88, 96, 196, 206
Gigondas; 220, Southern Rhone region, 173
Graves, 220
Grand cru Saint-Émilion, 120
Grenache, 220
Grüner Veltline, 22
Grüner Veltliner, Singerriedel or Achleiten 136, Australian grüner veltliner, 124

## H

## I

## J
Jura, white 161

## K

## L
Languedoc-Roussillon, 173

## M
Mâcon, 161
Merlot, 116
Montepulciano d'Abruzzo, 129
Mourvèdre, 64, 84, 206, 216

## N
Nouveau Beaujolais, 161

# O

Orvieto Classico, 196

# P

Petite Sirah; 124, California, 130
Pinot Blanc; 142, Alsace 188, Friuli, 140
Pinot Grigio, 47
Pinot Gris; 40, 96, Alsatian, 200
Pinot Noir; 36, 45, 49, 86, 102, 158, 174
 -California, 140, 200
 -French, 72, 134, 136, 159, 183
 -New Zealand, 38
 -Oregon, 198
 -White 42 (its real, look it up)
Port, 36, 84, 247
Pouilly Fuissé; 161, 194, 214, Fumè, 59, 60
Prosecco, 190
Portuguese red; Douro Reserva, 45

# Q

# R

Riesling;
 -Alsace, 17,
 -Dry, 47, 54, 59, 92, 94, 190, 192, 206;
 -Off-dry, 225,
 -German, 49, 159, 192
Rioja, White 204
Rosé; 14,
 -Provencal, 72, 154
 -Dry, 40, 60, 183
 -Dry French, 34
Roussanne, 70, 88

# S

Sake, 198, 204
Sancerre, 59, 76, 84, 145, 146, 186
Sauvignon blanc, 14, 100
Semillon, 142, 186
Soave, 86

Sparkling;
 -California; new world sparkling wine, 146
 -Prosecco, 190
 -Rose, 186
 -White, 92
 -Wine, 92, 100, 225
Syrah; 64, French 120

# T

# U

# V

Valpolicella Ripasso, 212
Verdejo; 145, Rueda Spain, 206
Vermentino; 154, Liguria, 145
Vin gris; crisp, 20
Vouvray; 164, 200, French, 49

# W

# X

# Y

Your Favorite Red, 247

# Z

Zinfandel; 164, 216, Amador County, 130, Dry Creek, 124

# REFERENCE & NOTES

| Product | Minimum Internal Temperature & Rest Time |
| --- | --- |
| Beef, Pork, Veal & Lamb Steaks, Chops, Roasts | 145 °F (62.8 °C) and allow to rest for at least 3 minutes. |
| Ground Meats | 160 °F (71.1 °C) |
| Ground Poultry | 165 °F |
| Ham, Fresh or Smoked (Uncooked) | 145 °F (62.8 °C) and allow to rest for at least 3 minutes. |
| Fully Cooked Ham (To Reheat) | Reheat cooked hams packaged in USDA-inspected plants to 140 °F (60 °C) and all others to 165 °F (73.9 °C). |
| All Poultry (Breasts, Whole Bird, Legs, Thighs, Wings, Ground Poultry, Giblets, And Stuffing) | 165 °F (73.9 °C) |
| Eggs | 160 °F (71.1 °C) |
| Fish & Shellfish | 145 °F (62.8 °C) |
| Leftovers | 165 °F (73.9 °C) |
| Casseroles | 165 °F (73.9 °C) |

# NOTES

Top Left: Jake taking a break to hang with the local cat mascot.
Top Center: Chef Nanette putting the final touches on cream scones.
Top Right: Gina preparing notes for next week's photoshoot.
Middle left: Chef Nanette and Gina plating the Stuffed Provençal Loaf.
Middle Center: Chef Nanette, Kevin and Oak tasting the beginning of the Radicchio Salad with Chestnuts Thyme and Prosciutto.
Middle Right: Jake starting the day by sharpening the kitchen's knives.
Bottom Left: Kevin enjoying a memorial day beer.
Bottom Right: Chef Nanette at the Bidwell Farmer's Market.

**Opposite Page**
Top Left: Jodi organizing the weekly schedule.
Top Center Left: Kevin enjoying a coffee break while contemplating Estabon's punchline.
Top Center Right: Peter posing for the camera.
Top Right: Estabon positioning the Tomatillo Shakshuka for a photo.

Middle Left: Diego prepping oranges for the Sweet Potatoes in Orange Shells.
Middle center Left: Jake placing the pheasant breast on the salt crust.
Middle center Right: Gina contemplating a sunny May day while preparing for the next photo.
Middle Right: A sprinkle of parsley goes a long way for the Scallops and Grapefruit recipe.
Bottom Middle Left: Chef Nanette at the Bidwell Farmer's Market with a basket of lettuce.
Bottom Middle Center left: Gina adding her magic touch to the Chestnut Cake
Bottom Middle Center Right: Roxanne paying attention to detail.
Bottom Middle Right: Chef Nanette presenting the Curried Mango and Tomato salad.
Bottom Left: Chef Nanette cutting the string on the Braciole.
Bottom Center Left: Oak enjoying a sunny day in Buffalo.
Bottom Center Right: Estabon making his point known.
Bottom Right: Jodi learning how to make whipped cream.

**AILEEN**

Sept. 15/97

DEAR NANETTE,
JUST WANT TO TELL YOU AGAIN HOW VERY SPECIAL YOUR "PRESENTATION" WAS; TO LOOK AT, TO TASTE, TO ENJOY. YES, IT WAS VERY BEAUTIFUL.
  SINCERELY
  AILEEN

---

May 28, 1992

Nannette
%Simply Delicious

Dear Nannette:

I am writing this letter to personally thank you for an incredible job on Maura's Bat Mitzvah. Everything was exquisitely done and the food was delicious. Your attention to details and insistence on perfection truly made her affair memorable. It was truly wonderful working with you and we look forward to any future occasions where our paths may cross.

I do not know Jack's last name but please extend to him our deepest thanks for a true winter wonderland. It was everything we hoped and expected, and everything he said it would be. The people could not stop talking about how beautiful the room looked. You two make a great team!

Thank you again for everything. We will be in touch.

Very truly yours,

---

Post Card

Nanette
New York

---

**JACQUELINE PH.D.**

It was a Fabulous Party — My mom is still glowing — and looking forward to her 90th!

Are you free Nov 29, 2001
  Thanks again from all of us, Jackie

---

### THE CULINARY INSTITUTE OF AMERICA 1946

This is to Certify That

**Nanette**

Has Successfully Completed

*A 5 Day Classical Cuisine Program*

Dated this **4th** day of **Aug.** 1989

And is Granted **3** Continuing Education Units

DIRECTOR                CHEF/INSTRUCTOR

Oct 18, 2010

Dear Chef Nanette,

Where to begin? First, by saying it was *fun* to work with you — a joy, really. Even if the food had been "pretty good", I would have been "pretty happy" with the whole experience, but the food was pretty off-the-charts & I am thrilled. If I'd known who I was listening to, I would have been a better listener, and I would have said ok to every suggestion you made!

I can't tell you how many compliments I received — I think *everyone* told me it was all amazing & then mentioned their own personal favorites.

---

December 29, 2000

Dear Nanette,

I am so sorry that I didn't think to tell you to send your bill to Connecticut after December 14.

Someone will be at Sutton Place on Thursday (Jan 4) & will send your books by Mobile Messenger. If this is not good (no one to receive them), please let me know how you would like them sent.

We look forward to enjoying another of your splendid meals when we are in NYC again.

I need to be more diligent in discussing high cost ingredients when we do planning. In my head, when you said "caviar & sweet potato," I thought low grade caviar -- It even occurred to me salmon roe, to go with the orange...

...menus that will please both Ted and guests — and me.

He says that I mis-quoted him when I said that your menu was the best I had served at a dinner party ever. He corrected me: It was the best *meal*, because I have often had great menus — but the chef found a way to mess them up!

One small change I might suggest for December 6: Substitute a more testosterone-compatible hors d'oeuvre (sp?) for the carrot one. I know you were considering our guest's allergies when you planned them.

Which reminds me that I want to check on allergies for Dec. 6. I don't want to ever forget that.

Nanette, you are a dream-chef-come-true! And you are a completely lovely person to boot. Eva...

---

**NEW YORK BARTENDING SCHOOL**
68 West 39th Street, New York, New York 10018   212 768-8460

**Licensed by the New York State Education Department**

This is to certify that

**NANETTE SMALLEY**

Has completed the introductory

**Hospitality Wine Certificate**

Having successfully completed the introductory course of study on the hospitality [...] and having passed the required test in wines & service of, is therefore entitled to rec[...]

IN TESTIMONY THEREOF:

WE HAVE AWARDED THIS CERTIFICATE ON THIS 24th DAY OF AUG[...]

Tom Sisson, Director